WELLINGTON'S NAVY

WELLINGTON'S NAVY

Sea Power and the Peninsular War, 1807–1814

Christopher D Hall

CHATHAM PUBLISHING
LONDON

STACKPOLE BOOKS
PENNSYLVANIA

Dedication
In memory of Simon Garrett

© Copyright by Christopher D Hall 2004

First published in Great Britain in 2004 by Chatham Publishing,
Lionel Leventhal Ltd, Park House, 1 Russell Gardens,
London NW11 9NN

And in North America by Stackpole Books, 5067 Ritter Road,
Mechanicsburg, PA 17055-6921

British Library Cataloguing in Publication Data
Hall, Christopher D., 1950–
Wellington's navy: sea power and the Peninsular War 1807–1814
1. Great Britain. Royal Navy – History – Peninsular War, 1807–1814
2. Peninsular War, 1807–1814 – Naval operations, British 3. Sea-power – Great
Britain – History – 19th century 4. Great Britain – History, Naval – 19th century
I. Title

ISBN 1 86176 230 5

Typeset by Servis Filmsetting Ltd, Manchester
Printed and bound by MPG Books Ltd, Bodmin, Cornwall

Contents

List of maps

Acknowledgements

THE LONG AND FREQUENTLY interrupted process of writing this book has seen me accumulate several debts of gratitude that I am happy now to record. First I must give grateful thanks to the Harold Hyam Wingate Foundation for the provision of a scholarship that enabled me to complete the necessary researches at the Public Record Office in Kew when disability prevented my going there in person. This financial support permitted my employment of Mr George Speight, whose diligent efforts ensured that a huge number of documents were investigated, photocopied, and sent to me for study.

My deepest appreciation goes to Dr Michael Duffy of Exeter University for his constant backing and encouragement, for manfully reading through the completed manuscript, and for his helpful suggestions thereafter. Valuable support also came from Professor Ian Beckett of Luton University.

The staff of Cornwall County and Truro City Libraries should also be mentioned for all their hard work in providing so many obscure naval tomes over the years. I also acknowledge my gratitude to Ken and Jennie Nicholls, both for allowing me access to their collection of books and for always being prepared to help in so many different ways.

Finally a word for my mother. She has endured the vicissitudes associated with the naval aspects of the Peninsular War for much longer than anyone has a right to expect. That burden at least should now be lifted.

CDH

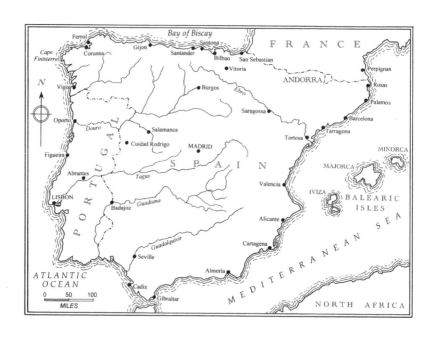

Introduction

'If it had not been for you English I should have been
Emperor of the east; but wherever there is water to float a
ship, we are to find you in our way.'
Napoleon to Captain Maitland, RN, July 1815.

IN HIS SEMINAL WORK on the history of British naval power,
Professor Paul Kennedy remarks on how this provided the
British army in the Peninsula with 'logistical support and added
mobility'.[1] True enough though this is, the comment does not
do justice to just how critical these elements were in that conflict
and pays no account whatever to the other numerous ways in
which control of the sea influenced the outcome of events on
land. It is all too easy to view the Royal Navy in the struggle
with Napoleonic France as only a defensive weapon, used to
prevent invasion and guard trade. If island Britain were to
pursue offensive operations on the mainland of Europe, at least
in those parts of it touched so extensively by water as the
Iberian Peninsula, then it was inevitable that the naval role
would amount to much more than the elements of supply and
mobility. In his failure to consider this Kennedy is by no means
alone, as no author has reflected at any length on the whole
multitude of naval activities linked to the protracted war in
Spain and Portugal. Such naval duties included attacks on
French maritime supply routes; the direct supplying and sometimes direct supporting of the Spanish guerrillas; the repeated
assaulting of French coastal batteries and strongpoints; the vital
task of helping to preserve the Portuguese and Spanish fleets;
the constant support of coastal fortresses under enemy attack;
and the assistance of British land forces in ways beyond the sole

I

provision of food and movement by water.

Compared to the large outpouring of work on the various land campaigns fought in the Iberian Peninsula there has been very little attention paid to its naval aspects. Just before the Great War Henry Shore published an extended series of articles covering part of the subject. These are revealing in many ways but only really concern themselves with major events and provide little background analysis. More obviously Shore only concerned himself with events in Portuguese waters and with operations linked to the main British army, no attention being paid at all to southern and eastern Spain.[2] The massive multi-volume work by Sir Charles Oman that details the Peninsular War on land does not ignore naval operations, but he was no naval historian, his facts and analysis are not always correct, and he was overwhelmingly concerned with events on land rather than water.[3] More recently, some American historians have started to examine aspects of the conflict's naval side,[4] but there has still been no attempt to draw together an overall account of how naval power shaped events in a long and bloody war.

The naval role must not be overstated. The actions of the assorted armies and generals, the ferocious persistence of the guerrillas, and the geography of the region were all crucial elements in determining the final outcome, along, indeed, with events outside the Peninsula itself. However, naval power was also an important element and this has hitherto been largely neglected. The object of this book is to correct this shortcoming.

CHAPTER I

Portugal, 1807–8

'From her geographical situation, paucity of population, &c.
it has long been obvious, that Portugal could oppose no
effectual resistance to an attack from France . . .'
The Naval Chronicle, vol XVIII (September–October 1807).

IN A PURELY MILITARY sense it is hard to conceive of any area
of Europe that was better suited for Britain to maintain a protracted land campaign against the Napoleonic Empire than the
Iberian Peninsula. Although there were other parts of the world
where British political and economic interests were more closely
concerned, the struggle in the Peninsula provided a variety of
benefits that could not be found elsewhere. The roughly 13½
million people who made up the Iberian nations in 1807 overwhelmingly came to loathe and despise the French who tried to
occupy their countries. Fired by such sentiments, the Spaniards
seemed able to raise a never-ending series of armies to challenge
Napoleon's forces. Usually disorganised and badly led, these
armies were frequently defeated but always seemed to spring up
again ready to continue the fight. At the very start of the conflict
at least one British journal, with startling prescience, advised its
readers: 'It is not ten defeats that will overcome the Spaniards:
and it should be remembered, that what may be lost by them in
the field, may be recovered by them in the mountains. . .'.[1] Such
an ally was a huge asset to a Britain willing to commit her own
limited number of soldiers to the theatre. Equally valuable were
to be the thousands of troops provided by the Portuguese who
became more or less willing British auxiliaries, boosting the
number of reliable soldiers that Wellington could put into the
field. Both nations also provided scores of savage guerrilla

bands that roamed the many inhospitable parts of the region, attacking French couriers and small groups of men and forcing the French to tie down tens of thousands of troops in garrisons. They served to keep separated French armies starved of information and intelligence, while simultaneously ensuring that Allied commanders were kept up to date on French movements. Britain further enjoyed the military benefits in the Peninsula flowing from French logistical problems that prevented them concentrating their superior manpower for a sufficient time to drive Wellington out, as well as from Napoleon's mistake in not going there in person after 1809 to take central control and stop the constant squabbling between French generals that often stymied their operations.

These factors allowed a capably-led British army to maintain itself on the European mainland for almost six years, gnawing away at the fabric of Napoleonic invincibility in a region where its own shortcomings, especially in the limited scale of its cavalry and artillery, were minimised. Standing alongside all of this, however, is the central fact that the Britain that fought Napoleon was primarily a maritime power and the Iberian Peninsula also provided her with the opportunity to employ her naval resources to maximum effect in support of a land campaign. Part of this can be immediately understood by merely glancing at a map. At its simplest, the Peninsula constitutes a rough square, three and a half sides of which were bounded by water, altogether comprising a coastline in excess of 1500 miles. As the French tried to extend their occupation, more and more of this coastline became vulnerable to seaborne assault and/or the seaborne supply of regular and irregular forces.

Nor did geography's impact on the value of naval power end with the extent of the coast. With the exception of Madrid, the largest city with a population of 167,000, most of the principal Iberian centres of population were situated on the coast. Of the other five larger Spanish towns with 50,000 or more inhabitants, only Seville was inland, all the others – Barcelona, Valencia, Cadiz and Malaga – were ports. Similarly, in Portugal the two most populous places – Lisbon and Oporto – were on the coast. This was significant in countries where most of the population was still rural, allowing naval power a greater say in the defence and possible recapture of the main centres. In Spain these places were also often separated by considerable distances. It was some 600 miles, for example, from Seville to Bilbao, while Madrid, in the centre, was 200–400 miles away from all the important peripheral towns on the coast. This was important in a region where there were few places that allowed people to travel more than 50 miles without having to cross a mountain. Although the Peninsula had many rivers, only four – the Ebro, Guadalquivir, Douro and Tagus – were navigable all the year round and then only in their lower reaches. Unless armies could use the sea for at least part of their movement, therefore, they were condemned to the roads for all transportation, as of course were all the combatants in the central areas. Some of the available roads in Spain, the royal roads that were constructed in the latter half of the eighteenth century, were as good as any to be found in Europe. These, designed to connect Madrid with the peripheral towns such as Corunna, Badajoz, Cadiz, Cartagena, Barcelona and Irun, were straight, 30–60 feet wide, flanked by retaining walls and built to the latest techniques. However, governmental lethargy had made their construction slow – parts of the network were still not completed by 1840 – and some sections were falling into decay even before the later sections were finished. Outside of such rare highways the armies were obliged to rely on the *caminos*, a series of primitive roadways or trails. These were solid enough in dry weather, but would turn into muddy morasses after rain. There were also the *carrils*, ordinary trails with two narrow bands of stone paving to accommodate cart wheels. These could be useful on level terrain, but in rough areas they degenerated into paths suitable only for pack animals. In Portugal the situation was no better and in many respects rather worse. The main roads, *ie* those fit for wheeled traffic, were equally few in number and confined to the sides of mountains: the obvious routes along the Douro and Tagus could not be built upon because the gorges where they thrust their way through the mountain belt tended to flood very quickly when it rained. The lesser Portuguese trails had all the restrictions and defects to be found in those across the border.[2]

The advantages accruing to the Allies of being able to use sea power to mitigate the problems of the Iberian road network and terrain should not be exaggerated, however. The Anglo-Portuguese and Spanish armies still had at times to campaign in very inhospitable areas, but they did nonetheless enjoy major advantages from the Royal Navy's control of the seas. For the greater part of 1808–11 Wellington's army operated within a comparatively short distance of the coast, enabling it to draw on a constant stream of supplies provided via maritime convoys. Thanks to these, huge stores of provisions were accumulated at Lisbon, to the extent where the Victualling Board could suggest at the end of December 1809 that supplies loaded on board vessels at Portsmouth and Plymouth be transferred to naval use. Only when Wellington had to campaign beyond a convenient distance from the coast, or from depots that could be formed and maintained by boat on the lower reaches of the Tagus, did his army suffer severe supply problems. A mere ten days of marching in pursuit of Massena in early 1811 left the Anglo-Portuguese army having to halt its half-starved troops while the supply train caught up. Nor was it merely a question of shipping supplies to various ports, but, while the French were compelled to rely on locally-procured food, the Allies could seek their supplies much further afield. Portugal could not feed itself under normal circumstances, let alone with thousands of soldiers present and all the disruption resulting from campaigns being fought across her. Foreign grain supplies were vital and they came by sea, largely from the United States but also from the Mediterranean basin, Brazil and Canada, with the British ability to block such imports playing its part in fomenting anti-French unrest in Portugal during its occupation in 1807–8. In 1805 the United States exported 125,000 barrels of grain to the Peninsula, a figure that had leapt to 835,000 barrels by 1811. On top of this, large quantities of meat were procured from North Africa, as well as from the Azores and Cape Verde Islands, the latter being sufficiently important for a sloop and a schooner to be sent to patrol their waters as late as 1812. Fish was another staple that had to be shipped to the Peninsula, the amount sent from Newfoundland to the Iberian and Mediterranean countries doubling between 1804 and 1815.[3]

Alongside provisions, the sea could also be employed in the movement of other more directly military items and a detailed illustration of how this flexibility assisted Wellington in the positioning of his siege train, particularly in comparison to the problems experienced by the French, will be provided in Chapter 4. That this facility existed at all, however, was only because of the Royal Navy's control of the seas. To secure this and to provide the constant and diverse support demanded by the various land campaigns required a substantial commitment of naval forces, as well as an administrative structure to maintain them. The ships and men so employed were to be the responsibilities of three separate commands. Of these one, the Portuguese station, was specifically created in 1808 in response to the French occupation of the kingdom and thereafter was maintained primarily to support Wellington's army. Initially the station's boundaries covered an area bounded by Cape Finisterre in the north down to Cape St Vincent in the south of the mainland and then out to 30 degrees West in the Atlantic, its southern border also taking in the Cape Verde Islands. In due course its commanding admiral would be based at Lisbon as a more or less permanent fixture. The command had the responsibility of supporting the army in Portugal, most particularly in respect of moving its supplies, reinforcements and replacements, and evacuating its wounded. It had also to oversee trade movements to and from the kingdom, to protect the outlying Portuguese islands, and to harass the enemy whenever the opportunity presented itself. Finally those ships of the line that came to spend so much of their time in the Tagus were to be kept provisioned and ready for up to five months extended sea service, the Admiralty in London viewing them as a reserve available to reinforce any warships from the Channel Fleet sent in pursuit of French squadrons escaping from Napoleon's western naval arsenals. The strength apportioned to the station to fulfil these duties varied considerably depending on the progress of events on shore. With the perceived threat of the Russian squadron in the Tagus, in the spring and summer of 1808 between ten and twelve ships of the line were present off the coast. A similar degree of force was maintained in late 1810/early 1811 in the face of the second French invasion of Portugal. At other times the squadron was much weaker, numbering only four ships of the line during 1809 and falling to just one or two from 1813 when the station was, comparatively speaking, becoming a backwater. The far-flung and disparate duties of the command did, however, demand the employment of a numerous force of smaller warships and it was a repeated complaint, as on every station, that there were not enough of them for the tasks in hand. After an initial period of being poorly-provided with such warships, from the summer of 1808 until the spring of 1811 the command generally controlled between ten and sixteen frigates and sloops. However, in early June 1812 the only significant alteration to the command structure was made when the Portuguese station's limits were extended to include Cadiz and Gibraltar, while shortly after its western limit was reduced to 15 degrees West, a separate squadron being formed to guard the waters around the Azores. Some individuals had been pressing for such a change for some time, though the idea had been resisted by the Admiralty. Indeed, at one point in 1809 they severely rebuked Vice-Admiral Berkeley in Lisbon for seeking the support of Villiers, the British ambassador and a mere civilian, for an extension of the command. That they did finally agree to a change was due to a belief that military operations in Portugal and southern Spain would benefit from a unified command over the relevant stretch of coastline. Ironically, within a mere two months of finally taking the step, Wellington's victory at Salamanca obliged the French to abandon southern Spain anyway. Nevertheless, the extension did bring greater responsibilities and a consequent increase in the number of warships under the command. By the middle of 1812 the station controlled some twenty-eight frigates and smaller vessels, the figure dropping to nineteen the following summer as the war moved farther away. Moreover, a large proportion of these vessels were brigs and schooners, smaller warships suited to coastal convoys and the maintenance of communications, which by then comprised the bulk of the station's work.[4]

Prior to the alteration mentioned above, the Spanish coastline from Cape St Vincent eastwards, up to the French border and beyond, was but one of the multitude of responsibilities assigned to the Mediterranean Fleet. In one respect at least, the insurrection that converted Spain from an enemy into an ally was a boon for the Royal Navy. In the years after Trafalgar a substantial squadron had had to be maintained off the great arsenal of Cadiz, in part because it was Spain's primary naval base but more particularly because it sheltered those French warships that had managed to escape the battle. Blockading the place during the first part of 1808 was tying down a force of about ten British ships of the line: by the end of 1809, with the French removed and the port not under threat, this force had declined to a single such vessel. Such relief, though, was short-lived; in early 1810 the French invaded Andalusia and appeared on Cadiz's landward side, so beginning a siege that was to last for more than two years. This necessitated a very rapid naval response to help preserve its security and by April 1810 there was a British squadron present of eleven ships of the line, two frigates and two bomb vessels. This number could be reduced after the initial danger had passed, but the squadron at the port still normally comprised four ships of the line plus smaller warships until the end of the siege in the late summer of 1812. Also near to Cadiz and on that section of the coast was the fortress of Gibraltar. This was both a centre for convoy traffic and for communications with the whole region as well as a long-standing British base for supplies and the repair of vessels. As such it had some limited potential for providing naval support in a crisis, as was to be witnessed in 1811–12.

East of Gibraltar there was, for most of the war, little need for any regular stationing of warships. Eastern Andalusia and the province of Murcia saw comparatively little of the French other than periodic raids, and the province of Valencia, apart from the quickly-repulsed effort in 1808, was not invaded again until the end of 1811. Consequently, no significant employment of warships was required until the latter period and the only point on this part of the coast that did engage consistent British naval interest was the Spanish arsenal at Cartagena, the possibility of its fall being a constant worry. In contrast was the situation off the coast of Catalonia. That province was to witness more or less constant campaigning throughout the war as the French sought to break the resistance of both its regular and irregular defenders. In naval terms, this meant constant employment for quite a strong squadron, the area seeing the deployment of one or two ships of the line and half a dozen frigates and sloops. However, with the bulk of the Mediterranean Fleet positioned to blockade Toulon, a duty significantly assisted once the Spanish revolt allowed the British once more to use Port Mahon as a forward base, the force off Catalonia could be quickly reinforced. It is hard to give a precise figure, but at any one time between a quarter and a fifth of the Mediterranean Fleet's warships would be directly committed to Spanish-related duties.[5]

Moving from the eastern to the northern coast of Spain, from Cape Finisterre, past Corunna and the naval base of Ferrol, to the Franco-Spanish border and beyond, the overseeing of naval operations was one of the responsibilities of the Channel Fleet. This made good administrative sense as that force merely had to stretch itself to the south from its primary area of operations off the western French naval bases. In doing so, however, it exposed the warships concerned to one of the most dangerous coasts for sailing vessels in the whole of Europe. During the summer the prevailing winds in this area are north-westerly, *ie* blowing towards the coast, and place warships sailing near to land in danger of the dreaded lee shore. This menace was espe-cially acute the farther east such vessels were, at the bottom of the Bay of Biscay, where they were liable to be hemmed in between the Spanish coast to the south and the French coast to the east. Square-rigged ships, in other words all ships of the line, frigates and sloops, were vulnerable because of their lack of manoeuvrability compared to smaller vessels such as cutters and schooners that carried a larger press of fore-and-aft rigged sails. During the winter months the prevailing winds shift round to the south-west, but this relief was more than offset by the prevalence of vicious storms that constantly made life a dan-gerous misery for the mariners concerned.

Given such circumstances, it is not surprising that this part of the Peninsula's coast tended to see much less naval activ-ity than elsewhere. In the summer of 1808, even with the Admiralty extremely keen to maximise its support for the newly rebellious Spaniards, there were only eight warships, six frig-ates, a sloop and an armed lugger, serving to the east of Cape Ortegal. This scale of force was to be maintained for the next few years, the only change tending to be the employment of two or three fewer frigates and three or four additional sloops or brigs. Only in 1812 did this alter, when a substantial squadron was formed to co-operate with the Spaniards ashore as part of Wellington's wider strategic offensive against the French. These months were to be the only occasion on which a ship of the line would be committed to extended service on this coast. After this, with the main Anglo-Portuguese army campaigning on or near the coast, the degree of naval support was obliged to become more extensive despite the dangers. By the autumn of 1813 the squadron numbered four frigates and no fewer than twelve smaller warships, mostly sloops and small brigs, the majority of them serving right at the very bottom of the bay in the vicinity of San Sebastian.

The only easier stretch of water for the Channel Fleet in its Peninsular duties lay in the short section of coast between Capes Ortegal and Finisterre. Here, during 1808–9, one or two ships of the line and a frigate were stationed continuously, the Admiralty being both eager to provide support for the Galician rebels but also, more pointedly, to keep an eye on the Spanish squadron based at Ferrol. Not until these vessels were moved in the summer of 1809 could the British warships be moved elsewhere, though Corunna itself was to witness very considerable naval activity during the famous evacuation and later over many years when it became the primary naval base for all the warships serving off northern Spain.[6]

These administrative arrangements served Britain well during the extended Peninsular struggle, nicely reflecting the different geographical circumstances pertaining and permitting the efficient use of available resources. Even when the one major change was made, the extension of the Lisbon station, this was not a response to any glaring military failure, but only an attempt to improve a system that was operating well enough already. That the arrangements did function smoothly was in no small measure due to the harmonious relations between the station commanders, the region being spared any serious command crises as responsibilities and egos came into conflict. No doubt in part this was due to the comparative proximity of the ultimate naval authority, the Admiralty in London, permitting problems to be dealt with in weeks rather than months, or indeed years in the case of the more distant stations of the period.

*   *   *

For Britain's navy, the Peninsular War may be said to have started on 30 October 1807. On that Friday orders were issued to Rear-Admiral Sir Sydney Smith to go to Plymouth, there to assume command of a squadron for service off the river Tagus. His task, in conformity with Viscount Strangford, the British ambassador to Portugal, was to assist the Portuguese royal family in their pending move to Brazil. Smith was further to ensure that no moveable part of the Portuguese military or commercial marine was to be left behind in the Tagus and was also to extend what protection he could to Britain's commercial interests in the country.[7]

These instructions comprised the first substantial British response to the steady deterioration in Portugal's international position over the preceding four months, a period of mounting tension that had begun on 19 July when Napoleon demanded that she close her ports to British vessels by 1 September or face a French attack. Such an assault had been feared in London during the previous summer, plans then being drawn up to send a squadron of warships and 10,000 troops either to defend the country or at least ensure that its royal family and fleet were kept out of French control. At that time campaigns in Germany and Poland had intervened to distract the French Emperor's attention, so granting Portugal a reprieve, but by the summer of 1807, his military endeavours triumphantly crowned by the Treaty of Tilsit and with Europe seemingly at his feet, Napoleon could once more concentrate on his Iberian ambitions. In early August, French threats started to take a positive shape in the formation of an army corps under General Junot in south-western France; on the 12th Napoleon demanded that Portugal declare war on Britain. By 25 September word had reached London that the Portuguese Prince Regent John, ruling in place of his insane mother Queen Maria, was prepared to flee to the colony of Brazil rather than submit to French rule. This intention was formally ratified on 22 October by a convention agreed in London between the British government and de

Souza, the Portuguese ambassador. Article Two of this document committed Britain to support and protect any movement by the whole royal family, or even just that of John's son, the Prince of Beira, to South America. To implement this six ships of the line were to be readied and sent to Portugal; furthermore 5000 troops were also to be sent upon the request of the Portuguese government, it being understood that part of this force would occupy the island of Madeira. Article Four of the convention also promised that Portugal would never cede, in whole or in part, her navy and merchant marine either to France or to Spain, stating that all such vessels would form part of any royal transfer to Brazil.[8]

From the British perspective this agreement was a matter of no small satisfaction. With Spain still a French ally, an assault on Portugal was not likely to be resisted for any length of time, even given the commitment of large numbers of British troops, a strategy the Cabinet was not prepared to risk at that time. This being so, the agreement mounted to a next-best option. At least all of Portugal's available maritime resources would be removed from Napoleon's grasp, while the exile of the royal family would provide a political barrier in Brazil to any French attempts to control Portugal's colonies via the motherland. Future British garrisoning of Madeira was a bonus that preserved a valuable Atlantic staging-post.

For Portugal, however, the matter was nowhere near so straightforward. A small nation placed between two ruthlessly competing larger powers, the Portuguese position was unenviable and Araujo, her chief minister from 1806, tried to pursue a policy of balancing appeasement, a process that frequently saw one official placating the British while another performed a similar function towards the French. Even as the convention was being signed in London, therefore, the British hopes for its smooth implementation were receiving setbacks. Word had reached Lisbon of Whitelocke's defeat at Buenos Aires the previous July and of the evacuation of the Rio de la Plata that followed it, a humiliating British defeat to be compared with Napoleon's triumphs. This naturally did nothing to make the Portuguese more receptive to British pressure and while de Souza was busy negotiating the convention in London the

Prince Regent was signing an order that banned British commerce from his country. This prompted a large and chaotic
exodus of most of the British business community and their
property from the kingdom, 60 ships leaving Lisbon on 17
October and being joined by 46 more from Oporto. This was
followed on 8 November by an order for the detention of those
British subjects still in the country and the confiscation of what
British property remained. Already, on the 5th, a British frigate
had been fired on by Portuguese batteries and on 10 November
Strangford asked for his passports.[9]

Smith's squadron finally sailed from Cawsand Bay on 11
November, consisting of the *London* (98 guns), *Elizabeth* (74),
Monarch (74), *Marlborough* (74), *Bedford* (74) and *Solebay* (32).
Off the Tagus these were reinforced by the three-decker
Hibernia (120), to which Smith shifted his flag, as well as the
Conqueror (74), *Plantagenet* (74) and *Confiance* (20). This was a
powerful force that was more than enough to overawe any
Portuguese naval assembly in the unlikely event of a sea battle
and it was commanded by a man who had already enjoyed an
illustrious naval career. Smith had come to prominence by following the expedition to Toulon in 1793 as a volunteer and then
supervising the destruction of the port's arsenals and shipping
upon its evacuation. He had followed this in 1799 by playing an
important role in the defence of Acre and then commanding a
small blockading squadron off the Dutch coast after the renewal
of hostilities in 1803. Promoted to flag rank in 1805, he had been
the junior admiral in the failed expedition to drive the Ottoman
Porte from its French alliance in 1807. Smith was one of the
naval 'characters' of the period, a man possessed of courage,
flair and imagination who was also viewed with suspicion by
some as a braggart and an awkward subordinate. When some
warships supposedly burned at Toulon were found to be still
intact, Nelson caustically observed that 'Great talkers do the
least, we see'. However, in this, his first significant independent
command, Smith's capacity for bluster would, if anything,
prove an advantage in his dealings with the Portuguese.[10]

By the time the squadron had reached its station off the Tagus
on 16 November, the Admiralty had already become aware of
Portugal's increasingly belligerent attitude and had, accord-

ingly, issued further instructions. If the Portuguese now refused to implement the convention Smith was, in co-operation with Strangford, to implement a strict blockade of the coast, attacking Portuguese shipping and, if possible, forcing his way into the Tagus and seizing the fleet. On the 22nd Strangford notified Smith that the time for hostile measures had indeed come and consequently the Tagus and the ports of Setubal and Oporto were declared to be in a state of blockade. Smith accompanied this by a suitably menacing letter to Araujo in which, despite the 'amicable object' of his mission, the admiral pointed to Portugal's evidently warlike intentions, particularly some defensive works being so obviously constructed at the mouth of the Tagus, and observed that these would make British hostility inevitable. Araujo's attention was also drawn to 'the recent example of Copenhagen' and to the danger of Lisbon suffering 'similar scenes of horror with the additional evils of famine, insurrection, and the presence of a foreign permanent garrison'.[11]

While the unfortunate Prince Regent had been contemplating this looming menace from his maritime flank, another had been forming on his landward border. By 12 November Junot, at the head of 25,000 men, had reached Salamanca, receiving orders the same day to push on with all possible speed to occupy the Portuguese capital. This Junot, living up to his nickname of 'The Tempest', hastened to do and by the 23rd the head of his increasingly disorganised and straggling command was at Abrantes, a mere 75 miles from Lisbon. Finally the Portuguese balancing act had to come to an end to a background of food shortages and mounting popular disorder in the capital, a tension heightened when the British squadron seized two vessels carrying provisions for the city.[12] The Council of State met on 24 November and the decision to flee to Brazil was taken. Smith believed that the naval blockade was the decisive element in this, though that view seems more a product of his vanity than anything else. Similarly unlikely is the oft-repeated tale of Strangford showing the Prince Regent a copy of the *Moniteur* in which Napoleon announced the removal of the House of Braganza: that he intended to divide up Portugal between France and Spain had been divulged to the Portuguese ambassador in

Paris as early as 23 October. More likely it was the simple fact of the French invasion of his country that made up the Prince Regent's mind. He seems to have been terrified by the sea, but had always stated that he would not bargain in the face of an actual invasion.[13]

Once the decision to go had been taken the whole process got under way with great speed, as it had to with Junot hurrying the last few miles to the capital with the least disorganised and exhausted elements of his command. It was fortunate that some activity aimed at readying the available vessels for sea had been going on in Lisbon's dockyards since as early as September, for now 15–18,000 panicking men, women and children sought to escape. In the resulting chaos families got separated and many people embarked without even a change of clothes into vessels that were only barely ready to receive them. All this taking place, moreover, in the teeth of miserable winter weather which, by the time the fleet was due to sail on 27 November, had turned into a violent gale, rendering the Tagus bar impassable and preventing the vessels' departure. During the whole of the next day they remained trapped, unable to leave until the wind veered to the north on the 29th when the fleet could cross the bar and join the British squadron. It was an escape by the narrowest of margins: as they sailed Junot's troops were actually entering the city. As it was, the French were able to open fire on some of the stragglers and three of them were compelled to heave to; fortunately the guns of Fort St Julien, which guarded the river, had been spiked or more would have been lost.[14]

Off the coast Smith received word from Araujo on the 27th that the departure was about to take place, news confirmed by a despatch from Strangford two days later that formally told him of the change in the Portuguese government's conduct. Smith responded by concentrating his marines in the *Solebay* in the hope of being able to seize Fort Bugio at the mouth of the Tagus. This position, he believed, could have been held for a long period against any assault, but again the weather intervened and a gale on 30 November put paid to any further thoughts of a landing. However, he enjoyed the consolation of being able to inform the Admiralty on 1 December that 'I had acted upon my instructions to their fullest extent' and had been joined, by then over 60 miles off the coast, by a fleet of eight Portuguese ships of the line, four frigates, three brigs and a schooner, there also being between 20 and 30 merchant vessels. Left behind were four other ships of the line, though three of these were mere hulks and the other had had her guns removed, as well as five frigates, two of which were so rotten as to be beyond repair. The haste with which the Portuguese had sailed was evident according to one observer in their 'wretched appearance' which 'resembled wrecks rather than men-of-war'. When Smith himself went to pay his respects to the Prince Regent aboard the Portuguese flagship, the *Principe Real* (80), the pair had to meet on the vessel's poop, the only place on the ship that was free of crowd and clutter. Apart from the fourteen members of the royal family, she also carried 398 other people besides her crew.[15] Generally the Portuguese vessels had 'multitudes of helpless men, women and children refugees and heaps of baggage (as at the evacuation of Toulon) on board, very few seamen, neither water or provisions for a voyage of any length. . .'. The latter situation seemed initially to threaten the plan of moving the whole to Brazil as the British did not have the capacity to provision so many people for any extended period. However, five days later, after enduring another gale that put a stop to any immediate preparations and doubtless massively increased the miseries of the unfortunates crammed into the ships, Smith could report that in the event most of the Portuguese would be able to sail for South America after all. Only one ship, the *Principe de Brazil* (74), was not in a fit state to make the voyage and would instead sail for England. The provisions in the remainder were more plentiful than Smith had initially reported and the British squadron was only required to part with comparatively minor quantities of bread, beef and pork to make up any shortfall. The *Hibernia* also supplied the flagship with an assortment of clothing, blankets and shoes. On 5 December the Portuguese fleet, less the *Principe de Brazil* and a brig that had separated in the gale, headed south towards Rio de Janeiro, escorted by the *Marlborough, Monarch, London* and *Bedford*, the whole arriving safely in January 1808. From the British viewpoint the operation was a narrowly won, though substantial, maritime success that deprived Napoleon of a significant increase in his naval means. The convention's terms were finally completed at the end of December 1807 when Rear-Admiral Hood led four ships of the line and four frigates acting as an escort to the 3600 troops that occupied Madeira. Smith, meanwhile, remained with the balance of his squadron to maintain a watch over the Tagus.[16]

Such a continuing blockade was a self-evident necessity. Despite the success of Smith's recent endeavours there still remained the unpalatable fact that Portugal itself, and most particularly the valuable Atlantic port of Lisbon, was now in French hands. This posed the threat of an extended coastline from which privateering attacks could be aimed on the passing trade arteries to and from the Caribbean, the Mediterranean and the South Atlantic; the possible future use of Lisbon by regular units of the French navy; and finally the equipping and use of those Portuguese naval elements that had had to be left behind in the wake of the royal family's flight. It was testament to French industry that by the time Lisbon was once again under Allied control there were found to be in the Tagus one ship of 74 guns and two others of 54 guns, all ready for sea, along with fourteen smaller vessels, three of which were frigates.[17] The Admiralty could not have afforded to ignore an enemy naval base of such potential, but further drawing their attention to Lisbon was yet another worry: the presence of Vice-Admiral Siniavin's Russian squadron consisting of nine ships of the line and a frigate. This force had formerly constituted Russia's naval muscle in the Mediterranean but, in the wake of the Russian defeats in Poland and Tsar Alexander I's concessions to Napoleon at Tilsit, the squadron had been deprived of any Mediterranean base and had been obliged to try and make its way home to the Baltic. For some time these warships provoked great alarm at the Admiralty, given the sense of uncertainty about the Tsar's future intentions. Although previously a British ally, Alexander I had become increasingly irritated by what he perceived to be a British failure adequately to support his military operations. For the moment under Napoleon's spell, the Tsar, after a fruitless attempt at mediation between the belligerents, completed a *volte face* by declaring war on Britain on 31 October 1807. Word of this did not reach London until early December, but already Russia was having to be viewed as a possible, and most unwelcome, enemy. As early as 14 November orders were sent to Smith telling him to prevent Siniavin's vessels sailing into an enemy port, he being permitted to use force if necessary to stop them entering the Tagus. This the admiral was unable to do. Just as the British squadron was approaching the Portuguese coast on 16 November, two of the Russian warships were entering the Tagus under stress of weather, these being rapidly followed by the other eight. Their arrival also posed a delicate problem for the Portuguese as their neutrality was broken by the presence of more than six belligerent warships, a situation resolved only by the removal of the powder from some of them and its storage on shore.[18]

Evidently by the end of November a certain desperation was starting to take hold in London as the Admiralty, in the dark about events in Portugal, was gripped by the nightmare prospect of some sort of Russo-Portuguese maritime union controlled by the French. Indicative of this was the decision on the 30th to instruct Vice-Admiral Collingwood to leave the Mediterranean Fleet and assume the command off the coast of Portugal. Four ships of the line were to be sent and he was to detain, *ie* fight, any Russo-Portuguese fleet he might encounter. If the Russians were met alone they were to be shadowed at first and not detained until they had passed Portsmouth; Collingwood was also to oversee the previously intended measures respecting the capture or removal to Brazil of the Portuguese marine. This projected transfer of the Admiralty's most reliable and respected commander (the Mediterranean Fleet was the largest maintained outside home waters and beyond anything approaching direct Admiralty command) was rendered unnecessary once word had been received that most of the Portuguese fleet had been removed from the equation. Even so, it was decided that so junior an admiral as Smith ought to be superseded by someone with more seniority in what was becoming an increasingly large and responsible command. Consequently, in early December 1807, Vice-Admiral Sir Charles Cotton was appointed to the Portuguese station. He had previously fought without particular distinction as a captain at the battle of the Glorious First of June in 1794 and, after promotion to flag rank

in 1797, saw service in both the Mediterranean and the Channel. He had then commanded the Newfoundland station and may well have been viewed as a 'safer pair of hands' than the more mercurial Smith. Such was the desire in London to see Cotton safely in charge of events that he was permitted to sail directly in the *Minotaur* (74). Not only had she been rushed from Chatham docks before her programme of repairs was completed, leaving her not fully seaworthy, but she was also supposed to have been the main escort for a troop convoy going to Portugal, in line with the normal policy of using warship transfers for this duty. The convoy concerned had been scattered in a gale but the Admiralty was unwilling for Cotton's departure to wait upon its reassembly. He finally appeared off the Tagus on 14 January 1808.[19]

Cotton's new command was not a comfortable one. His main force, consisting of nine ships of the line and a sloop, was concentrated to blockade the Tagus, with a sloop and cutter doing similar duty off Oporto and a frigate and sloop temporarily tied up escorting a convoy to Gibraltar.[20] The blockading vessels were obliged to take up positions off an exposed Atlantic coast, in winter, with no convenient harbours in which to seek shelter and repairs. They faced the arduous tasks of harassing the French occupiers of Portugal, blocking any naval operations they might attempt, and being prepared to meet any sudden sortie launched by the Russians. Yet all of this was initially imperilled by logistical problems. Cotton was obliged to inform the Admiralty on 24 January that his squadron was short of supplies, particularly water, and that he doubted if it would be able to remain at sea for more than five weeks. Seven days later the situation had deteriorated. Although the storeship *Hindustan* had appeared, she was largely full of naval stores and carried only enough bread to supply the squadron for one extra week. Moreover, Cotton had by then learned that the Rochefort squadron had escaped to sea on the 17th and it would put him in a very awkward predicament if any of his vessels were called upon to join in any pursuit. On 27 January he submitted a return of the provisions required by the squadron, this including requests for almost 480,000lbs of bread, over 136,000lbs of beef and 1650 tons of water. The central problem was the lack of convenient friendly harbours to provide supplies or shelter. In the middle of February Cotton had Berling Island occupied. This was a rocky outcrop almost 50 miles south of Figueira but was discovered to be little more than a fortified position that produced nothing, Captain McKinley of the *Lively* (38) reporting that it lacked shelter, had no anchorage, produced nothing and had no natural springs. Even the water that dripped down the walls in a cavern, the only local supply, dried up during the summer. The spot did have the advantage of being easily defensible and helped cover the communications with northern Portugal, factors prompting Cotton to have the fort occupied by some marines and to station the brig *Rapid* (14) to patrol offshore. However, in no way did this ease his logistical situation. The squadron had the option of taking water from the Bayonne Islands but, being close to Vigo where there were 2000 French troops, this could not be regarded as secure. Even when the risk was taken there remained the problem of time and distance: two ships of the line were sent to water there in February, the process depriving Cotton of their services for 15 and 17 days respectively. Even worse was the option of sending ships to the Azores for this purpose: such vessels would be out of the command for a month. Cotton faced the unpalatable dilemma of either weakening his squadron for long periods, or running dangerously short of water. Further compounding his difficulties was a shortage of fuel and candles, neither of which could be obtained locally.[21]

Not until the beginning of March did this situation start to improve, with the arrival of eight victualling ships from Plymouth. These allowed the squadron to be reprovisioned in all respects except water, fuel, candles and pursers' stores. By the end of the month, indeed, two victuallers that appeared could be sent on to service the squadron off Cadiz, Cotton's vessels being replete. At that time the water problem was also finally being solved as well, with the arrival of four transports loaded with that commodity. These were to be retained by Cotton to keep his vessels supplied from whatever sources were considered most suitable. It was the Admiralty's decided policy to keep its Portuguese squadron well provided for to maintain maximum efficiency and flexibility, a further eleven transports laden with coal and water reaching Cotton at the end of April and making his command provisioned in all respects for six months. Although he considered that four victualling ships attached to his command would meet all his needs, the Admiralty was determined to err on the side of excess, taking the view that any surplus provisions could be sent on to the Cadiz squadron and not wasted. Ultimately the supply problem would be solved by access to Portuguese harbours and the ability to form local depots: Cotton could send all the water transports home at the end of August, observing that sufficient quantities could then be drawn from Oporto. Nevertheless it reflects credit on the Admiralty's administrative machine that once it learned of the logistical problems off the coast it acted quickly to deal with them and ensure that its warships there would be effective.[22]

His supply problems only served to emphasise what Cotton considered to be a general shortage of warships for the tasks he had to perform. In February his command was weakened when Smith, newly appointed to command the squadron off Brazil, departed with two ships of the line and a sloop. The *Minotaur* also had to be sent back to Britain on account of her leaky and rotten condition and with the water problem being so pressing that vessels had to depart for long periods, Cotton was sometimes reduced during February and March to having only six ships of the line to contain any sortie by the Russian squadron. The duty of blockading the Portuguese ports was also rendered very difficult, he complained, by a shortage of small cruisers. He reflected early in February that this, combined with a series of gales that had driven the British ships off their stations, had allowed several Brazil ships, five or six American vessels, plus a number of Greek vessels, to enter or leave the Tagus in the previous weeks. At that time had only two small warships with him, the *Confiance* and the cutter *Cheerful* (10): the squadron's five other small warships were either out of action through accidents or were detached on other duties. This situation did improve as such vessels returned to him, though once again, as with the supply question, the Admiralty appears to have regarded the command as one of sufficient importance to warrant some priority as to resources. Even when, in April, the sloop *Haven* (16) was damaged in a collision and had to return home, and the schooner *Milbrook* (14) was driven from her anchors off Berling Island and wrecked, the Admiralty provided immediate replacements. By July 1808 Cotton's command had been increased to the level of a very powerful naval force, comprising ten ships of the line (two of them three-deckers), five frigates, six sloops and a cutter.[23]

With the Russians staying firmly in the Tagus and the French having few naval resources to hand, there was little chance during these months for the British crews to lock horns with the enemy. In February Captain Yeo of the *Confiance*, patrolling near to the mouth of the Tagus and hearing rumours that the Russians were about to sail, sent his cutter and jolly boat to row guard at the entrance. While so engaged the boats, with 16 men under Master's Mate Trist, encountered a French gunboat containing a 24-pounder and two 6-pounder cannon with a crew of 50. This was captured in fine style, the French losing three killed and nine wounded while the British escaped without loss. Trist had passed for lieutenant twelve months before and received his reward when Cotton appointed him in that rank to the *Alfred* (74). Two months later, though, the French had their revenge when boats from the frigate *Nymphe* (36) and the sloop *Blossom* (18) tried to cut out an armed vessel lying just above Belem. This failed completely, the frigate's captain, who led the assault, being killed while trying to board the enemy vessel and the attackers' boats falling into confusion. Two men were killed, including Captain Shipley, and two others were wounded. On the day after this defeat, 24 April, two British brigs were more successful off Faro in southern Portugal, capturing two Spanish feluccas and two gunboats and driving two other gunboats ashore. Even here, however, nemesis was just around the corner: on 25 May one of the brigs, the *Rapid*, was chasing two more feluccas off Cape St Vincent when she was hit and sunk by a shore battery, her crew being rescued by a nearby sloop.[24]

Of much greater significance than these minor actions was the simple menacing presence of the squadron, allowing both the observation of French rule and the encouragement of those Portuguese who wished to be rid of it. The intelligence stemming from this blockade, moreover, would have important consequences. Early in February 1808, the *Nautilus* (18) rejoined Cotton after escorting a convoy to Gibraltar. The sloop brought word that Junot commanded 32,000 French troops in Portugal, a figure that was close to the truth: he had some 26,594 soldiers in May once a 4000-strong draft of réplacements had made up the losses suffered in the exhausting dash for Lisbon. He also had present two Spanish divisions that assisted, amidst feelings of increasing discontent, in the occupation: these numbered a further 13,000 men. The particular problem for Cotton, and one he was never able to solve satisfactorily, was in discovering the dispositions of all these soldiers, a question of crucial importance as the commitment of British troops became a growing possibility. During the latter part of March and early April the squadron received a steady trickle of refugees wanting to escape the increasing harshness of French rule. Harriet Slessor, an Englishwoman who had stayed on in Oporto, remarked that:

> Numbers of Portuguese families have emigrated, and . . . they continue disappearing, and often in the night boats full go over the Bar, and are received by our King's ships, that are on this station, purposely to be informed of what is going on on shore.

On 5 April the *Hindustan* sailed for England carrying 173 such refugees. During the following two days a further 35 joined the squadron off Lisbon and then, on the 7th, the *Comus* (22) rejoined from closely blockading the mouth of the Tagus and brought an additional 175. The latter two groups Cotton planned to send to England in one of his water transports and, nervous in case hundreds more appeared to eat up all his provisions, he asked the Admiralty to send him two transports specifically to receive such people on board. In the event stern measures by Junot curbed the flow and by the middle of May only a further 82 had appeared, Harriet Slessor noting that 'there is penalty of death on any boatman that takes letters or anything else to convey them on board the Frigates'. The refugees would have provided a constant source of information, not least on the unpopularity of French rule, but their provision of hard, reliable military intelligence would have been limited.[25]

A better source, it seemed, was discovered early in June when news was received from Lisbon from a Briton by the name of Wilson, formerly a merchant there, who stated that there were a mere 4000 French soldiers in the city, this including both fit and sick. This was information he had obtained from one of the overseers responsible for baking their bread. Also present were 3000 Spanish soldiers and 300 Portuguese, neither group possessing much in the way of military quality. Six days later

Wilson escaped the city and was aboard the *Hibernia*, Cotton being impressed by him and repeating the news that Lisbon was poorly garrisoned and on the verge of revolt, though the Spaniards were now said to number 5–6000. On that day, 9 June, Cotton also heard that the Spanish province of the Asturias had risen in revolt and he took the opportunity of having a proclamation distributed, promising: 'All the assistance his Britannic Majesty's fleet can afford, shall be readily given to you and your generous allies the Spaniards, in the noble attempt to emancipate your capital from the severe oppression it has suffered since the French army marched into it.' Presumably he used the fishermen and vendors of fruit who held regular contact with his vessels to distribute this. As Harriet Slessor wryly remarked 'a good fee serves well, and all danger is forgot'. On 11 June a Spanish officer slipped out to the squadron and repeated that there were only 4000 French troops in the city, the Spaniards in Lisbon now numbering only 1200 but they having been disarmed by the French and confined aboard some ships. At his request Cotton agreed to warn the Spanish garrisons scattered along the coast about being similarly disarmed. The following day Cotton informed the Admiralty about the paucity of the Lisbon garrison, with the Spanish troops a factor that could now be discounted and a native population that was becoming more restive. His view was that:

> . . . five or six thousand British Troops, might effect a landing, gain possession of the forts on the banks of the Tagus, and by co-operating with His Majesty's Fleet give to our Possession the whole of the maritime means now collected in the Tagus.

He even proposed diverting troops which he believed might be on their way to Gibraltar to achieve this, if only his ships might fall in with their convoy. A week later, though, this aggressive optimism fell a victim to fresh information when word was received from an American that Junot was then supposed to be concentrating his forces in the capital and now had 10,000 troops present. This was confirmed on 28 June, as well as news that the French were now expecting a British attack.[26]

If Cotton felt that an opportunity had been missed he was not to be given time to dwell on it. The one piece of intelligence he had repeatedly received and which was correct was that the Portuguese were becoming more and more resentful of their rapacious and oppressive French conquerors. This sullen fury was finally given the opportunity to explode into action on 6 June when Balesta, the general commanding the Spanish troops at Oporto, heard of the rebellion breaking out in Galicia and received orders from the new junta at Corunna to march his troops home. This he immediately did, taking the French soldiers in Oporto with him as prisoners. The vacuum thus created in northern Portugal was rapidly filled by a native Portuguese insurrection, both in the city itself and in the adjacent provinces of Tras-os-Montes and Entre-Duero-e-Minho. The first intimations of these events reached the British squadron on 19 June when the sloop *Talbot* (18) off Oporto observed that Portuguese colours were flying over the city, her firing being answered by a friendly salute and an invitation to land. Her commander, Captain Jones, quickly accepted this offer and conferred with the Bishop of Oporto, the hastily-elected head of the Supreme Junta formed to co-ordinate the northern uprising. The prelate lost no time in writing to Cotton to seek the support of British troops. These the admiral did not have, but he did tell the Admiralty of the likely worth of a supply of arms and ammunition for the rebels. In the meantime, Captain Creyke of the sloop *Eclipse* (18), the senior officer off Oporto, sent a party of sailors to mount guns on a Brazil ship with the intention of employing the vessel as a floating battery to defend the bridge over the Douro in case of any French assault from the south. Creyke also spared 30 barrels of powder from his small vessel to help the insurgents. Rather more dramatic naval assistance became possible on 4 July when Cotton learned that the new rebels had seized Fort Catalina at Figueira, a work commanding the mouth of the River Mondego. This gave him the chance to respond directly to the assorted pleas for aid that he had been receiving, for with Fort Catalina only 30 miles from Oporto, the heart of the rebellion, and with communications between the two being good, Cotton believed that only a small commitment of force would be sufficient to secure the place while simultaneously serving as an earnest of Britain's desire to support the Portuguese. Accordingly, he instructed Captain

Bligh of the *Alfred* to occupy Catalina with 185 marines drawn from the squadron. Cotton felt that the presence on the ground of redcoats, even if marines rather than soldiers, could only serve to foster the rebellious spirit sweeping through the region, and he further hoped to foment matters by providing Bligh with 500 muskets and ammunition drawn from the squadron. Bligh was ordered to occupy the fort, provided he deemed such a step to be safe, and on no account was he to employ the marines on any risky ventures in the interior, from where a rapid re-embarkation might not be possible. Although being empowered to distribute both arms and a proclamation exhorting the Portuguese to throw off their oppressor, on no account was Bligh 'to commit the Faith of His Majesty's Government further than to the extent of the means within your power. . .'. The day after issuing these instructions, Cotton met two more Portuguese officers seeking aid, these coming from Lagos in the south of the kingdom, and the admiral provided another 100 muskets. He noted on 7 July that, since 22 June, he had received nine separate requests for help from various parts of Portugal and had provided 910 muskets plus ammunition, flints and suchlike. On the same day, Bligh successfully landed his marines at Fort Catalina, an enthusiastic Cotton sending him an additional 100 as a reinforcement within a week, believing that the mouth of the Mondego was the only place, other than Oporto itself, when an invading British army might get ashore safely. He thought, wrongly as it turned out, that 60 transports might enter the Mondego at any one time and that there was sufficient space for any number to anchor together. Such concern for a suitable landing place was no idle fancy on Cotton's part: he had received word on 9 July that an expedition was on its way.[27]

Back in London, the Cabinet had concluded by the end of June that the wave of rebellion and dissent that appeared to be sweeping the Peninsula, especially the revolt in the northern Spanish provinces of Asturias and Galicia, provided Britain with an opportunity to strike at Napoleon's armies. Accordingly, instructions were sent out to Lieutenant-General Sir Arthur Wellesley, commanding a force in southern Ireland,[28] to move with the aim of 'directing the efforts of the British Troops to the Expulsion of the Enemy from Portugal that the Insurrection against the French may thereby become general throughout that Kingdom as well as Spain, it is therefore deemed expedient that your attention should be immediately directed to that object'. The division that Wellesley was to lead consisted of 8762 infantry and artillerymen plus 394 cavalry, though there were only 180 horses for the latter. This force sailed from Cork on 12 July loaded aboard twenty-nine troop transports, nine ordnance vessels and storeships, one hospital ship, twenty-one cavalry ships, one transport carrying hay, and nine victuallers (three of them carrying oats). These seventy vessels were escorted by the *Donegal* (74) and *Resistance* (38), while Wellesley himself sailed ahead aboard the *Crocodile* (22) with the intention of discovering the exact state of affairs in northern Spain and Portugal and determining where, precisely, his troops should land.[29]

Aware of these developments, on 9 July Cotton dispatched the *Lively* north of Lisbon to try and intercept the convoy before it sailed too far to the south. With northerly winds prevailing off the Portuguese coast during the summer he was nervous about any loss of time too southerly a movement could cause. Cotton was by then firmly of the opinion that the mouth of the Mondego offered the safest spot for any disembarkation. Finally meeting on 26 July, Wellesley and Cotton agreed that any direct assault on Lisbon was far too hazardous to contemplate in the light of Fort St Julien and the other batteries defending the Tagus. The warships were unable to approach sufficiently closely to silence their guns. Nor were the various small bays to the north of the capital considered safe: only small numbers of troops could get ashore at any one time and there was always the risk on an exposed Atlantic coast of the surf getting up very quickly and interrupting the landings. Such a development would leave any units already ashore exposed to attack and defeat in detail. The two men therefore fully concurred that a landing at Mondego Bay under the protection of Fort Catalina was by far the safest option, the disembarkation beginning on 1 August.[30]

When it came to the business of amphibious operations, such as were to be witnessed along the Portuguese coast during

August and September 1808, the Navy's role went far beyond that of merely providing convoy escorts to the vessels transporting the troops to their landing points. At this time the practice when it came to moving British forces abroad was to employ civilian shipping hired for the purpose at the rate of so much per ton, the rate paid being determined by a variety of factors such as the availability of tonnage, the urgency with which it was required, the length of the contract, and the quality of the ships concerned, *ie* whether they had the copper sheathing on their hulls that rendered them safer and faster. Such vessels were usually adequate simply to transport troops to a given destination, though the resulting convoys, because of the numbers of vessels involved in moving any sizeable force, were invariably slow and unwieldy: one disgruntled commander lamented 'what can a convoy of 200 small brigs do, commanded by North Country skippers who will do nothing but what they like themselves. . .?'.[31] However, they were next to useless when it came to the matter of actually unloading their charges in conditions other than those provided by a nice, safe harbour. There were no such havens available on the Portuguese coast during the summer of 1808. With seamen always a scarce resource and owners having no desire to employ more than were absolutely necessary to crew their vessels, there was not the skilled manpower, let alone the provision of a sufficient number of ship's boats, to transfer troops from ship to shore with any degree of speed. For such services the escorting warships were expected to fill the void. Given such *ad hoc* arrangements, with all the dangers of tides and weather thrown in as well, it is hardly surprising that such landings were usually slow and fraught with problems and difficulties.

Because of such factors, the setting ashore of Wellesley's 9000 men at Mondego Bay took no less than five days to complete and for the sailors involved was to be only the start of what was to prove a long process. Just as the final units of this division were landed, another convoy arrived carrying just under 5000 troops under the command of Major-General Spencer. These too had to be ferried ashore, an operation not completed until 9 August. On the 19th and 21st, two further brigades appeared, between them numbering just under 5000 men, these being landed further to the south, at Maceira and near Mafra. Meanwhile, an even larger convoy had arrived at Mondego Bay, bringing Lieutenant-General Sir John Moore and over 11,000 troops, this force beginning its disembarkation on 22 August, only then receiving orders to re-embark and sail to the south. These instructions came in the wake of Wellesley's victory over Junot at the battle of Vimiero (21 August) and the resulting armistice negotiations that turned into the notorious Convention of Cintra.[32]

The dangers surmounted in landing some 30,000 men on a more or less open coast were numerous and its successful completion was a fine testimonial to the sailors concerned. Captain Malcolm of the *Donegal*, the officer who superintended much of the process, later observed that such undertakings on that coast during August and September would always be difficult because the Atlantic swell caused a large surf. Although some protection was afforded by the river flowing into Mondego Bay, it had a bar and that too possessed a heavy surf. Malcolm noted that during the several weeks that he served there, there were only four or five days on which the ships' boats could cross the bar in safety. What was fortunate, however, was that Mondego Bay was one of the few places between Oporto and Lisbon where the British could secure the use of large numbers of local craft, schooners and larger boats, whose crescent shapes made them better able to withstand the conditions. One witness to the landings gave unstinting praise to the naval personnel involved:

> Captain Malcolm, finding heavy surf breaking both on Figueras [*sic*] bar and the beach at Buarcos, immediately set the example to his men of jumping from the boat into the sea, and carrying the men and their canteens, etc., to the shore. The officers and men immediately followed so noble an example; and they continued on their arduous service for several days and nights. Frequently, owing to the surf, they were unable to return to their ships, and remained during he night in their wet clothes, on the ground.

Rendering the Mondego anchorage even less secure was the discovery that only some 20–25 ships could be anchored in the safer conditions of the river, and none of these could draw more than eleven feet of water.[33]

When the landing area was moved south to Maceira in the latter part of August, a step taken so that newly-arriving troops and stores could be landed nearer to Wellesley's main force, the problems got even worse. On the night of 20 August the prevailing northerly wind shifted to the south-west, placing the 230–240 vessels in the roads of Maceira on a lee shore. For safety's sake such vessels needed to get to sea and secure room for manoeuvre as quickly as possible, but only about half the fleet was able to do so. The remainder were obliged to remain at anchor and take their chance. The following day the wind veered back and upon his return Malcolm observed that about 60 vessels had lost their anchors in trying to leave.

> I have no doubt, had the breeze increased to a common gale, that many of the vessels would have been lost; they were then mostly reduced to their last anchor, and the bottom is very rocky. The transports, onboard which Sir John Moore's troops were, were very badly found, and not calculated to beat off a lee shore.

The boats that ferried the troops ashore at Maceira were constantly filled with water from the surf and about 20 of them were lost, together with six or seven men from the artillery and the King's German Legion. This at least was an improvement on the experience of those of Moore's command who had been briefly landed at Mondego Bay. There some 60 men had drowned when the growing swell overturned their boats. The day before he finally left Maceira on 30 August, Malcolm noted that there were only 30–40 boats in the whole fleet that were fit for service, this despite the efforts of the carpenters who had worked on them all through the previous night.[34]

For those conveyed ashore by such means, the experience could be terrifying. One who landed on 28 August recalled being carried in a flat-bottomed boat, the journey to the shore being through 'raging breakers' and a 'roaring storm of foam', the passengers crouching low in the boat and some closing their eyes. Once at the beach, they were dragged ashore by sailors stationed there for the purpose. The beach itself was a chaotic mass of soldiers, horses, sailors, guns, wagons, mountains of ships' biscuit, haversacks, hay, barrels of meat and rum and tents. Another witness saw how:

The weather had grown rough and the surf on the steep shore was of exceptional violence. A considerable number of boats were capsized during the landing, and it is only due to the courageous and untiring efforts of the seamen that such accidents were limited to so small a number. The English sailors, fired by the example of their officers, might be seen wading up to their shoulders in readiness to haul the boats up on to dry land the moment they were thrown ashore by the surf.[35]

As well as managing the actual landing of the troops, part of the naval resource off the coast was also employed to provide direct support and supply facilities to Wellesley's force as it advanced south from Figueira da Foz to the battlefield at Vimeiro. Bligh's *Alfred* escorted eight transports loaded with stores along the coast, Wellesley deliberately staging his advance along the more circuitous coastal road so that he could keep in touch with the ships. He wrote to Bligh on 20 August asking that the bread, ammunition, saddles and similar stores be landed at Maceira and stating that he intended to keep the transports close by in case it became necessary to turn the French flank by means of an amphibious landing. The victory over Junot rendered this unnecessary, but the general still acknowledged Bligh's support, an officer 'from whom we received some most essential assistance'. Some years later, when advising another commander, Wellington reflected upon his reliance upon naval support in 1808:

I kept the sea always on my flank; the Transports attented the movements of the Army as a Magazine; and I had at all times, & every day, a short, and easy Communications with them. The Army therefore could never be distressed for Provisions or Stores, however limited its means of Land Transport, and in case of necessity it might have embarked at any point of the Coast.

Naval support was also valuable in the wake of Vimiero when it came to helping the wounded. These unfortunates were moved the four miles to Maceira in carts, one accompanying doctor recording that although the beach was not approached before midnight:

On reaching the shore, we found a number of sailors, with lanterns in their hands, busily employed in removing into boats the wounded from Vimiera [*sic*]: it was highly gratifying to me to

witness the very attentive and humane manner in which this
service was performed by those kind-hearted honest tars, who,
during the whole of a very cold night, were working, nearly up
to the middle, in the wash of the sea . . . and, owing to their great
exertions, by ten o'clock next morning, I had seen the last of my
charges sent off to the hospital-ships appropriated for their
reception.[36]

The whole brief Vimiero campaign stood as an outstanding
example of how the Royal Navy could exert as profound an
influence upon the course of the war because of its amphibious
potential as by any great naval battle. During the first seven
months of 1808 Cotton's squadron had, in very trying circumstances, maintained a blockade that helped keep Junot as isolated on his seaward flank as the Spanish revolt had done on his
landward. It had, furthermore, helped spread the dissent in
Portugal that made the French occupation increasingly uncomfortable and had managed to secure one of the few places on the
coast where troop landings might be managed in something
approaching safety. Then, in many ways even more impressive
given the difficulties of co-ordinating military operations in the
age of sail, over 33,000 British troops had been deposited on
Portuguese soil in the space of five weeks. Moreover, these
troops did not start their movement concentrated at a single
point, but were brought together from places as diverse as Cork
in southern Ireland, Cadiz and Gibraltar in southern Spain,
Harwich, Ramsgate and Plymouth in southern England, and
from the island of Madeira.[37] Once such forces had been safely
transported, the accompanying naval warships had then
fulfilled the duty of overseeing their landing and providing
support during the campaign that followed.

In the immediate aftermath of Vimiero, the British army in
Portugal underwent two very rapid changes in leadership as first
Lieutenant-General Burrard and then Lieutenant-General
Dalrymple succeeded Wellesley as its commander, changes
prompted by the Cabinet's uncertainty about Wellesley in view
of his junior status on the army list. These alterations paralysed
the British campaign and when, the day after Vimiero had been
fought, Junot sought terms whereby he could escape the net that
seemed to be closing in on him, the offer was attractive to his

British counterparts. At that stage Moore's troops had still not landed and there seemed to be the prospect of hard fighting if the French had to be removed by force. An armistice was the consequence and for seven days the parties haggled over the details before the eventual Convention of Cintra was agreed on 30 August. Essentially these provided for the complete French evacuation of Portugal, they being removed in British vessels. More contentiously, the terms also protected all those Portuguese who had collaborated with the French and allowed the latter to go home with their loot.[38] Once such sensitivities were put aside, however, the agreement was a substantial strategic success, removing all of Portugal's military and economic assets from Napoleon's control and, in effect, transferring them to Britain. All of this, however, unfortunately omitted one remaining important element: the Russian squadron still in the Tagus.

When the basis of the Convention was passed to Cotton for his ratification on 25 August, he was far from happy at what he viewed as its overly generous terms to Junot's army, both respecting their safe removal to France and the retention of their plunder. Cotton could do little to amend these arrangements, which were the responsibility of Dalrymple, Burrard and Wellesley, but he took a more determined line when it came to the Russians, a more directly naval concern. He completely refused a proposal that Siniavin's vessels be allowed to leave Lisbon as if it were a neutral port and be given a generous head-start before any pursuit was mounted.

Throughout the period of the blockade of Lisbon in 1808, the British attitude towards the Russians had been ambivalent and at times, given that the two countries were supposed to be at war, decidedly odd. When he arrived off the coast Cotton brought with him despatches for Siniavin and the Russian consul in Lisbon from Alopeus, the Russian ambassador in London. He also carried a letter proclaiming amity towards Russia and expressing some irritation that Junot's decrees made the delivery of these missives difficult. From what information he could gather, Cotton was at least reassured that the Russians too felt no particular hostility towards their British 'enemies', indeed in February he learned that some British civilians were being given shelter from the French aboard the Russian warships. In the same month, two Russian officers visited the British squadron under a flag of truce, it being learned from them that their vessels were completely dominated by the French, they having occupied the old Tagus batteries and being busily engaged in building new ones. Via these officers, Siniavin let Cotton know that it was quite impossible for him to escape the river under the threat of such artillery. This all tended to suggest that the Russians did not pose a serious threat, but that could not be taken for granted when, for example, it was learned towards the end of February that the Russians were taking in large supplies of bread and it was feared that this might be a preliminary to their sailing.[39]

With Junot defeated and the French about to leave, Siniavin's squadron was rather left high and dry and he had little choice but to agree a separate convention with Cotton signed on 3 September. By this all the Russian warships, consisting of one vessel of 80 guns, six of 74 guns, one of 66 guns, one of 60 guns and a single frigate, were, with their stores, to be sent to England and interned until such time as there was an Anglo-Russian peace, at which point they would be restored to the Tsar within six months. All the 5685 Russian seamen and marines aboard the vessels would be returned to Russia without any stipulation as to their future service and at the expense of the British government. These were curious terms, it appeared, to be granted to an enemy fleet that was completely at one's mercy; even more so when it was discovered that two of the Russian ships were so unseaworthy as to be unable to make the voyage to Spithead even under British escort. The 'qualified detention' of the ships and the complete freedom for their crews made a total mockery of the supposed state of war between the two countries and was an outcome prompted by several factors. The crux of the matter was that the Cabinet had no desire at all, if it could be avoided, to engage in a serious shooting war with Russia, a nation so recently an important ally against Napoleon and one which, it might be hoped, could become so again. After much discussion among the ministers in London, this desire eventually took shape in the form of instructions sent to Cotton in April. As part of a wider hope for an agreement that would have removed all remaining Portuguese military and civil vessels from the country in return for a lifting of the British blockade, Cotton was told that the Russian warships would have to be surrendered to him, up to a time six months after an Anglo-Russian peace, but that their crews might return home without stipulations as to their future service. The similarity between these proposed terms and those eventually negotiated with Siniavin are obvious. That the Russians had aided British citizens in Lisbon and done nothing directly to support the French, plus the fact that they had entered the Tagus before the departure of the Prince Regent and had committed no act of hostility against the Portuguese, all encouraged the granting of liberal terms.[40]

Initially the agreement signed was greeted with raised eyebrows at the Admiralty, where there seem to have been concerns that the agreement to restore the Russian vessels might form some sort of precedent for the future. It might be pointed out, however, that such worries had not influenced their instructions of 16 April. On 27 September Cotton acknowledged an Admiralty rebuke of the 17th which had complained that the terms he granted to Siniavin were too lenient and he may thereafter have felt some unease about his position. Six British ships of the line and a frigate under Rear-Admiral Tyler had left for Spithead as an escort for the Russians on 12 September and by the middle of November a rather woeful-sounding Cotton was wondering if he too should return home as he had received no orders from the Admiralty since Tyler's departure. Eventually he left Portugal in the *Hibernia* on 10 December, his fears for his future career proving groundless. By the time he reached Spithead in January the court of inquiry, set up to investigate the Convention of Cintra and appease the popular fury sparked by the agreement, had already reached its decision. All the opprobrium stimulated by its shortcomings had been heaped on the luckless Dalrymple and Burrard. Both Wellesley and Cotton, men with powerful political allies, escaped censure and were free for future employment, serious political damage also being avoided by those who drafted the orders that Cotton had followed so closely in his agreement with Siniavin.[41]

CHAPTER 2

The Spanish Revolt, 1808–9

'Wherever the people have put themselves in action, they
have proceeded to the end with a resolution and courage
which shew a determination to free their Country from its
invaders . . .'
Vice-Admiral Collingwood, 3 July 1808[1]

IN STRATEGIC TERMS the most crucial factor bearing upon
events in Portugal was the uprising in Spain. It was this that had
left Junot's corps isolated and exposed to attack. Naval power
had played a prominent role in bringing about Junot's eventual
defeat and although, initially at least, it did not have the same
impact on Spanish developments, nevertheless its influence
should not be ignored.

Whereas Napoleon had applied a mixture of bullying and
brute force in his efforts to control Portugal, his plans for Spain
were of a rather more subtle nature. In part this was prompted
by Spain's position in 1807 as a French ally, one that had for
years been providing massive financial aid for Napoleon's treasury and whose naval means had boosted France's own: of the
Combined Fleet's 33 ships of the line at Trafalgar in 1805,
almost half, some 15 in all, had been Spanish. However, Franco-
Spanish relations were not without their tensions. Napoleon
doubted the reliability of a kingdom whose royal family were
Bourbons and resented what he viewed as the limited support
his ally could be prevailed upon to provide. In Napoleonic eyes
Spain appeared a second-rate military power run by a feckless
and incompetent government, a nation crying out for a dose of
French reform. As the Bourbons had assumed the rule of Spain
in the eighteenth century, so might the Bonapartes in the early

nineteenth. The Emperor's assessment of his ally was undoubtedly true in many respects. Spain was in theory ruled by the ignorant King Charles IV: in reality the power was wielded by Queen Marie-Louisa's shifty lover Manuel de Godoy, the Prince of the Peace. Under Godoy's rule the endemic corruption of Spanish public life became more organised and more venal than ever, its society becoming increasingly fractured between the Court, with Godoy and his creatures on one side, and the remaining courtiers, nobility and populace on the other. Godoy's corruption extended to his being in French pay, but he was an auxiliary whom Napoleon, with reason, mistrusted. In October 1806, just as the French Emperor was launching his campaign against Prussia, Godoy, seemingly caught up in the general anticipation of a French defeat, issued a proclamation that sounded suspiciously like a call to arms against the French. The rapid Prussian collapse prompted Godoy into some equally speedy backpedalling, but an infuriated Napoleon had been given a clear insight into his ally's reliability. Attempting to appease this wrath, the Prince of the Peace quickly obeyed an imperial summons in March 1807 to send 15,000 of Spain's best troops northwards, to the Baltic coast, to help guard French communications during the concluding stages of Napoleon's successful campaign during the summer.

Once his eastern affairs had been settled at Tilsit, Napoleon, as stated in Chapter 1, began to increase the pressure on Portugal. If the military element of this, Junot's force, was to be allowed to go into action, it was evident that Spanish permission would be required to allow French troops to cross their territory. This was secured in October by the Treaty of Fontainebleau, a document that purported to divide Portugal between Godoy and Napoleon in return for permission for French regiments to cross Spain and for 16,000 Spanish troops to help garrison the occupied kingdom. In reality the agreement was more about Godoy allowing a further 40,000 French soldiers to be introduced into Spain in case Britain sent forces to aid Portugal and Junot required support. In the event these troops, and their number was to increase to over 100,000 men, were to be little more than a Trojan horse awaiting the time when Napoleon decided the moment was ripe to take over the whole country. This process finally began in February 1808 when the French took possession of a whole series of northern Spanish towns and fortresses: Pamplona, Barcelona, San Sebastian and Figueras were all seized and the Emperor's troops completely controlled the Pyrenean passes. By early May Charles IV and his heir, Prince Ferdinand, had been called to meet Napoleon at Bayonne and compelled to abdicate all their claims to the Spanish throne, the craven royal family, with Godoy in tow, being removed to exile in France. Joseph Bonaparte was declared King of Spain in their place, but now the smooth process of usurpation began to go wrong. Madrid had been occupied at the end of March but many Spaniards, xenophobic in general and specifically resentful of the atheistic and arrogant French who were so blatantly stealing their country, started to react. There were minor disturbances in the capital on 1 April that were put down, but these were followed by a much more serious outbreak on 2 May when rioting Spaniards surged through the streets slaughtering any isolated Frenchman they could find. This disorder was in turn brutally crushed by the French garrison and hundreds of civilians were killed. This was just the beginning. The news of the Bourbons' removal only fanned Spanish fury and by the end of May revolts were breaking out all over Spain. Francophile governors were murdered and provincial juntas established in Valencia, Seville and the Asturias, these sending out messages of defiance and starting to raise armies. By early June every province of Spain was arming and Napoleon had a full-scale war on his hands.[2] These shifting and confused events were naturally followed with the keenest interest by an assortment of British observers. In the early months of 1808 Spain remained the enemy she had been for the previous four years, though there was at first the highly alarming possibility of the current Spanish lethargy being replaced by Napoleonic vigour and plans were initially laid to try and limit the threat that a fully Napoleonic Spain might pose. To help maintain Gibraltar's security it was proposed in January that Ceuta should be seized, a capture that would also help guard the supplies drawn from North Africa by the squadrons off Lisbon and Cadiz. Expeditions were also readied in Britain for attacks on Spain's empire in the Americas, preparations that would eventually allow Wellesley's force to be quickly redeployed for Portugal instead. On 17 May Castlereagh, then Secretary of State for War, issued orders for the use of some of the troops stationed at Gibraltar for an attack on the six Spanish ships of the line stationed at Port Mahon, Collingwood being given the final say in the enterprise as the man on the spot. However, just a week later the momentous changes prompted by the Spanish insurrection finally began to have their impact on the Cabinet's military thinking. On the 25th Castlereagh informed Dalrymple, at that time governor of Gibraltar, that all attacks on Spain and her forces were to be stopped in the light of that nation's new hostility towards France. In a second despatch of the same day, copies of which were sent to Collingwood, Cotton and Rear-Admiral Purvis commanding the squadron off Cadiz, it was made clear that in future Spain was to be regarded as an ally, that co-operation with the Spaniards was now the order of the day, and that, with an eye to the possible future collapse of the present uprising, dissident Spaniards were if possible to be moved to their colonies where they might provide a barrier to the spread of French influence. Castlereagh also expressed profound concerns about the future security of Cadiz.[3]

Off that port the change in Spanish sentiments had already begun to have its effect. With Spain so obviously becoming more unsettled by the day, in the middle of May Dalrymple had sent Spencer with 2500 troops to join Purvis and be ready to take advantage of any opportunity that the commotion then gripping Cadiz might offer. Such thoughts were directed primarily towards the destruction of Vice-Admiral Rosily's French squadron, which had been sheltering in the port since Trafalgar, but at first these aspirations seemed overly optimistic. The two British commanders sent a proclamation into the city declaring that they were willing to support any insurrection, but the only response was the movement of all the warships in the harbour to more secure positions. To try and encourage the Spaniards, the transports carrying Spencer's troops were anchored closer to the inshore squadron: the conditions off Cadiz allowed the blockading warships to ride at anchor rather than face the exhausting routine of tacking back and forth as was required off ports like Brest and Toulon. However, Purvis observed on 29 May that the only desire among the Spaniards seemed to be one of placating the French and two days later Spencer's troops sailed back to Gibraltar, only to be immediately recalled when two representatives from the junta at Seville appeared and sought to discover what aid the British were willing to provide. Purvis pressed them to hand over Rosily's ships as a preliminary step, but this was refused as they were now regarded as legitimate Spanish prizes. On 2 June two British officers, one naval and one from the army, landed at Cadiz and returned with a paper requesting permission to send word of the revolt to the Americas, asking to be granted freedom from British attack, and in return promising that the French warships would be reduced once this had been agreed. The next day Purvis conferred with the senior naval and army officers present and returned a partial agreement. Spanish emissaries would be conveyed to Britain and news of the uprising would be sent to the colonies. Furthermore, British merchant vessels would be given access to Cadiz and the Spanish coasting trade would not be molested. However, the Spaniards were urged to neutralise Rosily's squadron immediately and were told that no British aid would be forthcoming as long as the French flag flew over the harbour. Morla, the Captain-General of Andalusia, replied agreeing to all of this, seeking help in dealing with the French ships and requesting British protection for some of the coastal harbours and in preventing the French forces in the Algarve from crossing the Guadiana to threaten Cadiz. Purvis reported on these developments on 6 June, his actions nicely anticipating the instructions that were being sent to him from London: two days previously Castlereagh had written telling the admiral that the destruction of Rosily's squadron was to be his first objective and that nothing should be left undone in pursuit of it. Castlereagh urged him to work closely with Dalrymple and to be prepared to send Spanish officers to the New World to spread anti-French propaganda. Rarely can subordinates have so well anticipated the wishes of their political masters in what was a very delicate and sensitive situation.[4]

Any thoughts that British forces would be allowed to enter Cadiz in the wake of Morla's concurrence were to be quickly dispelled, however. Although some of Spencer's troops, together with two ships of the line, a frigate and a sloop, were sent along the coast to Ayamonte on the Portuguese frontier to try and restrict any possible French movement, no enemy formations were encountered and Collingwood believed the whole process was just a blind on the Spaniards' part to keep the British occupied. After this, as noted in Chapter 1, Spencer and the troops that could be spared from Gibraltar were transferred to Portugal in the hope of more useful employment. Back at Cadiz on 10 June, having first sunk two ships in the channel above and below the luckless French squadron, the Spanish batteries opened up a heavy fire on Rosily's vessels, there also being plans to increase the fire by the creation of a massive battery of thirty 24-pounders firing red-shot shot. Purvis observed that the next day the French were flying a flag of truce, finally capitulating on the 14th after some vain efforts to secure more favourable terms. If the Royal Navy had played no direct part in these proceedings, at least the Admiralty could reflect with satisfaction on the fact that by the middle of June 1808 not only had the Spanish fleet changed sides, but that the French marine had lost the services of seven ships of the line: the same loss it had sustained, for example, at the Glorious First of June in 1794.[5]

While these events had been unfolding at Spain's chief naval arsenal, matters elsewhere were having a profound influence upon how the general conflict would develop. The French military position in the wake of the revolt in Madrid in May was that there were substantial forces around the capital and in the northern provinces guarding communications with France. Further troops were attempting to secure Catalonia, and Junot of course was becoming more and more isolated in Portugal. In an effort to crush the growing insurrection, Napoleon, misinformed as to the intensity of the revolt, despatched two powerful columns from the central mass. One, under General Dupont, marched south towards Cordova and Seville; the other, commanded by old Marshal Moncey, tried to restore control of Valencia and Cartagena. The first of these met with complete disaster, Dupont incompetently allowing himself to be surrounded by the Spaniards and surrendering his whole force at Baylen on 19 July. Almost 20,000 soldiers laid down their arms, a massive blow to Napoleon's prestige and to his position in Spain. By the terms of the capitulation these troops should have been shipped back to France in an arrangement similar to that to be agreed at Cintra the following month, though in the event Spanish popular fury would not have allowed such a step and their leaders hoped to use the British as an excuse to avoid honouring the deal. Collingwood reported back to the Admiralty that Morla had approached him – verbally – to make obstructive noises respecting any French repatriation and the Admiralty was quite willing to connive in such a process. Perhaps oddly, the ministers in London seemed to possess consciences of a more fragile kind, Castlereagh eventually telling Collingwood that passports would be granted for the return of Dupont's men but that Britain would, doubtless with the due pomposity of those retaining the moral high ground, protest to the Spaniards at the request. As it was, no Spanish official was prepared to risk life and limb by suggesting that the hated enemy should be released and the miserable prisoners were condemned to spend years of captivity in abominable conditions.[6] Alongside the destruction of Dupont's force, the French also suffered defeat when Moncey's advance on Valencia was rebuffed and he was obliged to retreat to Madrid around the time of the Baylen disaster. By early August 1808 the French were in full retreat from central Spain as well, Madrid being abandoned and, to the north, their first siege of Saragossa being lifted as the imperial forces withdrew behind the Ebro to await the arrival of reinforcements led by Napoleon himself.[7]

For the moment these developments ensured the security of Cadiz, though in the long term it was to remain a lingering concern. All those who had any serious say in the formulation of strategy in London were keen to see British troops providing a reliable backbone to the arsenal's garrison. Unfortunately the Spaniards were equally determined to resist such a step, even after the initial euphoria of the national revolt had subsided: given that Britain had spent much of the preceding 200 years at war with Spain and her empire this attitude was not altogether surprising. For the British it was much more directly a question of preserving the safety of Cadiz as long as possible and, as always much more to the point, making sure that the warships stationed there did not fall into French hands. In this respect the surrender of Rosily's squadron had not eased British fears as the warships were still at Cadiz, only now under a different flag. The port still, therefore, contained a maritime prize of immense worth if only Napoleon's armies could take it. Early in February 1809 a British frigate escorting eleven transports reached the port, these carrying three battalions under Major-General Mackenzie which, it was hoped, would help garrison the place. However, as with Spencer's troops the previous summer, the Spanish authorities would not allow them to land. Mackenzie was informed that he could disembark them at the nearby small harbour of Puerto de Santa Maria if he wished, but, not being allowed access to Cadiz itself, he kept them aboard the transports. The caution of Spanish officialdom may well have been wise as towards the end of the month there was considerable unrest in the city when a unit composed of foreigners – Poles, Swiss and others – was moved into it. Purvis wryly observed that the Spaniards would not permit British troops in Cadiz but did reinforce it with their own. The place seems to have been even more xenophobic than other parts of Spain and any disorder involving British troops and the locals could, no doubt, have done serious harm to Allied relations. At least the British squadron was being allowed to provide some seamen to help in the business of rigging the Spanish warships and to prepare them for sea. Two parties, 300 strong, were busily engaged in this laborious task and there was plenty for them to do. Of the eleven Spanish ships of the line in the port in early February, only three 74s, the *San Lorenzo*, *San Justo* and *San Raimond*, together with the 64-gun *San Leandro*, were ready for sea. The remainder were in a varying state of unpreparedness ranging from the *Santa Anna* (110), which was masted but not rigged, through to the *Conde de Regala* (100), which was still in dock and seemed to be rotten. By the following month, however, the Spaniards no longer seemed willing even to accept this aid, Admiral Alava, the port's naval commander, declining Purvis's offer of help with the pointed comment that the British might be required for 'other Services', *ie* away from Cadiz.

British nerves over the arsenal's security were not helped by the awareness that by early 1809 it contained some 15,000

French prisoners, a legacy of Baylen and Rosily's squadron. Some 3–4000 of these unfortunates were confined in hulks situated alarmingly close to the under-manned Spanish warships. Such worries only slowly began to be addressed. The Spaniards were prepared to accept help in moving some of the prisoners, the eventual transfer of 5000 of them to the Balearics in April seeing the 15 transports required being escorted by a single Spanish frigate and four British warships. At the same time, three Spanish ships of the line moved captive French sailors to the Canaries, Purvis providing three of his own ships of the line as escorts. Such movements, combined with the greater security enjoyed for the moment by Cadiz, reduced the scale of British naval force that was immediately required and, as well as the movements above, two other British ships of the line were sent to Cartagena to assist the Spanish warships there. By November 1809 Purvis had only his own flagship, the *Atlas* (74), and two smaller warships present.[8]

Beyond Cadiz the Royal Navy played no part in the main Spanish successes during the summer as the operations of Dupont and Moncey came nowhere near the coast. However, its influence was very profoundly felt in the other region where the French made strenuous efforts to assert their control: Catalonia. Geographically this was one of the more difficult provinces for Napoleon's soldiers to secure despite its proximity to France, its inland area being both mountainous and dissected by numerous rivers that had gouged out isolated valleys. In such terrain both regular and irregular units could constantly operate without being completely crushed however frequently they met with defeat. Only on the coastal plain could French authority hope to be more firmly established and yet it was here, along the 200 or so miles of Catalonian coastline, that naval power could have its impact. Alongside the terrain the French also faced another abiding strategic problem. At the end of February 1808 they had, by a ruse, bloodlessly seized the citadel of Barcelona, so gaining control of the second most populous place in Spain, a city of over 100,000 people, and the most important political and commercial spot in Catalonia. Without Barcelona no French claim to rule the region would be credible, and yet with it came the logistical nightmare of trying to feed its citizens and the substantial garrison required to hold it. The general uprising during the summer swept Catalonia with a fervour that fully matched the other parts of Spain. This put Duhesme, the local French commander, in an essentially isolated position with 12,000 troops in Barcelona surrounded by a hostile countryside, the small number of regular Spanish troops present in the province being boosted by the arrival of 5000 more brought, under British naval protection, from the Balaerics – a further 1200 from there also being sent to help defend the stubborn fortress of Saragossa. Particular problems for the French were the Spanish occupations of Gerona and Rosas, the first a small but very strong fortress astride the main road running from France to Barcelona, and the other a small fortified port situated on the coastal road that ran from France to the Catalonian capital. Gerona was beyond the reach of naval support, but nevertheless its intrinsic strength was sufficient to repel all French efforts at capture during July and August. This made control of Rosas and the coastal road all the more important and it was here that British ships could make their first impression.

In July General Reille, having assembled 3–4000 men in Perpignan, tried to take Rosas, which was then held by only 400 troops who had a mere five guns to defend the port's landward side. However, Reille was thwarted by a combination of guerrilla attacks on his landward flank and by the opportune arrival on the 22nd of a British frigate and sloop, these being joined the following day by the more powerful *Montagu* (74). The ships' appearance convinced him that he would be unable to take Rosas and he immediately started to withdraw to the French-controlled fortress of Figueras some ten miles to the west. Otway, captain of the *Montagu*, briefly landed his ship's marines to hold the port and free the Spaniards to harrass the French withdrawal. 'The Fortress of Rosas,' he considered, 'in its present ruined, and miserable state, is incapable of making much resistance, and I consider its chief protection a Man of War in the Bay.' He remarked on the Catalan loathing of the French but also upon their lack of leadership, arms and ammunition. The *Montagu* remained off Rosas for three weeks, supporting its retention by the Spaniards and, according to her log, providing some limited aid within her means in the shape of 20

47

barrels of powder for Rosas and 21 boxes of case shot for Gerona. Collingwood acknowledged in October that it was necessary to keep a warship permanently stationed in the bay there, he believing that Rosas would have fallen in July without naval support. Fortunately for the convenience of his naval dispositions, though, the spot was a good one for vessels to take on water and they could be relieved on a shuttle system once each was complete.[9]

While this primary coastal strongpoint was being defended, other warships were engaged in attacking the French along the coast from Barcelona northwards. Chief among these was the frigate *Imperieuse* (38) under the command of the dashing Lord

Cochrane. In the middle of June, after refitting his vessel at Gibraltar, he received orders from Collingwood to support the Spaniards by all the means in his power, an instruction that anticipated similar orders from the Admiralty to the fleet's commander that would not be issued for another three weeks. As the *Imperieuse* sailed along the coast she called in at the various harbours on her route, hoisting Spanish and British colours and being greeted with great enthusiasm. At Cartagena the ship was visited by a party of senior officers and Cochrane was invited ashore by the governor. Off Barcelona the frigate sailed just out of reach of the shore batteries and, still flying Spanish and British flags, fired a twenty-one gun salute, Cochrane observing that the streets were empty, save for French soldiers, but that the rooftops were covered with cheering Spaniards. Following these morale-boosting stunts, Cochrane then got down to serious business. Near Mataro he landed a party of marines and blew up the coast road at several points, then attacking two batteries of brass 24-pounders and, having driven off the gunners, seizing the pieces and taking them back to the ship. On 29 July *Imperieuse* was anchored off the castle of Mongat, ten miles up the coast from Barcelona, when some local guerrilla leaders came out in a boat to seek Cochrane's help in attacking the little fort. He agreed and during the night again landed his marines to blow holes in the road on either side of the castle, leaving it surrounded by 800 guerrillas and without hope of relief. On the 31st *Imperieuse* stood in close to Mongat and began to bombard the place, its garrison quickly seizing the opportunity to surrender to the British and avoid the clutches of the enraged Catalans. Cochrane took 71 prisoners and 80 muskets, handing the latter over to the guerrillas; the castle, after being thoroughly looted, was blown up. Not only was this a sharp local success that indicated the value of the guerrillas when provided with naval support, but the damage to the road would cause enormous problems for the French the following month. Attacked by a Spanish force, on 16 August the French attempt to take Gerona had, for the moment, to be abandoned. Some of the besiegers returned to France while Duhesme led the remainder back to Barcelona. With the coast road so effectively blocked and being under constant guerrilla attack, Duhesme eventually had to abandon his artillery and proceed to the city via some difficult mountain tracks. His exhausted and demoralised troops finally marched into Barcelona on 20 August, the first French attempt to subdue Catalonia having failed completely.[10]

Spearheaded by the *Imperieuse*, the coastal attacks continued in the wake of these successes. From the beginning of August to the middle of September Cochrane ravaged his way along the French coast just beyond the Spanish border. Signal posts were destroyed and batteries engaged, the guns from some of the latter being seized. On 7 September, now joined by the *Spartan* (38), the *Imperieuse* captured three small coasting feluccas off Sète; the next day a signal house and telegraph in Saintes Bay were attacked and destroyed along with two vessels sheltering under their protection. On 12 September two customs houses near Montpellier were blown up and on the following day six more coasting vessels were taken. The ports of Sète and Agde were bombarded and attacked with rockets, though to little evident effect. This mayhem caused disruption and fury among the French, damaging morale, dislocating the movement of supplies and obliging troops to be switched to coastal defence duties rather than service in Spain. Collingwood reported that 2000 troops had been transferred from Figueras to try and fend off such assaults.[11]

Duhesme's disorganised flight back to Barcelona in August marked a temporary delay in French operations while Napoleon, who now recognised that winning control of Catalonia was not going to be an easy task, ordered up reinforcements. By the end of October these had appeared and 25,000 troops were concentrated in the Perpignan-Figueras area under the able command of General St Cyr. His task, above all else, was to preserve Barcelona and, with Gerona still unlikely to fall without a long and tedious siege, he felt he must also clear the coastal road to the Catalan capital by capturing Rosas.

The town itself, a place of only about 1500 inhabitants, consisted of little more than a single street running along the shore, its length protected by nothing more than a ditch and an earthwork. At one end of these was a weak redoubt and on the other a citadel. The latter was the main defensive position, but had been damaged during a previous siege in 1794 and never properly repaired. A mile to the south-east of the town, on a rocky promontory that formed part of the bay, stood further protection in the shape of a detached work, Fort Trinity, that had been constructed to protect any shipping in the bay. Rosas' Spanish garrison numbered about 3500 men supported by 58 guns, against whom St Cyr directed half of his command. When the French appeared the naval vessels off Rosas consisted of the *Excellent* (74) and the bomb vessel *Meteor*, these immediately making their presence felt by bombarding the French as they took up positions around the town on 7 November. At the request of O'Daly, the Spanish commander, Captain West of the *Excellent* bolstered the defence by landing all of his marines as well as a naval officer and 50 seamen. These proved their worth the next day when West led a sortie to relieve a party of Spaniards who had sallied out of the fortress and become surrounded, he having the somewhat novel experience for a naval officer of having a horse shot out from under him during the sharp little action that followed. On the 9th further British support was provided when West learned that a breach had been made in the citadel, he positioning the *Meteor* to flank any assault on the gap and stationing two launches with carronades to cover the beaches. In the event no French assault materialised and the breach was repaired in three days, a British officer and 40 seamen being provided to help in the process. With constant heavy rain making life difficult for the besiegers, there was no further activity of note until 15 November, when 700 men tried to storm Fort Trinity. Its garrison of 80 Spaniards and 25 British marines beat this off with comparative ease and at some cost to the assailants, West nevertheless moving 30 more of his redcoats into the position as a reinforcement. Substantial French progress did not resume until their heavy siege artillery began to arrive from Perpignan on the 16th, they then forming batteries to hammer Trinity and the citadel. By that time the naval force had been reinforced as well with the appearance of the bomb vessel *Lucifer*, though her duel with the batteries bombarding Trinity had to be abandoned when the vessel was hit three times. On the north-western flank the defenders were more fortunate, heavy fire from both *Excellent* and the citadel silencing one battery when a lucky shot exploded its powder magazine. Overall, however, the French continued to make steady progress, opening more parallels and establishing more batteries which obliged the warships to retire from the shore. The bomb vessels, with their higher trajectories and consequently longer range, could still fire effectively, but by the time *Excellent* left Rosas on 21 November West was coming to the conclusion that, though Trinity might hold out, the citadel would soon fall.

West's replacement as the senior naval officer present was Captain Bennet of the *Fame* (74). This was to be a backward step for the defenders as Bennet showed himself to be a man of a dispirited and pessimistic disposition. His first suggestion was that the much-battered Fort Trinity be abandoned, he considering that in general the Catalans were 'inert and worse than useless'. A sortie by the garrison against the Puig-Rom, a hill near to Trinity upon which there were several French batteries, was defeated on 23 November, Bennet attributing the failure to the 'very dastardly conduct of the Spaniards'. The British lost a man killed and four others wounded in the attempt and Bennet's negative approach was made crystal-clear when he asked O'Daly to reinforce Trinity so that the British marines might be withdrawn! Fortunately for the Allied cause, at the same time that Bennet arrived so had Cochrane with the *Imperieuse*, he displaying a greater resilience both by overseeing the repair of Trinity's walls and putting heart back into its defenders. Bennet was grudgingly prevailed upon to hand over 50 barrels of powder to the Spaniards, though his request to O'Daly for their careful use was probably not appreciated. On the 26th the town itself was finally stormed by the French in the teeth of stubborn resistance, a heavy bombardment of the remaining buildings being inadequate to drive them out again. However, the citadel continued to be bravely defended, the warships landing over 200 newly-arrived reinforcements plus additional supplies of powder and provisions during the night of the 27th–28th. Despite this the defenders' prospects continued to look gloomy, worsening as the construction of more French batteries, now along the waterfront, rendered ship-to-shore contacts both difficult and dangerous. Efforts to evacuate the garrison's sick and wounded were thwarted when one of the boats was hit and an attempt to land a Spanish courier with despatches was also prevented, two British seamen being killed and Bennet complaining of the 'idleness and inaction of the Spaniards'. On 30 November another assault on Trinity was beaten off, largely through the efforts, according to Cochrane at least, of the 80 seamen and marines from the *Imperieuse* who had replaced those from the *Fame*. Both *Lucifer* and *Meteor* continued to provide supporting fire during these operations, but nothing could preserve the citadel from the relentlessly encroaching trenches. On 3 December O'Daly launched an attack on the trench lines but this was beaten off: next day the citadel surrendered. There was now no longer any point in prolonging Trinity's resistance and on 5 December Cochrane withdrew his men, the fort being blown up while their embarkation was covered by fire from all the warships in the bay, these having just been joined by the *Magnificent* (74).

Given the citadel's dilapidated condition and the power of the French force sent against it, the resistance maintained by Rosas reflects great credit on its defenders and provided the first illustration in the conflict of how vital naval support could prove in the defence of coastal strongpoints. Not only was St Cyr's attempt to clear the coast road to Barcelona held up for a month, but the strategic/pressure was maintained by continual attacks on the maritime supply route to the city. On 29 November Bennet seized an opportunity to send six of his boats to attack five French supply vessels in Cadagues Bay, just up the coast from Rosas. One of the enemy was captured, though the others had gone. There were other reports of 15 more such vessels assembling just across the Franco-Spanish border at Port Vendre, these being under escort and just awaiting the opportunity to slip down the coast. Evidently some of these had moved south, for on 30 November, when Bennet sent his boats back to Cadagues Bay, they took another five prizes.[12]

Following his success, St Cyr next set about relieving Barcelona, the city having been menaced on its landward side for some weeks by a force led by Vives, the Captain-General of Catalonia. The latter had done nothing to succour Rosas and had launched no assault on Barcelona either, but the city could never be secure with a force in excess of 20,000 men lurking outside it. Significantly, St Cyr decided not to try and use the coast road in his approach (such had been the damage inflicted by Cochrane that whole stretches had been destroyed), but instead felt compelled to march past Gerona, a manoeuvre obliging him to leave his artillery and baggage behind. The risk paid dividends when, having shuffled past the fortress, he advanced and routed Vives' command at Cardadeu on 16 December, Barcelona being relieved the next day. Throughout most of the following year the military situation in Catalonia would remain essentially the same. A large proportion of the available French forces would be tied down in the protracted siege of Gerona, its continuing resistance impeding their communications along the province's primary road. The remaining troops would be equally restricted by the need to prevent any Spanish relief of Gerona while simultaneously maintaining communications with Barcelona. Most of the province, particularly the central mountainous region, remained under Spanish control and, with Barcelona and Rosas occupied by the French, the chief port remaining under Allied control was now the fortress of Tarragona in Catalonia's south-east corner. Seaborne supplies and reinforcements could be brought in via that port while at the same time the British navy devoted much of their time to impeding French supplies being moved along the coast during 1809.

In the shape of the indefatigable Cochrane, this process had continued during the last weeks of 1808 when the *Imperieuse* had been warped into Cadagues and a convoy of eleven vessels carrying wheat for Barcelona had been seized, a battery also being destroyed while two escorting vessels were scuttled by their crews. Cochrane drove off the harbour's garrison with his frigate's guns and then proceeded to remain in the place for ten days, refloating and repairing the two scuttled vessels, an armed xebec and a cutter. The wheat he sold to the local Spaniards so as to provide an immediate distribution of prize money to his crew: this avoided the usual deduction of an agent's percentage, but came with an awareness on his part that the grain would be immediately sold back to the French![13] Against this sort of success, however, was the unpalatable fact that a complete interdiction of French coastal movements was impossible given the vagaries of weather, when ships could be blown off their stations for days at a time, and the necessity for vessels to leave period-ically for provisions, water and/or repairs.

During 1809 the best efforts were made to maintain the blockade of the coast and keep up the pressure that had been applied during the latter part of 1808, this duty chiefly falling on the senior officer present off Catalonia, Captain Mundy of the frigate *Hydra* (38). He was an experienced commander who had served with distinction off Cadiz and Catalonia in 1806–7 and his squadron to maintain the blockade usually consisted of another British frigate and two or three sloops, these on occa-sion being supported by a Spanish frigate. To judge from the *Hydra*'s log, Mundy was not a commander whose capacity for annoying the enemy was in the same league as Cochrane's, but he was certainly diligent. In April 1809, for example, *Hydra* and some of her consorts were constantly stationed directly off Barcelona, frequently at anchor off the city or near to it, weather permitting. Each evening, again depending on the weather, Mundy would send in one or more of the *Hydra*'s boats 'armed in shore' to try and prevent vessels slipping into the port during the hours of darkness. The boats, containing perhaps ten or a dozen seamen, remained on the shore patrol throughout the night and returned to the frigates early in the morning. During that month only one merchant vessel was intercepted and burned, and such a close watch would strongly suggest that, with days of calm weather, little in the way of provisions were reaching the city by sea.

With their supplies running low, the French were finally pro-voked into a more desperate action and on the afternoon of 26 April *Hydra*'s lookouts spotted a large enemy force comprising five ships of the line, two frigates and a corvette escorting a convoy of 16 merchant vessels. These had managed to slip out of Toulon unobserved by any of Collingwood's warships and there is some suspicion that he was remiss in not anticipating such a step. The first the admiral knew of the operation was on the 29th when, with the main body of his fleet watering at Port Mahon, he learned of the resupplying of the Catalan capital. The French, fully aware of the risks they were running, stayed only a mere 18 hours in Barcelona while the precious cargoes of corn and flour were unloaded, and then headed back to Toulon under all sail. Collingwood managed to intercept a couple of stragglers from the convoy, but the bulk of the French force returned home safely. This was a galling defeat experienced at a moment when Barcelona was starting to feel the pinch of starvation and when St Cyr had been obliged to move the bulk of his forces stationed to cover the city away from its environs in order to try and spare its supplies. The *Hydra* and the other small warships had fled northwards to a position off Blanes when the French force appeared and quickly reimposed the blockade, but it would be months before it would start to bite once again.[14]

Stung by his failure in April, Collingwood was much more alive to the possibility of a repeat French performance in the autumn of 1809 as Barcelona's supply situation again started to reach a critical level. In October the admiral abandoned his usual blockade position off Toulon and moved to a station between Cape St Sebastian and Minorca, directly on any likely route to Barcelona, in the belief that another resupply mission was likely. Two frigates were left to observe Toulon and on 21 October one of these sighted a squadron of three ships of the line – *Robuste* (80), *Borée* (74) and *Lion* (74) – and two frigates escorting a convoy of 20 other vessels, all of them heading to sea: as in the previous April the French were commanded by Rear-Admiral Baudin. Collingwood was informed the next day that the French were out and, assuming that they were heading for Catalonia, he set about their interception. This was achieved on 23 October, Baudin, realising that he could not fight the whole Mediterranean Fleet, instantly abandoning the convoy, which was left to steer in confusion to the north-north-west. The French warships hastened off to the east-north-east, hotly pursued by Rear-Admiral Martin at the head of the eight fastest sailing ships of the line in the British fleet. Two of Martin's warships parted company during the night, but with the remaining six – *Canopus* (80), *Renown* (74), *Tigre* (74), *Sultan* (74), *Leviathan* (74) and *Cumberland* (74) – Martin sailed northwards, guessing that Baudin would be intent on reaching the sanctuary of his home port. The assessment proved correct, four of the French vessels being spotted to the north-north-east early on the morning of the 24th (one of the French frigates had sailed independently for Marseilles). Martin crowded on all sail in an effort to come up with the enemy but was unable to do so before nightfall, the pursuit then having to slacken off near the mouth of the Rhône because of the proximity of what was a lee shore. Next day, the 25th, the enemy was again sighted, now creeping along the coast in a final effort to escape. Martin once more crowded on sail and tried to engage, but the *Robuste* and *Lion* avoided battle by running themselves ashore at a point about six miles north-east of Sète. The *Borée* and the remaining frigate, though pressed, managed to find shelter in Sète's little harbour, they later making their way back to Toulon. During the evening of 26 October the French set the two grounded ships on fire and both blew up.

Meanwhile the abandoned convoy had headed directly for the coast of Catalonia, five of its number being snapped up by the *Pomone* (38), one of Collingwood's observing frigates. Eleven others, consisting of seven merchantmen and four armed vessels, sought shelter in Rosas Bay under the guns of Fort Trinity and the batteries there. Once the pursuit of the French warships had been completed by Martin, Collingwood turned his attention to these vessels. Having first sent a frigate to reconnoitre the enemy's position on 29 October, the following day he appointed the experienced and aggressive Captain Hallowell to lead a detached force to attack it. As well as his own vessel, the *Tigre*, Hallowell also had the services of the *Cumberland* along with three frigates and three sloops, although heavy weather delayed the eventual assault until the evening of 31 October/1 November. Anchoring the five larger warships some five miles from the bay, Hallowell sent in their boats, armed and manned, and accompanied by the sloops to deliver the attack, an event the French had anticipated and resisted with determination: their vessels had twice the numbers defending them than the British had expected, had boarding nettings rigged to hinder the attackers, and were supported by constant fire from the shore batteries. By daylight seven of the convoy, including a 600-ton storeship armed with 16 guns, had been burned and the remaining four had been captured. However, the attackers paid a heavy price for this success, losing 15 dead and another 50 wounded, French losses probably being heavier still.[15] This was a major victory in the battle to keep Barcelona hamstrung for provisions, but the scale of force required to destroy the convoy in Rosas Bay and the losses suffered in the action were indicative of the sort of problems that could be encountered as the French sought to make their coastal movements more secure. All along the Mediterranean coast there were anchorages some nine to twenty-one miles apart. These were guarded by strong batteries, giving a high level of protection to any vessel seeking shelter. On all the hills along the coast there were telegraph posts that passed on information to the convoys about what enemy warships were in the area, when they had been sighted, details of their course, and so on. If it was safe to do so, the convoy would sail: if not, it could wait. They did not sail at night, in foggy weather or if the wind was fresh. In short, they would stay put if there was any discernible risk. Writing in November 1809, Collingwood considered that the only time to attack such convoys was at night, which had been managed with some success, but, even when a covering fort was destroyed, one twice as strong to replace it would be built in a short time. 'Their Commerce is retarded, and Convoys sometimes stopped from one to three weeks, but an opportunity will at last open to them, and they wait it patiently.'[16] The days when a single warship like the *Imperieuse* could cause mayhem along a comparatively unprotected coastline had gone, and, as will be illustrated in a later chapter, assaulting convoys when they were sheltering in protected anchorages could be a bloody business.

Shortly after the action in Rosas Bay, the situation in Catalonia underwent a profound strategic change with the capitulation, on 11 December, of Gerona. Not merely did this free thousands of French troops for service elsewhere in the province, but it opened the possibility of supplying Barcelona overland via the main central road from France. In future the Royal Navy would find it even harder to undermine the French logistical arrangements, both from improving coastal defences and the overland alternative, and would be called upon to provide much more extensive support for the Catalans as the French assault on them began inexorably to gather momentum.

*   *   *

Off Spain's northern coast the initial Admiralty reaction to the French takeover of the country was to issue instructions on 10 May 1808 to Admiral Gambier, commanding the Channel Fleet, to station a squadron of warships off the naval arsenal of Ferrol equal in force to the vessels there. Interestingly, the ships in Ferrol were all Spanish and it was the prospect of a dose of Napoleonic vigour being applied to them in the shape of overt French control that prompted the view that the port needed watching. Accordingly Gambier sent two of his ships of the line, the *Defence* and *Gibraltar* (80), to assure the blockade, a step approved by his masters in London.[17] Very rapidly, though, such defensive precautions began to be overtaken by events as the threat of a Bonapartist Spain turned into a revolt that offered the chance of seriously damaging Napoleonic power. On 12 June George Canning, the Foreign Secretary, was writing to the Asturian deputies sent to seek British help to assure them that everything possible would be done to support their cause, military supplies being dispatched to Gijon and warships moved to stations off the coast to prevent French sea-borne landings. The following day Gambier was told to ensure that two frigates that had been appointed to cruise between Bayonne and Cape Peñas to intercept any French supply movements also did all they reasonably could to aid the insurgents. Furthermore, no Spanish vessels sailing between ports that appeared to be hostile to the French were to be molested. On 14 June, perhaps urged on by Canning's keenness to take advantage of Peninsular developments, the Admiralty ordered that another frigate as well as an armed lugger be sent to the northern coast, telling Gambier to add as many of his own command's frigates and cruisers 'as can be spared'. By the time he received this instruction on the 21st Gambier was recording that there were three frigates and a sloop off that coast, with another three frigates and a lugger on their way; two ships of the line and frigate were watching Ferrol; and two other frigates were cruising off Cape Finisterre. Such a substantial force required the overseeing presence of a flag officer, a position that was filled the following month when Rear-Admiral De Courcy, one of the junior Channel Fleet admirals, was sent to Corunna in the *Tonnant* (80) with instructions to take command off northern Spain. The *Tonnant* would replace the *Gibraltar* and all British officers were told to be 'respectful, friendly, & conciliating' in their dealings with the Spaniards.[18]

In northern Spain the midsummer months of 1808 were to be as confusing and uncertain as they were in the rest of the country, the chaos generated by the uprising prompting rumour and doubt about exactly what was happening and where. Under these circumstances Captain Atkins of the *Seine* (32), at that moment the senior officer present on the coast, anchored in the Bay of Santander on 20 June and was the first to inform some Spanish officers who came aboard of the altered state of Anglo-Spanish relations, news they were delighted to hear. Atkins reported that there were 20,000 men in the area ready to fight but that a quarter of them lacked arms; they were also short of ammunition and money. Within a week of his visit Santander was seized by the French, though not before parties from the *Cossack* (22) and *Comet* (18) had been landed and, with the locals' co-operation, spiked all the guns in two of the forts defending the port as well as blowing up a magazine containing 500 barrels of gunpowder. With the uprising spreading rapidly, the occupation of Santander was destined to be very brief, the French evacuating the place in the middle of July, and the British being able to give their allies a boost on the 17th when the *Unicorn* (32) took a French-controlled Spanish schooner off San Sebastian. This was a valuable prize as she carried a cargo of 3000 muskets, which Atkins immediately had distributed among the rebels.[19]

Although the French had scattered the armies of Castile and Galicia at Medina de Rio Seco on 14 July, their overall strategic position was completely undone by the disaster at Baylen and the retreat from Valencia. These defeats forced an evacuation of Madrid on 1 August and a general retirement behind the Ebro whilst awaiting the arrival of reinforcements from France, their general position rendered all the more gloomy by their setbacks in Catalonia and their failure to take Saragossa. While the Spanish forces slowly moved north in the French wake, the Biscayan provinces also seized the opportunity to revolt (6 August), though this was to prove premature as no help from the other provinces was forthcoming and the French still maintained powerful forces in the region. The only support that could be offered to the new rebels came from the British cruisers off Bilbao. On 14 August, informed that the enemy was approaching the city and that its inhabitants were desperate for arms, the three warships in the vicinity – *Iris* (36), *Unicorn* and *Cossack* – between them managed to muster some 150 muskets. Aware that Francophile elements were spreading anti-British propaganda, Captain Tower of the *Iris* resolved to land with the arms himself in an effort to counter any ill-impression. On the 15th the frigate could not cross the bar at the mouth of the river Nervion upon which Bilbao stands and so Tower was obliged to travel the ten miles up river by ship's boat, another following behind with the muskets. He observed that the road leading from Bilbao was choked with fleeing refugees, one retreating Spanish regiment telling him that the city had already fallen. This was not true and Tower pressed on, being warmly received despite the small number of arms he was able to offer. Bilbao actually fell the next day, Tower then having to go by land to Santander to rejoin his ship: the boats were unable to return across the bar in the teeth of a strong north-west wind. Just as the city fell the *Seine* appeared escorting a transport loaded with more arms and ammunition, the two vessels narrowly avoiding capture.[20]

The problem of finding secure harbours to land supplies destined for the Spaniards was to plague British captains throughout the Peninsular War, the difficulty being particularly acute at a time of such military fluidity as pertained in northern Spain during the late summer/early autumn of 1808. It was self-evidently desirable to land any stores as close as possible to the units that were to use them, but that also often meant in close proximity to the fighting with a consequent hazard to the shipping. Bilbao itself graphically illustrates the point: occupied by the French on 16 August, it was briefly liberated by the Spaniards towards the end of September before being lost once more; then continuing Spanish advances in the Biscay province obliged the French to evacuate it once again on 11 October. Finally, Napoleon's general counteroffensive hustled the Spaniards out of the city at the end of October, leaving it under the occupation it was to endure for many years. Nor was this sort of uncertainty about events on land the only problem for naval officers, for as summer turned into autumn the weather in the Bay of Biscay became more malevolent, further affecting the scale of naval support that could be provided. Atkins learned that Bilbao had been evacuated by the French on 21 September and appeared the following day with the *Seine* and *Cossack* in the hope of being able to land arms, ammunition and money. Such was the weather that no arms at all could be got ashore until the 26th and then only a small number. By then he learned that the French were returning and decided to employ some Spanish coasting vessels to move the remainder to Santona, much farther to the west but at least out of any immediate danger. The next day Bilbao was captured again, but Atkins could at least reflect that most of the local coasting craft had been moved to safety. He picked up a Spanish commissary on 28 September and took him to Santander, though once again the weather intervened and the Spaniard was unable to be landed until 3 October. Then the *Seine* sprang a leak and had to return home, the gales also damaging the *Unicorn* and obliging her too to return to England for repairs while the *Iris* also had to depart to be revictualled and refitted.[21]

These gales prompted Gambier to remind the Admiralty that the northern coast was extremely dangerous during the autumn months because of the combination of foul weather and no accessible harbours. He wondered if square-rigged vessels like frigates ought to continue serving there, particularly as in his opinion the Navy could do little to help the Spaniards in the region. Initially the Admiralty concurred and issued orders on 18 October that no frigates should in future be stationed to the east of Cape Machichaco. Even before this was issued, though, Captain Digby of the *Cossack* was writing to Gambier from Santander that General Blake, commanding the Spanish troops in the Bilbao area, had requested a naval diversion along the coast between San Sebastian and St Jean de Luz. Digby considered that any such operation should be confined to the smaller, more manoeuvrable craft such as luggers or cutters, an opinion he shared with Captain Tower. For the moment any such thoughts were academic due to the incessant north-westerly gales that continued to lash the coast: *Cossack* left Santander on

13 November with a convoy of transports for Corunna but the journey, of only some 250 miles, took no less than twelve days and then she did not arrive with all her charges still present. Nevertheless, with the fighting in northern Spain becoming ever more intense, it was becoming evident that, whatever the risks, naval support could not be withdrawn without the danger of appearing to desert the Spaniards in their hour of need.

By 1 December the Admiralty was worried that Napoleon's troops might try to move provisions and military stores along the coast beyond Bayonne, perhaps to Bilbao or some small harbour nearby. In the light of this, their instruction of 18 October was suspended and Gambier told to station a suitable squadron of frigates and small warships to prevent any such movement. They also wanted Bilbao to be strictly blockaded. Gambier duly moved the sloop *Foxhound* (18) and brig *Attack* (14) to that section of the coast, planning also to send the brig *Conflict* (12) and, when she had completed her refit, the *Iris*.[22]

Under all these circumstances, the impact of naval power on the land campaigns was inevitably limited, for all the enterprise displayed by the captains concerned. In one respect, however, the Royal Navy was able to make a substantial contribution to the effectiveness of Spanish resistance and this came in the shape of the troops from the Baltic. As noted earlier in this chapter, Godoy had been prevailed upon to send 15,000 of Spain's best soldiers to northern Germany in the spring of 1807. For Napoleon the transfer both strengthened his line of communication along the North Sea coast while he campaigned in Poland, while simultaneously removing a potential source of resistance to his future plans for the Peninsula. By the spring of 1808 these troops had not been returned home and remained scattered in small groups around Jutland and the Danish islands, the whole in theory being under the command of the Marquis de la Romana. For many weeks they were kept in a state of ignorance about Napoleon's machinations in Spain and not until 24 June did they learn of the replacement of the Bourbons by Joseph Bonaparte. The British government knew of their presence in northern Europe and was also aware, in the light of the general revolt in the Peninsula, that their loyalty to Napoleon might be suspect. In a plot-line worthy of a novel, a

Scottish Catholic priest named Robertson, a man who had lived in central Europe before being expelled by the French, was sent as a secret agent to sound out Romana. The latter, a friend as it happened of the Asturian deputies who had gone to Britain seeking help, was eager to escape from French control and join the uprising. Experiencing some difficulty and personal danger, Robertson successfully managed to get in touch with Romana and passed word on to Rear-Admiral Keats, commanding the British squadron off the Danish coast and islands, that the Spaniards wanted to change sides and return home. By the end of July, ignorant of their officers' intentions, the Spanish rank-and-file were becoming increasingly restive, a state of mind the French too were beginning to notice. Marshal Bernadotte, the area commander, tried to make the Spaniards swear an oath of loyalty to King Joseph and in so doing sparked off a mutiny in two of the regiments which Danish troops had to quell. This gave a clear warning of future trouble and Romana had to move quickly before reinforcements appeared and the whole of his command was disarmed and imprisoned. Fortunately, as these events were occurring, a Spanish envoy appeared in the Baltic, sent from London to co-ordinate arrangements between Romana and Keats for the troops' evacuation. On 7 August the Spaniards on the island of Fyn revolted and captured the port of Myborg; the surprised Danish garrison put up no resistance but a brig and cutter in the harbour refused to surrender and had to be stormed by men from the *Edgar* (74) and *Superb* (74), one British officer being killed and two men wounded. Next day the Spanish forces in Jutland also rose, most of them taking a number of fishing vessels and, under the escort of the brig *Snipe* (4), transporting themselves across the water to join their compatriots on Fyn. There Keats and Romana had concluded that Myborg could not be rendered sufficiently secure and that all the troops would be safer if moved to the small island of Langland. Local fishing boats were seized and parties from all the British warships landed to fit them out as ferries: at this point Keats was, for the sake of mobility, flying his flag from the sloop *Hound* (12). During 9–11 August all the Spaniards were carried across to Langland, a few other escapees from the mainland joining the main body over the following days. By 27

August the whole force, numbering 9000 men, had been further moved to secure Allied territory in Gothenburg, Sweden. Back in London the preceding day had witnessed a flurry of orders from the Admiralty instructing that 42 transports and store-ships be moved from the Downs, Portsmouth, Deptford and Harwich to Yarmouth. They were all, once assembled, to sail under the sloop *Racoon* (16) to the Great Belt to collect Romana's troops and take them back to Spain. *Racoon* and two other escorting sloops shepherded the convoy out of Yarmouth on 31 August, reaching Gothenburg six days later. There the vessels remained, embarking the Spaniards and helping to victual the transports, until 13 September when the whole, now comprising 54 transports and four escorting warships, set sail for the voyage south. This proceeded more or less without inci-dent until the end of the month when the convoy, deep in the Bay of Biscay, was struck by a two-day gale and scattered. At one point *Racoon* had only nine transports in company, though the number had risen to 22 by 8 October when she put into Santander, crowning an unpleasant few days by running aground as she entered the harbour. Fortunately the remainder of the transports also survived the storm, making their way either to Santander or Santona in the course of the following week. None of the troops had been lost in transit and they were immediately supplied with British arms upon their arrival. Thanks to this singular example of naval power in action, the Allied cause had been strengthened by 9000 troops just before Napoleon was about to launch his counterstroke in November.[23]

In circumstances that were rather less dramatic, the early autumn of 1808 also saw the scale of Britain's land commitment to the Spaniards being increased. Following the recall of the officers responsible for the Convention of Cintra, command of the British army in Portugal had fallen upon Sir John Moore. With the French across the border in Spain in full retreat, the Cabinet had decided to commit a force of about 35,000 men to aid the Spaniards in the complete expulsion of the enemy from their country. Having left a garrison of about 10,000 troops in Portugal, Moore set out with some 20,000 men for Salamanca in the middle of October. The Cabinet intended to reinforce his command with further units sent out from Britain, these landing in the first instance at Corunna and then marching to join Moore's force and so forming a 35,000-strong army. The first section of this reinforcement, comprising 12,691 rank-and-file, was assembled at Falmouth from troops moved from Ireland and southern England. Loaded into upwards of 200 transports and under the escort of the frigate *Endymion* (40), the force sailed in September and reached Corunna on 14 October, immediately running foul of a severe case of Spanish xenophobia when the Galician Junta refused to let them land. Writing from Corunna ten days later, De Courcy lamented that:

> Considerable difficulties have for a long time obstructed the landing of the British Troops at this place, and, were a judgement to be formed from appearances, it might be said that they scarcely seem acceptable to the Spanish Nation.

It was Cadiz all over again, British resentment being fuelled when the force commander, Major-General Baird, heard that a 1500-strong Spanish force marching from Oporto to Burgos had been turned about and marched back with all speed to the previously undefended Ferrol. The local authorities were prepared to let the troops ashore in small parties, but such a parsimonious attitude was rejected and not until the 25th was the question finally settled when a courier arrived from Madrid bearing expressions of belated goodwill from the Central Junta and permission for the troops to land. This was just as well as De Courcy already believed that the disembarkation would take a fortnight and Baird's command was increased yet further during the first two weeks of November by the arrival of another 5414 troops, these coming primarily from southern England.[24]

With Baird's force thus delayed in its landing, and then additionally frustrated by a lamentable shortage of logistical support in Galicia, it was to be some time before it could begin to advance towards the planned link-up with Moore. Even when Baird did finally get on the move, progress along the wretched roads, made worse by the deteriorating weather, was very slow: when he reached Astorga on 22 November Moore was still over a hundred miles away at Salamanca. What was much worse was that by then the forward Spanish armies had suffered a crushing series of defeats by the reinforced French, now led by

66

Napoleon in person. On 11 November Blake's army had been routed at Espinosa and sent reeling back towards Reynosa; the day before a smaller Spanish force had been all but destroyed at the battle of Gamonal and the French were pouring back into Spain. On 23 November the principal remaining force, Castaños' 'Army of the Centre', was scattered at Tudela and only narrowly avoided encirclement. By 4 December the French were back in Madrid and the Spanish armies Moore was advancing to support were shattered, retreating remnants. In this predicament, Moore first considered retiring back to Portugal, but, receiving an – entirely false – report that Madrid was determined to resist any occupation and that Romana was busily rallying the forces beaten at Espinosa, he decided instead to advance and strike at Napoleon's lines of communication with Burgos. Moore hoped to force a withdrawal from Madrid and his plan seemed all the more feasible when a captured despatch suggested that some of the French formations in the vicinity of Burgos were scattered and vulnerable. The whole scheme was a gamble. Indeed, as one author has observed, it was potentially lethal as the French in Spain were three times as numerous as Moore believed them to be. As the British moved northwards Napoleon quickly appreciated what Moore was about and set off to fall upon his rear with 80,000 men. Moore's and Baird's commands had finally united to form one army on 19 December and five days later, just as he was preparing to assault the French northern forces, Moore learned of the danger that was materialising behind him from the south. He immediately turned in retreat towards the one remaining direction of safety: to the west, to the coast, and to the Royal Navy.[25]

While these dramatic events had been unfolding De Courcy had remained at Corunna to oversee naval operations off the northern coast. With a prescience that did them credit, the Admiralty seems to have regarded it as important to maintain an uninterrupted command structure in the area, presumably with the thought of facilitating any naval support that circumstances might require. Certainly when Gambier wanted to move De Courcy and the *Tonnant* to either L'Orient or Rochefort, so as to relieve the blockading warships there more regularly, the Admiralty turned down the request. As events on land began to take on a more ugly appearance, the possibility that the army might have to be evacuated took shape, though the port from which the troops would be lifted had not been settled. Corunna was an obvious possibility, but by the end of November French advances in the north of Spain seemed to make a British retreat to the south, to Vigo, more likely. De Courcy had the latter place examined at the end of November with this possibility in mind and following representations from Baird he decided to move the transports at Corunna to Vigo in preparation. Overall the admiral preferred the prospect of an embarkation at Corunna, provided its guarding batteries could first be destroyed as a security measure, despite its being crowded with shipping and its vulnerability to being sealed for days at a time by adverse winds. He was worried, though, by both the shortage of available transport tonnage and the smallness of his own command: at that moment, on 25 November, this consisted of his flagship and three frigates. [26]

By 1 December his situation, which he believed to be rather exposed, had improved somewhat. For one thing, he had learned that Moore and Baird were going to unite their commands, a concentration that could only help the deteriorating military position. He had also good news in the shape of the *Minerva* (32), which had escaped from Santander, occupied by the French on 16 November, with 237,000 dollars sent out to fund Spanish resistance. What with other monies returned by British warships, the *Tonnant* had become something of a floating treasury, having aboard her 107 casks each containing 5000 dollars. Finally he could also record the steady transfer of the transports to Vigo, *Endymion* having departed Corunna with 62 of them on 26 November, *Cossack* leaving with a further 42 on the 27th, and *Minerva* escorting 41 on the voyage south on the 28th. A final body of 32 would also soon sail under the wing of the *Champion* (24), leaving only 26 remaining at Corunna, along with the *Tonnant* and *Unicorn*, to move the sick and the ordnance stores. That additional naval resources might be urgently required off north-western Spain was by then also prompting the Admiralty to send substantial reinforcements to Vigo: on 2 December *Alfred* and *Jupiter* (50) were sent, to be followed six days later by *Victory* (100), *Ville de Paris* (110),

Barfleur (98), *Implacable* (74), *Plantagenet* (74), *Resolution* (74), *Audacious* (74), *Mediator* (32) and *Hindostan*. With these vessels went instructions that made it clear that the primary worry at the Admiralty was that the French Brest fleet might escape and fall upon the assembled transports at Vigo. De Courcy was to employ these reinforcements to prevent such a disaster and was, if he heard that the Brest fleet was at sea and had sailed south, to send some of them in pursuit, but only in such numbers as to ensure the transports' safety. This was a continuation of the strategy observed previously when strong reinforcements were sent to Cotton off the Tagus: such warships had on-the-spot duties but were also regarded as a permanent reserve to counter any French naval moves. Although doubtless welcoming such a strengthening of his command, they did make De Courcy's situation more awkward in one respect as his instructions assumed that he had moved his flag to Vigo as well. This he had neither done nor wished to do for fear of making the Spaniards feel deserted. His reluctance was appreciated in London and he was allowed to remain *in situ*, the command at Vigo being vested in Rear-Admiral Hood, he arriving the middle of December with yet more reinforcements, his own flagship the *Zealous* (74) and the *Norge* (74).[27]

The big question for the naval officers still remained to be answered: from where would they be required to conduct the pending evacuation? During the latter part of December and during the first days of January Moore's army retreated westwards through increasingly severe winter weather, conditions that only worsened as the troops climbed into the Cantabrian mountains, the cold becoming acute, the commissariat collapsing and much of the army degenerating into a rabble. Although the 3500 men of the two light brigades were sent off towards Vigo, Moore did not decide until 5 January where the main point of embarkation was going to be. On that day he received a report from Colonel Fletcher, his chief engineer officer, that opted for Corunna, chiefly on the grounds that Vigo did not offer positions from which the boarding could be covered.[28] Having made up his mind, Moore sent an aide to gallop to the leading units to tell them, on reaching Lugo, not to march for Vigo as their orders had previously instructed, but to head instead for Corunna. The aide delivered the message to Baird, but the general entrusted its further transmission to a dragoon who proceeded to get drunk and lose the despatch. In consequence, not only did part of the army make a completely needless march along the road towards Vigo before it was recalled, but, potentially much more serious, word of where the evacuation was to occur was delayed from reaching the naval commanders. While the army headed for Corunna, the transports remained at Vigo.[29]

Not until 9 January did word finally reach Hood, via an exhausted courier, that the transports would have to be moved. Hood, a member of an extremely distinguished naval family, had an agreeable and gentle manner that concealed a character of steely determination and resilience. Now he did not dither and immediately issued orders for the fleet to weigh, despite the fact that the wind was blowing directly into the bay and so hard that not a transport could move. The warships, however, were working their way out to sea in less than half an hour and, once round the point, speeded north to Corunna to announce that the transports were to follow. It would be another 48 hours, though, before the gale subsided sufficiently for the transports themselves to sail, hustled and harried by the *Endymion* as their escort. Remaining behind at Vigo were the *Alfred* and *Hindostan*, together with sufficient transport tonnage to gather up the two light brigades: Hood, who had remained at Vigo, wrote on the 13th that 4000 troops had embarked there and that it was thought a further 300 stragglers would appear over the next couple of days, together with £100,000 in gold and its 200-strong escort. These were all eventually lifted without undue difficulty.

The bulk of Moore's army, 'harassed and fatigued' according to De Courcy, finally reached Corunna on 11 January and began an anxious wait for the transports. As they did so, their almost equally exhausted French pursuers, now led by Marshal Soult as Napoleon had returned to Paris, closed in. Excepting those cannon in the town itself, De Courcy had already had the guns and their carriages in all the batteries around Corunna spiked and thrown over the cliffs. Similar treatment had been handed out to other batteries on the western shore of Betanzos Bay. He had shrewdly calculated that the French, having been obliged to advance through mountainous terrain in the middle of winter, would be unlikely to have any heavy artillery with them, but feared that any such shortage might be quickly rectified. Also destroyed, and a great deal more dramatically, was a huge store of gunpowder that was blown up on the 13th: the artillery officer responsible exploded a building containing some 1500 barrels, not realising that next door to it stood another magazine containing thousands more. The enormous double explosion shattered every pane of glass in the town and caused two menacing black palls of smoke to rise over the harbour. Several people were killed by falling debris. On 14 January, to the immense relief of everyone, *Endymion* and her convoy of transports arrived, though on the same day the French also appeared and it was immediately apparent that the evacuation would have to be managed in the presence of the enemy.[30]

The French were in no fit state to attack at once and Soult elected to pause while his men recovered and many stragglers could rejoin their units. This gave Moore the chance to embark part of his army and during the 14th and 15th all of the cavalry – but only some of their horses – as well as most of the artillerymen, 52 of their pieces and all of the sick and injured were taken on board. Some of the infantry were also embarked, Moore leaving the bulk of them, some 15,000 men with nine pieces of artillery, to hold the high ground immediately to the east of the port. This part of the withdrawal proceeded very smoothly. Prior to its commencement the army officers had been issued with tickets specifying the name and number of the transport their men were to board and even those units that were to embark at night were able to march without any delay straight to the harbour, there to board the barges and launches of the warships and the flat-bottomed boats of the transports drawn up in readiness to receive them. The careful Hood, whose responsibility it was to oversee the arrangements, had even issued orders for all the houses leading down to the harbour to be illuminated so that their light would shine on to the streets. The worst feature was the fleet's inability to carry off more than a handful of the army's horses and draught animals. More than 7000 of these wretched creatures were stabbed or flung into the sea amidst scenes of the greatest distress. By the early afternoon of the 16th Moore was coming to the view that he might not be attacked when finally the French assault began. After severe fighting the French attack on the British centre, the primary point of Soult's effort, was beaten off, other manoeuvres against the right flank amounting to little more than skirmishing. By nightfall the French efforts to pin the British down had petered out in failure, though Moore himself had been mortally wounded in the fighting and Baird severely. All told, the British suffered about 800 casualties and the French perhaps 1400. Most important of all, though, the evacuation could proceed largely unhindered.[31]

Through the night the remainder of the infantry were slowly withdrawn to the waiting ships, a rearguard staying behind to keep camp fires burning on the hills around Corunna to try and deceive the enemy. How far the French can have been surprised at daybreak to discover that most of the British had gone may be wondered at, though there still remained about 2600 troops in the port itself. The French tried to close with this rearguard but were held off by the fire of guns situated on the walls on the neck of the isthmus where Corunna stands. More troublesome were the French batteries now placed on the hills across from the harbour to the east. They began a long-range bombardment of the shipping, which did little material damage but prompted a panic among the civilian transports and there was a desperate attempt to weigh anchor and escape. One observing army officer scathingly wrote that they 'acted with a degree of idiotic disobedience not unusual nor incompatible with the character of the masters of transports'. Because of the enemy fire, however, it was thought to be no longer practicable to continue the evacuation through the town and it was planned to maintain it via a sandy beach near the lighthouse at the head of the isthmus. Unfortunately this was quickly rendered impossible as the weather intervened and a gale blew up. With several boats having capsized in the surf and some men having been drowned, this attempt was abandoned. Despite the enemy fire, therefore, the town continued to be the embarkation point.

As they had been throughout, the warships' crews remained at the heart of all this effort, maintaining the wearisome task of rowing back and forth just as they had been doing for the previous three days. Indeed, their burden was becoming heavier all the time for in their panic some 80–90 transports had cut their cables and run to sea, many without any troops aboard. In his official despatch on the evacuation De Courcy referred to the 'fright and mismanagement' of the civilian masters – words that were carefully expunged when it was printed in the *Naval Chronicle* – which caused nine vessels to be run ashore. Two of these were saved, five were bilged and the other two burnt, their flames at least providing light for the removal of the final elements of the rearguard during the night of the 17th–18th. Embarking them was the responsibility of Captain Carden of the *Ville de Paris*; he even managing to gather up about 70 stragglers who had broken into some wine cellars and in a drunken stupor missed their places in the boats. By the morning of 18 January the process was complete and the whole fleet was standing out to sea, the naval personnel, many of whom had had no food in two days of unremitting toil, now having to work their ships home. One grateful soldier wrote:

> Considering everything, our embarkation was very ably conducted and we were very much indebted to our friends in the Navy for the easiness of our transition from the land to the sea; and all was conducted with the utmost coolness and determination.[32]

De Courcy left the *Minerva* and a schooner off Corunna to inform any incoming vessels that the port was now under enemy control and with the remainder of the fleet headed back to England, though the voyage was not to be a pleasant one. The gale continued into the Bay of Biscay and many of the transports were scattered over hundreds of miles of sea, though by the same token the strong south-westerly winds did make for a speedy passage home. Many of the warships had had to collect men abandoned by the transports and were jam-packed with people. On the *Ville de Paris*, for example, there were 2300 soldiers and women plus her crew of 850 officers and seamen. Major-General Leith came home in Hood's flagship and wrote afterwards that the *Zealous* carried 'a very motely group' of 423 men from no fewer than 25 different units. Half of these came from the 6th Foot and the remainder even included 15 French prisoners of war. Between 29 and 31 January most of the ports along the south coast of England from Falmouth to Dover witnessed the arrival of assorted vessels wanting to land their ragged, bearded and filthy human cargoes, some of them, to add to their misery, having contracted typhus during the voyage. Only two transports failed to complete their journey, striking rocks off the treacherous Cornish coast with the loss of 293 men from the 7th Hussars and the King's German Legion.[33]

It is hard to exaggerate the importance of the Navy's achievement in overseeing the evacuation. The rescue of some 26,000 soldiers, the backbone of the only field army that Britain could muster, was, in strategic terms, as crucial to the war with Napoleon as Trafalgar. Although Soult's initial assault on Moore's army on 16 January was beaten off, had the British been unable thereafter to escape there can be little doubt that, as more and more French formations appeared, they would have been compelled to surrender in a repeat of the terrible disaster at Yorktown in 1781. Complete catastrophe had been narrowly avoided, De Courcy admitting, in another sentence removed from the public printing of his despatch that: 'Had the Wind been otherwise than Southerly the whole would probably have been lost.' The Board of Admiralty also seemed fully aware of the danger that had just been avoided as they insisted that the moment De Courcy reached Plymouth he come immediately to London and report on the whole operation. This the admiral duly did, negotiating heavy floods and broken bridges to travel to the capital via Exeter, Bath and Oxford. An Admiralty that was generous in relief granted his claim for the journey's expenses, £95 12s 0d, in full.[34]

Even before the fleet bringing the army home had begun to arrive steps were being taken to try and maintain some sort of naval pressure upon the victorious French in northern Spain. On 26 January, knowing that the enemy would soon have possession of Ferrol and the warships there (the fortress happened to surrender that very day), orders were issued to Captain Adam of the *Resistance* to sail with his frigate and the *Arethusa* (38) to try and prevent any stores being delivered to Ferrol or Corunna along the coast. Two sloops were already operating off Cape Peñas and Adam was to take them under his orders as well. Two days later his squadron was expanded by the addition of the *Unicorn* and *Iris* together with a corvette, two more sloops, a brig and a cutter. These vessels, assisted by the winter gales and the nature of the coastline, started to make any sea-borne supply movements by the French very difficult. On 8 March *Resistance* chased an armed schooner and a chasse marée into the small harbour of Anchove, to the east of Cape Machichaco. That night the frigate's boats made a five-hour row through a sea that was calm for once and attacked both the vessels. The defensive fire from the schooner and a four-gun battery on a height overlooking the pier initially delayed the attackers, but soon both vessels and the battery had been stormed without loss. The chasse marée was carrying cloth for the Santander garrison and both it and the schooner were burnt. A few days later a group of sailors and marines from the *Arethusa* destroyed batteries mounting 20 guns at Lequitio, a French sergeant and 20 men being captured. A small chasse marée loaded with brandy was captured in the harbour and the day after two more chasse marées also carrying brandy were taken as well, the cargoes being destroyed and the vessels being restored to the Spaniards from whom they had been requisi-tioned. *Arethusa*'s depredations continued until 20 March with the destruction of more batteries, some signal posts and the taking of a vessel carrying wool to Bayonne. At the end of the month the two frigates joined forces to send a boat force to attack Andarrua, another small harbour where three chasse marées carrying provisions had sought shelter. The attackers first eliminated the protecting batteries and then, having thrown the guns over a cliff, went on to capture the vessels, which were taking brandy to Santander. A fourth vessel was learned to be a little way up the river and that too was captured. The attackers suffered three men wounded, one seriously. The assaults continued into April, the sloop *Wild Boar* (10) patrol-ling off Cape Machichaco taking a French schooner making her way from Corunna to Bayonne.[35]

Such successes were a heartening indication of French vul-nerability, both suggesting that the northern coast could reward the commitment of warships to it and be sufficiently blockaded to prevent the movement of naval supplies to Ferrol. By early

May the ships engaged in these duties had declined in number and the Secretary of the Admiralty informed Gambier:

> My Lords deeming it to be of the utmost importance that a most vigilant look out should be kept along the Coast of Spain from Cape Finisterre to Bayonne in order, if possible to prevent a single Vessel of the Enemy from throwing in supplies to any part of the French Army, and also for the purpose of seizing any opportunity which may occur of distressing the Enemy and of assisting the Spaniards in cutting off small parties of the French, or of annoying them by any other means in their power, I have their Lordships Commands to signify their direction to you to augment the Force on the Coast of Spain accordingly . . .

Gambier, an uninspiring commander who seems to have been very reluctant to see his ships operating off so tricky a coast, acknowledged receipt of this instruction and listed those warships on that station as consisting of the *Resistance*, two sloops, two cutters and a brig. The Admiralty was providing the *Endymion* and to her Gambier added the frigate *Amazon* (38) to cruise between Capes Peñas and Finisterre, the *Amelia* (38) frigate to patrol between Capes Peñas and Machichaco, and a sloop to operate in the most dangerous waters of all between Cape Machichaco and Bayonne. Early in June yet another sloop was ordered to the northern coast after she had completed the escort of a transport carrying arms to Gijon.

The same month also witnessed the first important example on the north coast of the military returns to be won by joint operations between Spanish land forces and British warships. At the end of May 1809 the French General Bonnet had attacked Spanish forces in the Asturias from his chief base at Santander. Marching with 5000 men as part of a wider offensive against the province, Bonnet left his lines of communication exposed to attack. Early in June, after a rapid march through the mountains, a Spanish force under Ballasteros descended upon Santander and took its garrison completely by surprise. Some of the French fled overland, but others sought to escape by sea. This was prevented by the presence of the *Amelia* and another frigate, the *Statira* (38), which were able to capture the three corvettes and two luggers in which the enemy had sailed. For the moment the possibilities suggested by this neat piece of co-operation were not followed up, in part perhaps because two days after his success Ballasteros was counterattacked and routed. In the longer term, however, as will be shown later, the French in the northern provinces were shown to be extremely exposed to such combined assaults, with sometimes profound ramifications.[36]

From the very beginning of the Spanish revolt British naval power and the lack of any corresponding French maritime muscle had an important effect. Rosily's squadron at Cadiz was doomed because of the combination of Spanish hostility and its inability to escape the blockading British. Immediate Anglo-Spanish tensions proved a portent of problems to come, though the potential value of naval support was quickly made clear at Rosas during the summer and autumn of 1808. For Napoleon's strategic prospects in Catalonia the dead weight of keeping Barcelona supplied was to prove a lingering problem, the essential weakness of the French navy again being shown in the autumn of 1809 when the supply run of a substantial convoy encountered complete disaster once the British were aware of the movement. Such resupply efforts would not be abandoned by the French in the future, but they were never secure and increasingly they would have to rely on other means to keep Barcelona functioning.

Off northern Spain the combination of a treacherous coastline, winter weather, and the speed of Napoleon's offensive at the end of 1808 severely limited the effectiveness of the British warships nevertheless sent to the region. Even so, the very welcome appearance of 9000 troops rescued from the Baltic was a welcome fillip to the Allied cause and the evacuation of Moore's army was to be vital for its future. Neither operation would have been feasible without British control of the sea.

CHAPTER 3

Portugal, 1809–12

'No bed of roses I can assure their Lordships.'
Vice-Admiral Berkeley, 26 March 1810[1]

AT SPITHEAD ON CHRISTMAS Day 1808, Vice-Admiral George Cranfield Berkeley raised his flag on the *Conqueror* preparatory to taking up his appointment as the new commander of the Portuguese station. It was a position he was to hold throughout the most difficult period of the Peninsular War for Britain, not returning home and to retirement until 1812. With the exception of one notorious incident Berkeley is almost unknown in history, yet he was to be one of the most significant naval officers involved in the conflict in Spain and Portugal.

Born in 1753, the second surviving son of the Earl of Berkeley, young George first went to sea in 1766 and thereafter pursued both a naval career and one in politics. He tried and failed to win a parliamentary seat in 1774, but was finally successful in 1783, becoming a member for Gloucestershire and remaining so until 1810. Promoted to post captain in 1780, he distinguished himself at the battle of the Glorious First of June in 1794 when he was one of the few captains to obey Howe's orders to engage the French closely. Afterwards he was rewarded with a gold medal for the action. Reaching flag rank in February 1799, he again served with the Channel Fleet and for a brief period commanded a squadron off Rochefort. Up to 1806 his naval career had been marked by steady if unspectacular progress, doubtless assisted by the considerable political interest he was able to wield. Not only was he an MP in his own right, but he was related to the powerful Grenville family, to Earl Bathurst the President of the Board of Trade, and to the

Duke of Richmond, the Lord Lieutenant of Ireland. In that year, recently promoted to vice-admiral, Berkeley was given the command of the North American station. To judge from his correspondence, as well as from his portrait where a florid, heavy expression rather glowers at the onlooker, Berkeley was an officer intolerant of opposition and those elements that stood in the way of national and service interests. Unquestionably one such barrier at that time was the flagrant way in which the authorities in the United States connived at the desertion of seamen from British warships. With trained manpower at a premium, such losses were a constant concern for all British naval officers and Berkeley was no exception. On taking up his position at Halifax, his response to the problem was blunt and direct: he instructed his captains to stop and search American vessels for such deserters, an order that flew in the face of US sensitivity and asked for trouble. It came in June 1807 off Hampton Roads when the USS *Chesapeake* refused a request for a search by HMS *Leopard* (50), the British warship opening fire and causing the deaths of four of the American frigate's crew and wounding many others. Anglo-American relations teetered on the brink of war for weeks afterwards and Berkeley found himself recalled.[2]

It was a testament to the strength of his political influence that within eighteen months of the encounter off Hampton Roads he was being offered the Portuguese station. For two (American) historians Berkeley was 'a man of rather mediocre ability', but such an assessment perhaps owes more to residual wrath over the *Chesapeake* incident than anything else. In fairness, however, another American writer who has examined Berkeley's career more carefully has concluded that he was a thorough professional who 'knew his business around a ship, port or dockyard'.[3] During the three-and-a-half years he held the Lisbon command Berkeley was to display a high degree of resilience and determination in circumstances that were often stressful and difficult. For all that, in 1811, when he was offered a much more comfortable billet as flag officer commanding at Plymouth, his sense of duty prompted him to decline the post, feeling that the Portuguese station was too important to abandon, especially when there was still a chance that the Allied forces in the country might have to be evacuated. While in Lisbon, not only did Berkeley handle his direct naval responsibilities with competence, he was also able to establish very harmonious working relations with Wellington, a crucial factor given the importance of inter-service co-operation and no easy task bearing in mind the army commander's stiff-necked aristocratic arrogance: no doubt Berkeley's own noble pedigree helped. At one stage Wellington would grumble that he was 'teazed to death' by the admiral's activity, but ultimately wrote in the warmest terms of his naval colleague. 'It is impossible for two Officers to be on better terms than we are. I have always found the Admiral not only disposed to give every assistance in his power, but to anticipate and exceed our wishes in this way.' That Berkeley's tenure of command was extended for six months beyond the three-year norm was probably in part due to Wellington's earnest support.[4]

The Admiralty's orders to their new commander instructed him to employ his frigates and smaller warships to protect trade and harass the enemy while keeping his ships of the line provisioned for five months and ready to support any detachments from the Channel Fleet pursuing French squadrons escaping from Brest. He was also told to do all that he could to support the army in Portugal and was to discover if there would be any use for armed vessels or boats employed in the Tagus, supplying such craft if necessary. Furthermore he was also to be prepared to send detachments from his command to Cadiz should he receive any requests for help in getting the Spanish fleet to sea.[5]

On his arrival in Lisbon on 14 January 1809 Berkeley discovered that matters were far from satisfactory with his new command. To start with it was immediately apparent that the force at his disposal, *viz* the *Ganges*, four frigates and two sloops, was quite inadequate to the duties that were demanded, and even his retention of the *Conqueror*, which was supposed to have been sent to Cadiz, did little to improve things. The shortage was all the more acute as it seemed highly likely that the evacuation of Lisbon might be required in the near future. At that moment Moore was in full retreat to Corunna and it was not unreasonable to assume that in the wake of this Portugal might be abandoned. This would mean the removal of about 10,000 British troops and the convoying of the large number of transports in the Tagus: at the end of the previous month these had numbered 158 vessels set aside to carry the troops themselves, their horses, ordnance, baggage and even decayed stores. Alongside this there was also the question of removing the remaining Portuguese vessels left over from the flight to Brazil. These numbered three ships of the line, four frigates, four storeships and four other vessels. Most of these were seaworthy but would require manning and escorting, while those that were too rotten to sail, together with stores in the naval arsenal that could not be moved, would have to be destroyed.[6]

Berkeley was disappointed when none of the warships involved in the Corunna operation were thereafter transferred to him, his situation instead becoming worse when one of his frigates was damaged and had to be sent home and when, in March, Vice-Admiral Duckworth appeared off the Tagus in pursuit of a French squadron from Brest and Berkeley felt obliged to strengthen his force with the *Conqueror* and a frigate. He would also have added the *Ganges* to Duckworth's squadron but was aware that to have done so would have left him without a single ship of the line, a situation which 'would leave me without the means of compelling the Portuguese Ships to put to sea. . .'. He had also suffered a setback in the shape of the two Russian warships left behind from Siniavin's squadron: it had been hoped to use them as transports to boost the tonnage available for any evacuation, but unfortunately both had been found to be too rotten and unseaworthy.

There were also problems in Lisbon stemming from a shortage of supplies for naval use. The dearth of provisions could in part be rectified by drawing from those held in army transports in the Tagus, and Berkeley also issued orders for local purchases to be made, but more awkward was the condition of some of his ships, which he complained were down to their last set of sails and were also short of cordage. The Admiralty Office responded by observing that any shortage of provisions would have been caused by the prevailing westerly winds preventing victuallers leaving English ports at that time: during January–February one cutter, in the teeth of south-westerly gales, took 28 days to sail from Falmouth to Lisbon. More pointedly, they also rebuked Berkeley for not specifying precisely which of his warships required sails. 'It is impossible,' he was acidly informed, 'from such general statement . . . to take effectual measures for supplying the wants of the ships under your command.' It was also at this time that Berkeley was even more severely mauled by an Admiralty furious that he had sounded out Ambassador Villiers over the question of extending the limits of the Portuguese station (see Chapter 1). Nor were they pleased with him for failing to make arrangements to send some despatches to Cadiz, documents that were supposed to have gone in the *Conqueror* and which, doubtless because of his shortage of vessels, had been held up. All in all it was an uncomfortable start to his new command.[7]

While Berkeley's initial worries centred around likely developments in the vicinity of Lisbon, where the British forces were concentrated, he also had matters demanding his attention in northern Portugal. Early in February 1809, following the Corunna evacuation and with Galicia (theoretically) occupied by Marshal Ney's VI Corps, Soult moved his II Corps south with the intention of re-occupying Portugal. Vigo was easily taken *en route*, but the French quickly found their progress slowing in the face of winter weather, difficult terrain and fierce guerrilla resistance, an opposition encouraged by a small regular force kept in the field by Romana but out of French reach in the high mountains. Guerrilla activity isolated French garrisons and prevented any sort of regular communication between them. The burden of combating this resistance primarily fell on Ney's formations, but Soult too had problems as he pressed on into northern Portugal in March. Organised resistance was brushed aside, but the French controlled only the ground on which they stood and were repeatedly harassed by the guerrillas, the whole corps becoming isolated from the other French units in Spain much as Junot had been the previous summer. Nevertheless, by the end of March Soult had reached and stormed Oporto, seizing a large quantity of British-supplied armaments and stores and 30 merchant vessels. However, a commercial disaster had been avoided as most of the fleet of ships, long weather-bound, carrying between 8000 and 10,000 pipes of port wine valued at £400,000 had got out of the port a few days before the city fell.[8]

Naturally such developments caused alarm in Lisbon, Berkeley worrying at the end of February about a Russian corvette at Vigo which he feared the French would man and operate, they also having seized three gunboats in the port and now being able to employ the place as a base for privateering. Under the circumstances he felt compelled to send the *Venus* (36) frigate to support the much-battered *Lively* which had been patrolling off Oporto since January. By 21 March Coutts Crawford, *Venus*'s captain, was writing from off Vigo to report that the Spaniards had the port closely blockaded by land and were imploring him for help. He believed that the added presence of the *Lively* might prompt the small and beleaguered French garrison to surrender and in consequence McKinley hastened to join his colleague, the two warships landing arms and ammunition as well as some of their ships' guns. On 27 March one of Vigo's gates was battered in and the garrison surrendered the following day to avoid an assault. McKinley took charge of about 1300 prisoners, the Anglo-Spaniards also seizing horses, wagons and money. Instrumental in this success, warships were to be similarly important shortly after when, on 14 April, a French column appeared. By that time the British had been substantially reinforced by the arrival of three more frigates, the *Fisgard* (38), *Amazon* and *Niobe* (38). Bolton, the *Fisgard*'s captain and the senior officer present, landed 213 marines gathered from his vessels as well as 50 seamen to help man Vigo's citadel. This force he provisioned for a fortnight and he also landed all the arms he could spare for the Spaniards. To his disappointment the French made no effort to attack the castle, which he regarded as very strong, and instead quickly retired. The British marines remained in Vigo until July, by which time there were no French forces in its vicinity.[9]

As a point of communication with the Galicians Vigo was extremely valuable and within a month of its capture 800 muskets and 100 kegs of ball cartridge had been landed there. It also offered the Spaniards the chance of procuring some heavy artillery for Romana's small force in the hope that an attack on Corunna might become viable, McKinley, once again the senior officer present, being approached on 22 May with a request for 22 assorted pieces of ordnance along with carriages, powder, shot and the like. Berkeley could not provide an artillery train on such a scale, but could report in June that he had sent the Spaniards two transports containing a mortar and four assorted cannons as well as a mortar vessel. However, he was sceptical about Spanish military arrangements and directed McKinley to make sure that the train was landed only if a siege of Corunna was directly in the offing. Otherwise it was to be retained aboard the transports and kept at Vigo or one of the small islands off the port. In the event Ney, much harassed by the Galicians, voluntarily evacuated Corunna and Ferrol on 22 June, rendering a siege unnecessary.[10]

Before most of these events had taken place, moreover, the Allied cause in Portugal had enjoyed an even more dramatic success. On the evening of 22 April Arthur Wellesley landed at Lisbon to resume the command of the British army. His arrival was a significant moment for it marked the British Cabinet's determination to try and defend Portugal rather than submit to a tame evacuation in the wake of Moore's retreat. The preceding weeks had seen the British army more than double its previous numbers in the kingdom due to a combination of reinforcements sent from Britain and the return of unwanted formations sent to Cadiz. Comprising over 40,000 British and Portuguese soldiers, the force at Wellesley's disposal was sufficient for him to strike at Soult's isolated corps with the aim once again of driving the French out of the country.[11]

For the Navy the decision to fight on in Portugal had equally significant ramifications as it was apparent both that it would be closely involved in the support of future land operations and that Berkeley's command would have to be substantially reinforced for it to do this effectively. At first Berkeley found himself hard-pressed to meet the needs of normal trade protection and cruising, let alone Wellesley's requirements. The day after the general's arrival Berkeley told the Admiralty that he had been asked to convoy troops from the Tagus to Gibraltar, the transports then returning with other soldiers; to transfer horse transports to Cork and then return them with a regiment of cavalry; and to send home to England such transports as Wellesley deemed superfluous. To manage all this he was having to take under his orders any warships that happened to call as Lisbon while performing other duties. Thus the *Tribune* (36) was to be used to convoy home the trade, the horse ships and the unwanted transports, she being instructed by him to go on to Cork once she had handed over the trade and empty transports to any passing cruiser she might meet. In the event, even this *ad hoc* arrangement did not work out as, under pressure from Wellesley, on 25 April Berkeley agreed to send the *Tribune* with the horse ships alone and directly to Cork to prevent any unnecessary delays in the arrival of the cavalry regiment. The trade and transports would have to wait. His shortage of warships was to be a constant source of worry for Berkeley. Countermanding Admiralty orders given to vessels not under his command was an uncomfortable thing for any admiral to do, yet '. . . without those infringements which I have been compelled to make upon those ships which have accidentally called here, I should not have been able to have fulfilled any part of my duty'. The Admiralty was not unsympathetic to his plight, though, fully endorsing his issuing of fresh orders to visiting warships and, more significantly, taking steps to bolster his command. On 11 May no fewer than nine further warships, sloops and small brigs, were ordered to join him and by the beginning of July the Lisbon station comprised four ships of the line, four frigates and thirteen sloops and brigs. This was a great improvement, but as the station's responsibilities seemed always to be growing, particularly the diverse and constant demands for convoys and for the movement of despatches, there was a continual battle between Berkeley and the Board of Admiralty about the strength of his command. By early August the admiral was writing that the *Comus* was soon to leave with 40 transports and the Lisbon trade, at which point he would not have a single warship in the Tagus. Only two others were anywhere close to being within easy distance of his call and they were observing the Russian corvette in Vigo and patrolling between that place and Cape Finisterre. It was with particular irritation in March 1810 that he acknowledged an Admiralty rebuke written the previous month expressing their displeasure at his acceptance of a Portuguese offer to fit out a schooner and a lugger. His need for small warships was acute and made all the sharper by the requirement to maintain regular communications with Cadiz. To rub salt into the wound the only new vessel sent to him from Britain, the schooner *Whiting* (4), arrived full of defects and in need of repairs. The Admiralty later expressed its satisfaction with Berkeley's conduct, effectively withdrawing their complaint.[12]

To return to the spring of 1809, very particular efforts were to be demanded of the station to support a land campaign that would take place in close proximity to the coast and away from the main supply base at Lisbon. Even before 2 May, when Wellesley joined the bulk of his army which was concentrated at Coimbra, Berkeley had ordered the *Nautilus* to cruise off Oporto (16 April) and with the campaign underway he added the frigate *Semiramis* (36). Logistical support for the army was provided in the shape of transports for 3–4000 men along with victuallers, forage ships and vessels carrying ordnance stores and suchlike moving up the coast to Figueira and the mouth of the Mondego, from which point supplies could be ferried up river to Coimbra. All of these were placed under the protection of the sloop *Port Mahon* (18). The pre-planning for the campaign stated that should the army advance from Coimbra then these vessels could move northwards to Aveiro, a point only 16 miles from Oporto itself. This permitted comparatively easy supply arrangements, for vessels to be on hand to receive the sick and wounded, and for the return of troops to Lisbon by sea within 48 hours should circumstances demand it and provided the winds were fair, which was usually the case. If operations went well there were also plans for French prisoners of war to be moved to Vigo where McKinley could make arrangements to hold them on one of the offshore islands until transports arrived to take them to Britain. Finally Berkeley also provided the brig *Jasper* (14) together with a mortar vessel and four armed flatboats to guard the provision boats at Santarem and to try and prevent any French crossing of the lower Tagus.

The weather served to delay *Port Mahon*'s convoy, it sailing for Figueira on 27 April but being struck by a gale and immediately having to return to Lisbon. It did not depart again until 5 May, by which time Wellesley was busily advancing on

Oporto. He hustled a surprised Soult out of the city on the 12th and forced the French into a precipitate and disorderly retreat over the mountains and back into Spain, a withdrawal that cost Soult many casualties and all of his guns. Back in Lisbon this strategic triumph was, ironically, accompanied by a military scare as news arrived that on 14 May Marshal Victor's I Corps had captured Alcantara, a move that seemed to be threatening the Portuguese capital at a moment when Wellesley was committed to the north. The available Allied troops were moved to cover the approaches to Lisbon and Berkeley responded to the emergency by landing all his marines to release soldiers from the capital's citadel. As well as the small flotilla of armed vessels on the lower reaches of the Tagus, he also provided ten flatboats armed with carronades and crewed by 200 seamen ready to move up the river. These seamen were also employed to move heavy cannon to guard likely crossing points. Actually Victor's whole manoeuvre was merely a reconnaissance designed to feel out the forces in front of him. Once he had discovered that no immediate invasion of Estremadura was likely, Victor withdrew and the whole crisis blew over. Nevertheless the episode did illustrate the willingness of Berkeley to employ all of his available resources in a crisis and fully to back his army colleagues, a factor that would be repeated later on in infinitely more dangerous circumstances.[13]

Following his triumph against Soult, Wellesley advanced into Spain with the bulk of his available British troops, the plan being to co-operate with Cuesta's Spanish Army of Estremadura in the destruction of Victor's corps. The resulting campaign consumed June, July and much of August and, although marked by Wellesley's Pyrrhic victory at Talavera on 28 June, was a strategic failure. The British army, indeed, narrowly avoided encirclement by superior French forces moving down from the north and Anglo-Spanish relations were sorely stretched in the welter of animosity and ill-feeling which followed the retreat. The general Allied failure was then finally capped on 1 August when the Spanish Army of La Mancha was hammered at Almonacid. These events were well beyond the reach of naval participation, but for Berkeley the summer was marked by important services by some of his vessels outside the borders of his station.[14]

As has already been noted, the much-harassed forces of
Marshal Ney in north-western Spain were obliged to evacuate
the ports of Ferrol and Corunna on 22 June. The French had
been unable to gain any maritime advantage from their six
months' control of the Spanish Ferrol squadron, lacking as they
did the materials, provisions and manpower to make the warships operational. Nor had they been able to bring these in from
outside, the war-torn state of northern Spain not permitting
movement by land and the British blockade preventing any use
of the sea. Throughout these months the two ports had been
watched by the *Defiance* (74), her captain, Hotham, also having
the support of one or two frigates. Their presence represented
continuing Admiralty worries about the fate of the Spanish
warships, a matter that had even got so far as being briefly raised
in a debate in the House of Lords in March. On 24 June, uncertain about the precise state of affairs in Galicia, Hotham sent a
flag of truce ashore purportedly to gain information about some
captured British soldiers and their transport, though the real
reason was his wish to discover the extent to which the French
retained control of the area. From this he concluded that as far
as Corunna was concerned the enemy was not actually present
in the port, but were only exercising a theoretical control.
Hotham immediately seized the opportunity to land a party of
130 marines and as many seamen from the *Defiance* and the frigates *Amazon* and *Indefatigable* to destroy all of Corunna's
seaward batteries in an action reminiscent of the precautions
taken by De Courcy at the end of 1808. Hotham reasoned that
the port might soon be used once again by a British force and
that it would be that much more secure and available for them
if its seaward defences were neutralised. The landing party's
destruction of 114 guns and mortars would, he hoped, both
overawe the Spaniards and provide them with an alibi for lethargy should the French return. Garcia, Corunna's governor,
vigorously complained about the attack, but Hotham replied by
pointing out that the French were still supposed to be in control
of the place and piously expressed the hope that the Spaniards
there would soon return to the Allied cause, offering to lift the
blockade of Corunna and Ferrol as an inducement. Two days
after the raid a similar blow was aimed at Ferrol, Parker of the

Amazon landing at the port to be received with great enthusiasm by the bulk of the population, only its governor and senior government officials being cool and distant for fear of future French reprisals. Of particular concern was the fort of San Felipe, which commanded the entrance to Ferrol and was held by a force loyal to the French. Hotham responded by landing 200 seamen and marines under Parker's command. This force, marching under a banner inscribed 'For Fernando 7°', was greeted as a saviour and San Felipe was taken with little trouble, the castle's commander being arrested and transferred to the *Defiance* while the former incumbent, himself arrested by the French, was released and reinstated. For all of this success and enthusiasm, though, Hotham was still careful to neutralise much of the castle's defensive capability, its 68 guns being spiked and all its powder being transferred to the arsenal. The blockade of Ferrol was then formally lifted and by the end of June the two ports were garrisoned by a Spanish force of about 11,000 men.[15]

Hotham cautiously made no mention in his various dealings with the Spaniards of the prime source of British concern, the warships at Ferrol, for fear of arousing their suspicions about British motives. Fortunately this tantalising question, with the port having been occupied once already, was on Spanish minds as well, on 10 July the Admiralty received word that De Castro, the Spanish representative in Lisbon, had raised the issue of the vessels' future with Villiers. No second invitation was needed and within a few days Berkeley was told to send all his ships of the line to Ferrol in order to help ready the warships for transfer to the greater safety offered by Cadiz. On the same day orders were sent to Hotham to provide all the aid he could manage with the same objective in mind. At that time the squadron that was the cause of all this concern consisted of eight ships of the line, seven frigates and an assortment of smaller warships and many gunboats. There were also two ships of the line under construction, though it was indicative of the chaotic state of Spain's administration – only worsened by the war – that they had been on their frames for six years. The arsenal was completely bereft of building materials, relying in normal times on oak from the Asturias, fir from the Pyrenees and iron from Biscay, none of which could be moved through a war zone.

On the more positive side, Hotham could at least report that those warships which were serviceable would be able to be equipped quite swiftly as most of the ship's furniture was in store in the arsenal. Only one 64-gun vessel and a frigate lacked such items and their immediate needs could either be made there or provided from the British warships. Much more of a problem were the three ships of the line, the *Mexicano* (112), *San Fernando* (84) and *Atlas* (74), and the frigate *Pellor* (40), that were found to be in need of substantial repairs before they could possibly venture to sea. Not only were there no materials in moribund Ferrol, but yet another indication of the collapse of Spain's naval administration was the fact that the dockyard's artificers had not been paid for seven months. Hotham took it upon himself to procure 12,000 dollars from a British commissioner in the region to hire a body of seamen and labourers, but was nervous about possible future trouble as the wretched dockyard workers had come to view the warships as some sort of pledge for their arrears of pay. Some 400,000 dollars would be required to meet this and a petition for such a sum was, with the support of Romana, submitted to the Central Junta. Yet another shortage afflicting both Ferrol and Corunna was a lack of provisions and that the French had taken all the stocks of powder, small arms, medicines and surgeons' equipment. Here again assistance would have to come from the British vessels, though at least on a brief voyage to Cadiz such shortcomings were not likely to be serious and the vessels would be able to carry their guns.

Back in Lisbon Berkeley received his instructions to send support to Ferrol on 30 July, he immediately dispatching the *Norge*, which was in the Tagus, northwards and ordering a sloop to deliver similar orders to the *Triumph* (74) and *Zealous* which were on a cruise. This left his flagship, the *Barfleur*, which was unable to leave Lisbon at once as many of her crew were away manning flatboats moving soldiers up the Tagus. The *Barfleur* was not finally able to sail until 4 August. The last of the quartet to reach Ferrol – the *Triumph* – appeared on 25 August and brought with her a nice problem in naval etiquette. Her captain,

Linzee, became the senior officer on station and therefore assumed the command from Hotham. However, the latter, an officer belonging to the Channel Fleet, was a detached commander in his own right appointed to oversee his own small squadron, *viz Defiance, Indefatigable, Amazon* and *Amelia*. In the event the matter was resolved sensibly with Linzee directing matters at Ferrol itself while not interfering with Hotham's other responsibilities. Indeed, the whole process was to reflect great credit on the diligence and tact of all parties concerned, both British and Spanish. While the British crews undertook the lion's share of the immense labour involved in readying the Ferrol squadron for sea, they were fully supported by Admiral Vargas, the officer appointed by the Central Junta to co-ordinate the Spanish side of the operation.

By the end of August three of the Spanish frigates had been able to leave for Cadiz and the details of the work still in progress showed that 892 seamen from the British warships were being employed on the other vessels on the 26th. Their duties aboard the massive *Principe de Asturias* (120) included the bending and storing away of cables, the receiving of spars, the fixing of sail booms, and the receiving of running rigging and stores. At the same time other men aboard the *Conception* (120) were taking in guns, binding cables and suchlike while others on the *San Telmo* (74) were storing casks and booms and loading shot and tar. A frigate, the *Diana* (36), was being unmoored and prepared for sea and the *Santiago la America* (64) was being moored alongside a sheer hulk in preparation for getting in her masts. Through most of September and the first half of October this scale of effort was maintained, Hotham writing of the 'activity, exertions, and cheerfulness of the British Officers and Seamen who were employed in it . . .' and the Admiralty being sufficiently impressed to pay bonuses to the crews at the rate that would have been paid had they been fitting-out British vessels.

Ever-needed supplies were also forthcoming to render the Spaniards mobile, the *Defiance* and the *Norge* providing more than four and a half tons of bread between them during August despite an overall shortage that obliged Linzee to put all five British vessels on a two-thirds bread allowance: by the end of the month *Barfleur* had only 22 days of bread remaining aboard, a particular shortage compared to her consorts which spoke volumes for the speed with which she had been sent to Ferrol. *Zealous* was slightly better off with 31 days' supply while the others had stocks sufficient for just under eight weeks. This problem was fortunately eased in September when a transport laden with bread arrived from Lisbon. Linzee's vessels also made up the Spanish shortfall in a range of other items such as flour, pease, rice, rum and iron hoops. Nor was Vargas abandoned by his own government as in August the Central Junta sent him 25,000 dollars to help the equipping and in September the *San Lorenzo* (74) arrived from Cadiz with a further 100,000 dollars and 80,000 rations.

Thanks to all of this, progress was gratifyingly swift. Writing on 20 September Hotham could report that the *Diana* had sailed from Cadiz on 28 August, the *Principe de Asturias, San Telmo* and *San Julian* (64) had departed on 10–11 September, and the *Conception* on 16 September. The *Iphegenia* (36) frigate was evidently earmarked for local duties and had been transferred to Corunna, while the *Santiago la America* and the frigate *Lavinia* (40) were due to leave Ferrol once the wind permitted. Five smaller warships had also been brought into service, either having sailed for Cadiz or being due to leave shortly. The only four substantial warships remaining at Ferrol were those requiring extensive repairs to make them seaworthy. One of these, *Atlas*, could possibly have been moved in due course but only after jury masts had been rigged and once she had been caulked; even then, however, she would not have been able to stand the weight of her guns: for the moment she was being employed in the less-than-glamorous role as the support for a sheer hulk.

The final movements of the Spanish vessels was also to be managed without the potential diplomatic embarrassment that could have been caused by the question of their possible escort for the voyage south. Loaded with equipment from the Ferrol arsenal and with minimal crews, the warships would have been capable of little resistance had they been attacked. Yet to have accepted formal Royal Navy protection as if they were nothing more than lumbering merchantmen would have been an affront to Spanish pride. When consulted on the matter, Berkeley suggested that his own ships accompany the Spaniards, not as escorts but out of respect and because they were so poorly manned! Without being aware of this opinion Vargas also seems to have come to the same face-saving conclusion. Early in September he reaffirmed that no formal escorts were required, but if 'casually it should happen' that British and Spanish warships departed together, then 'I would avail myself in this particular . . . of the goodness of the British Nation. . .'. As the four ships from Berkeley's command returned to their station in mid-September, they in this fashion provided protection for some of the larger Spanish warships at least as far as the Tagus. Thereafter the Spaniards sailed alone and did arrive safely, the great irony being that only a few months after reaching the supposed sanctuary of Cadiz that port itself was to be under siege and in great peril.[16]

While the large warships were so onerously employed at Ferrol, the remaining vessels of the Portuguese squadron were busily engaged in the various duties of cruising, convoy protection and despatch delivery as Berkeley oversaw the day-to-day responsibilities of his command. At one point, such was the distant employment of all his ships, the admiral was even vexatiously obliged to fly his flag in the Tagus from the *Abraham Newland*, a transport. He also personally investigated the possibilities offered by the river as a means of moving supplies up-country, grumbling that the Portuguese accounts of its conditions were too contradictory to be relied upon. Although shallow, the Tagus proved to be navigable for flatboats up to a distance of 90 miles, as far as Abrantes. This was of great value to the army's commissariat department as any waterborne movement was preferable to the cumbersome and slow-moving carts that had to be used on land, the army commander expressing his appreciation of Berkeley's arrangements. The river could also be used for moving troops, both healthy and sick, removing the need for exhausting marches. For example, in June 1809 Wellesley asked the admiral for any flatboats that could be spared to move two newly-arrived regiments up the Tagus as far as Valada. Naval vessels also continued to be involved in the movement of supplies to Figueira during the summer, Berkeley expressing particular glee at the beginning of June when the arrival of the sloop *Doterel* (18) enabled him to ship 20,000 pairs of much-needed shoes up the coast within a few hours of the request for them arriving. The onset of winter, however, made the route more difficult because the high bar at the mouth of the Mondego became even more awkward to cross despite the use of small schooners particularly placed there for the service.[17]

Increasingly, as 1809 moved into its autumn months, the question that dominated British thinking was whether the campaign in Portugal would be able to be sustained at all in the future. In the wake of the collapsed Talavera campaign came the unwelcome news from central Europe that the Franco-Austrian war, raging in the Danube valley since the early spring, had ended with Napoleon once more triumphant. For the Allies in the Peninsula this meant that French resources could now be concentrated south of the Pyrenees, with there almost inevitably being a renewed and reinforced attempt by Napoleon to conquer Portugal. The British army's commander, raised to the peerage as Viscount Wellington after Talavera, believed that although the Portuguese frontier was too extensive to be defended, nevertheless the country could still be preserved given certain preconditions. Wellington planned to make use of all Portugal's military means – regular, militia and guerrilla – to bolster his British troops while he pursued a strategy of retreating towards Lisbon in the face of any substantial invasion. The French would be obliged to advance through a countryside where limited natural resources had been further reduced by the devastation of a 'scorched earth' policy, so wrecking the enemy's practice of relying on local means to feed his troops. Once the Allied forces had reached Lisbon they would occupy a system of previously-prepared fortifications, these becoming known as the Lines of Torres Vedras. Orders for their construction were issued to Wellington's chief engineer, Colonel Fletcher, in October 1809 and, when fully completed, were to comprise some 53 miles of man-made defences situated to enhance and strengthen the natural ruggedness of the local terrain. Stretching in two lines to the north of the capital, with the sea to the west and the Tagus to the east, the defences meant that Lisbon stood at the base of its own little fortified peninsula. Wellington intended to take the bulk of his forces into these positions and force the French either to make costly assaults on him or be compelled to retreat through simple starvation.

Wellington's strategic prescience in analysing the elements that would determine the forthcoming campaign is deserving of the highest praise, but it is all too easy to view the way it unfolded as being in some way inevitable. Seeing the Lines as an impenetrable barrier that would completely block the French advance is not difficult in hindsight. One writer describes the fortifications as 'this Maginot Line of the Napoleonic era', they being 'impregnable by the standards of the day'.[18] This may be true enough, but neither Wellington nor his political masters in London could have trusted the fate of Britain's only effective field army to the probable strength of a group of fortifications alone. The crucial factor permitting the army to sit and wait for an attack to be delivered by a much stronger enemy was the knowledge that if things went wrong, as could always happen in war, then the troops had every chance of being evacuated by sea in safety. It was the Royal Navy's provision of this maritime insurance policy that permitted the Cabinet to allow Wellington to test his theory that Portugal was defensible. Without it one cannot for a moment imagine that the risk could have been taken and from the very start Wellington was fully aware that an evacuation might ultimately be necessary. In the same month that he issued the orders for the building of the Lines, he also sought Berkeley's advice about where any embarkation should take place, wondering about the merits of Peniche, Setubal, Paço d'Arcas on the Tagus and the bays to the east of St Julian. The latter were the most suitable and it was significant that behind the two main fortified lines north of Lisbon a third, defending the St Julian position, was also created to allow a small rearguard to cover any final withdrawal to sea.

The man primarily responsible for supervising any embarkation would be Berkeley, his immediate concern being to provide sufficient tonnage to move all the troops that might require lifting. In the event, by November 1810, there were over 90,000 soldiers of various nationalities behind the Lines and to these would doubtless have been added hundreds of Portuguese civilians keen to avoid another dose of French occupation. Although the voyages from Lisbon would have been comparatively short, to either England or Cadiz, nevertheless space would still have to be found for such a multitude. It was ironic that for much of the summer of 1809 Berkeley had been busy returning transports to Britain whenever possible in an effort to ease the pressure on the Transport Board in London. By September 1809 there were only 84 vessels of 25,310 tons remaining in the Tagus, 48 of which were scheduled to go home, most by the next convoy. The remaining tonnage was utterly inadequate for even a modest evacuation, let alone a large one. Nor at that stage could the admiral look to his warships for any significant capacity, there being only four ships of the line in his command. Fortunately the French threat was slow to materialise, although as early as February 1810 Berkeley was becoming ever more aware of the danger at a moment when his resources seemed to be diminishing. Most of his transports had left the Tagus to move an Anglo-Portuguese brigade to Cadiz and by then he also had only one ship of the line remaining on station.

During March the Admiralty set about addressing this weakness by returning his command to its former establishment in terms of large warships by the addition of four ships of the line, although one of these, the *Norge*, was rendered temporarily unserviceable when she hit a rock while entering the Tagus. The resulting damage allowed three feet of water to enter her hull every hour and she had to be sent to Gibraltar for repairs. At the same time the shortage of transport tonnage was emphasised when Colonel Fisher, the artillery commander in Lisbon, discovered that after the heavy ordnance and some stores had been loaded there was still, in his area of responsibility alone, a shortfall of over 2000 tons of shipping. An anxious Wellington stressed that he wanted 'everything in such a state that we may either go or stay, according as it may be expedient, in view of the force by which we shall be attacked'. The following weeks saw the situation start to improve as the government back in London exerted itself to rectify the deficit. By early May an embarkation plan had been drawn up in Lisbon and this noted that 128 transports had been set aside for receiving the various regiments, with another 84 vessels to lift off the staffs, the sick and the stores.[19]

These preparations were coming to fruition as the pending French invasion finally began to take shape. Massena, the marshal appointed to command it, took up his duties in May and, after the siege and capture of the border fortress of Ciudad Rodrigo, the advance into Portugal commenced in July. Wellington administered a bloody nose to the invaders at Bussaco at the end of September, but in general continued to fall back in an orderly fashion towards Lisbon, the last units of his army safely entering the Lines on 10 October. A few days before this Berkeley reported that, thanks to the exertions of the seamen present, all the transports and stores at Figueira had been removed in case of a sudden French attack. Although Massena seemed fixed on Lisbon, Berkeley also felt that an increased naval presence at Oporto would be valuable, the brig stationed there accordingly being reinforced by a frigate and two sloops. Now that the moment of greatest danger was at hand he was also able to enjoy the reassurance of commanding a very powerful squadron. Once again the Admiralty, as it had been for the Corunna evacuation, was fortunate that its means were required off the Peninsula during the winter months when it was obliged to withdraw its major vessels from the Baltic, so again providing a reserve to enable its ships to be moved to the south. By November 1810 Berkeley had no fewer than eleven ships of the line under his orders in the Tagus, a force providing a sub-stantial measure of security against any sudden French naval assault that might be launched in support of Massena, as well as the tonnage and thousands of seamen to assist any evacuation.[20]

With over 250 transports moored alongside all the warships large and small, plus the constant comings and going of trade convoys, the Tagus must have presented a dramatic spectacle by the end of the year. For Berkeley it was a stressful period, one made all the more difficult by the running battle he endured to try and preserve some sort of control over the trans-ports' crews. With scores of vessels lying idle there were all to many opportunities for some of their number, in all totalling some 4000 men, to get up to mischief. A furious Berkeley reported a series of crimes ranging from robbery to murder committed by these individuals, noting that the Portuguese authorities wanted nothing to do with them unless the offences had been committed on shore. If they had occurred on water they regarded them as a British naval matter: in one cited case two seamen from a transport stole £100 from a regiment's baggage and then deserted. The Admiralty, rather unhelpfully all things considered, suggested that the admiral try to control any criminality by threatening impressment. Berkeley pointed out that such a step would break the contracts under which such vessels had been hired and might render them unable to perform any future service. Nor was he at all keen on the notion of a transfer to a King's ship being regarded as some sort of punishment! Miscreants could have been sent back to Britain for trial, but such a process would have had little immediate deterrent value in the Tagus. The admiral wanted the transports to be put under a letter of marque and so under military discipline, allowing courts martial on the spot to deal with offenders. Such a radical step, however, did not meet with Admiralty approval and it was perhaps significant that when a seaman from a transport at Messina in Sicily was tried in this fashion it prompted immediate protests from the Transport Board. The whole thorny problem was, consequently, never satisfactorily resolved, only the eventual break-up of the fleet easing Berkeley's predicament.[21]

Nor was this his only concern respecting the transports. Many of them were in a very poor state of repair, some having just had the copper sheathing on their hulls patched over and being quite unfit to carry troops. In consequence Berkeley ordered the whole to be surveyed, a step that infuriated some of the vessels' owners who tried to get the admiral removed from his command. In September he considered that: 'The state of the transports is too dreadful to be known publicly, and might almost occasion a mutiny in the army, if they knew to what rotten and dangerous ships they were consigned.' Such masses of shipping were unwieldy to move, unreliable in a crisis (as had been shown at Corunna), and were often structurally unsound. Yet despite all this, the tonnage was enormously expensive for the government to hire, the costs of those vessels appropriated to Peninsular service in 1810 alone coming to almost

£1,300,000, or in excess of 10 per cent of the whole cost of the war for Britain in that year.[22]

The ideal solution to the problem would have been the provision of properly-prepared vessels manned by naval crews, *ie* the creation of a fleet of formal troopships in the modern sense of the term. The notion of such a force was nothing new and even a civilian such as Spencer Perceval, the Chancellor of the Exchequer, had badgered the Admiralty about its potential worth, not merely in financial terms but also in respect of flexibility, reliability and security.[23] Unfortunately there were also snags, most pertinently when it came to the questions of where the Admiralty was to obtain such vessels and the crews to man them. Custom-building troopships would have been a process both extended and expensive and the only alternative to this was to convert old, existing warships, retaining some of their guns and a portion of their crews and keeping them under naval command and discipline. Such a step would reduce the number of warships available for more general duties, but the Admiralty, when finally instructed to implement the schemes for such vessels in March 1810, compromised by converting some of the more ancient 64- and 50-gun warships that were increasingly unable to stand in line of battle against larger opponents, as well as a few of the older frigates. By the summer of 1810 over a dozen such ships were entering service, though their numbers of course were insufficient to replace the lumbering fleets of merchant vessels for the movement of large forces of troops. The new troopships had a total lift capacity of only perhaps 6000 men for the shorter voyages associated with Peninsular operations, but they did provide for the moving of smaller numbers of troops more rapidly and securely. They were destined to play a prominent part in Iberian naval operations and were first employed in September 1810 when three battalions of infantry in England were moved out to Portugal, nine of them, with a lift capacity of just under 4000 men, being put under Berkeley's command. The value of these troopships was more clearly illustrated when two of them, the *Diadem* and the *Regulus*, shipped the almost 1000-strong 1/23rd Foot from Halifax, Nova Scotia, to Lisbon in 34 days in October–November. When the same unit had been moved in conventional transports to Canada in 1808,

99

the voyage had taken 56 days, during which one transport had rammed another and one had got separated, taking even longer to complete the journey.[24]

While the Navy fulfilled its primary role of maintaining the army's constantly available escape-hatch during the autumn and winter of 1810–11, Berkeley was also providing Wellington with many other valuable services. According to Wellington's own despatch, naval personnel gave useful support to Lieutenant-Colonel Fletcher in the monumental work involved in constructing the Torres Vedras fortifications. But the army commander also sought naval aid in rendering them fully effective by requesting some men familiar with Popham's code of signals to man the signal stations that formed a part of the Lines. There were five such stations in all, the chief among them being on a high point immediately above the village where Wellington had his headquarters. The seamen concerned, led by a lieutenant from the *Barfleur*, seem to have taken up their posts as early as July 1810, a long time before the French appeared, and certainly became highly proficient in their duties. They were eventually able to pass a message from one end of the Lines to the other, a distance of 29 miles, with unerring accuracy in a mere seven minutes.[25]

Such signalling facilities in no sense marked the end of naval contributions to the defence of Lisbon. In June, when requesting the signallers, Wellington also asked for some armed vessels to operate on the Tagus between Alhandra and the capital and for gunboats to guard the coast between Mafra and Maceira. Coastal security was provided as part of the station's normal duties, but Berkeley responded to the question of controlling the Tagus by forming a flotilla of armed launches and flatboats drawn from all the assembled shipping, the flatboats in the event being found particularly useful in both moving troops and forming bridges, Berkeley requesting the Admiralty early in 1811 to send him some more. This flotilla was manned by seamen and put under the command of the admiral's nephew, a lieutenant on the *Barfleur*. The arrival of the French in October prompted the vessels to move up the river to Alhandra, a transport armed with two of the *Barfleur*'s 18-pounder cannon going with them. The force was soon engaged in duels with the enemy along the river's edge and on the 13th an attack was directed on the town of Villafranca, the French being driven from their positions by cannon fire and pursued inland for some distance. In this action the French lost General Saint-Croix, 'its most brilliant and energetic cavalry officer', killed when he was cut in two by a shot from one of the British vessels.[26] Towards the end of October the flotilla was strengthened by men from the fleet serving on land as well and by 6 November three artillery pieces had been established in a mud fort on an island in the Tagus opposite Salvaterra. From there another was soon placed on another island farther up the river opposite Santarem, then the main base for the whole of Massena's army. Fire from five assorted cannon was opened upon Santarem on 12 November and four days later 42 of 'Congreve's infernal rockets' were also aimed at the place, four actually managing to hit Santarem and as many exploding among the British. These batteries were manned by over 200 seamen and marines prior to their withdrawal in early December.[27]

Early in November Wellington had asked Berkeley for the loan of some officers familiar with Congreve rockets as it was his intention to move some of his cavalry under Major-General Fane across to the southern side of the Tagus to observe French movements as well as to try and destroy bridging materials that Massena was supposed to be assembling at Santarem. Wellington was extremely keen to prevent any French crossing of the Tagus and the possible link-up between Massena's command and that of Soult in southern Spain. Fane's 1500-strong force was passed over the river and, although the eventual rocket attack did little damage, it did make it clear to the French that any attempt to cross the river would not only be opposed by the flotilla, but would also face immediate assault once ashore on the opposite bank. As it was, the French were confined to the increasingly barren territory on the northern bank, Massena finally being compelled to pull his men back into the more fertile area between Santarem and the River Zezere in the middle of November when it became apparent that Wellington was not going to evacuate Lisbon without a fight. The Allies only slowly became aware of this partial withdrawal and Wellington continued to worry in case the French managed to cross to the southern bank. To block any such move, the flotilla was called upon to effect an even larger trans-riverine movement when Lieutenant-General Hill was instructed to lead 14,000 men to the southern side. The crossing was overseen by Rear-Admiral Williams, sent out to Berkeley as a junior flag officer in the light of his squadron's growing size, and was completed without a hitch, Wellington telling Lord Liverpool that 'in every instance I have received the most cordial and friendly assistance from Admiral Berkeley and the officers and men of the squadron under his command'. When Massena proved unable to cross the Tagus himself, Wellington was for many weeks to have in the back of his mind the possible necessity of requiring a return of Hill's detached force to the main body. Here again the flexibility provided by the flotilla was a huge asset. Although the vessels were briefly withdrawn from service in the middle of December, this was during a sustained period of wet weather that rendered active military operations highly unlikely. The French withdrawal provided an opportunity for the boats to be cleaned and Berkeley observed that a single tide would be sufficient to see them up river once again. As late as January 1811 Wellington was continuing to speculate about the possible need for Hill's force to be moved back to the northern bank and was concerned about how such a transfer might be managed given the swollen state of the Tagus. He fretted about embarkation and landing points and the influence of tides, relying heavily upon Berkeley's advice:

> The knowledge which you can give me on these points, and of the length of time which the passage will probably take, will enable me to form a disposition of the troops on the left of the Tagus, which, at the same time that it will secure the objects there, will make it certain that I shall not want them in the lines, if the enemy should think of making another movement upon us.[28]

A final assistance for the army came in the shape of the short-lived naval brigade, a body of 500 sailors and a similar number of marines drawn from Berkeley's fleet. Wellington floated the idea for such a force on 10 November, proposing that they should occupy the fortified positions around Lisbon, particularly St Julian and Cascaes, so as to relive army formations for more active duties. Berkeley had already in part anticipated this sort of request and had formed a provisional marine battalion drawn from his warships, having it constantly drilled throughout the summer. Some of those who made up the naval brigade were already serving on the islands up the Tagus, but the whole notion was making the Admiralty nervous. Worried that the Toulon fleet might seize the moment to make mischief at Lisbon or Cadiz, they were concerned to ensure that all the Portuguese station's warships were kept in a state of constant readiness for sea and wanted them to be properly manned at all times. Such effectiveness included the vessels' marine complements, although they did agree to their serving ashore if there was a dire need. To try and ease any problems such views might cause, however, the Admiralty did send out a complete reserve battalion of marines for service ashore and in the Tagus as a replacement. On the spot in Lisbon the two commanders effectively arranged a compromise to circumvent at least some of the inconvenience that the Admiralty's worries were likely to cause. The seamen serving on land were returned to their ships in December although the marines remained ashore, Berkeley reassuring his nervous superiors that he had never lost sight of the possible need for a rapid return to their vessels in an emergency and that this could be managed in half-an-hour if necessary. On Christmas Day Wellington responded to rumours that Massena was about to be reinforced by moving the 2/88th Foot, the last regular formation in Lisbon, up to the forward positions. The reserve marine battalion was moved to a position a few miles north of the capital, while the ships' marines remained in the city, quite literally holding the forts. Early in January Berkeley was again even prepared to put seamen ashore, landing 250 of them to help the marine artillery to hold Fort St Julian and the fortified positions in the vicinity of the harbour entrance.[29]

Gradually the sense of crisis engendered during these weeks began to ease as Massena first made no attempt to break the Lines and then retired to Santarem, still making no effort to engage the Allied forces and expel them from the country. Finally, with his army starving and with no hope of reinforcement or resupply, the tenacious marshal was compelled to retreat back to Spain. As it happened, the honour of discovering this move fell to the Navy, some gunboats reconnoitring Santarem on 5 March observing the departure and quickly passing the news back to Wellington's pickets. Ten days later, in full retreat, Massena felt obliged to destroy most of his baggage and wheeled vehicles to lighten his army and speed its progress. With operations now moving decisively away from Lisbon, Berkeley ordered that in future provisions should be landed at Peniche or Figueira, instructing his cruisers to tell any victuallers they encountered to sail to those harbours. Once there they were to provide local commissaries with any provisions that were required and only then were they to proceed on to the Tagus. The admiral suggested that convoys coming from Britain follow the same procedure, though he warned that to do so they would have to consist of small vessels able to cross the shallow Figueira bar.[30]

The French retreat prompted a rapid change in the whole naval situation. On 20 March Wellington agreed to a substantial reduction in the transport tonnage that needed to be retained in the Tagus. Each division of infantry or cavalry would therefore have its baggage held in a single transport. Sufficient tonnage was to be kept on hand for an immediate lift of 3000 infantry and 300 cavalry and the vessels employed as hospital ships would also remain. Finally Wellington also offered to land the bulk of his ordnance stores, with the exception of the battering train and its stores, and place them in a depot at St Julian. Should a withdrawal be necessary in the future he wanted four jetties constructed so that these items could be quickly re-embarked: he asked Berkeley to co-ordinate with Fletcher on their construction. Thanks to these arrangements Berkeley could report by the end of March that 148 transports of 45,764 tons were soon to be sent back to Britain, leaving 108 vessels of 29,723 tons remaining in the Tagus to meet the army's continuing needs – 42 of these vessels were victuallers and storeships. Berkeley was doubtless delighted to see the back of the troublesome transports and their crews, though the accompanying reduction in the strength of the Portuguese station's warships was much less welcome. On 30 March he was ordered to send Williams and five of his ships of the line back to England; also to be sent home were the marine battalion and a marine artillery detachment that had seen some months' service in Portugal. Within a month further instructions were received in Lisbon telling the admiral to return all of his ships of the line except the *Barfleur* and the *Elizabeth*, the injunction to return the marine battalion being repeated. Berkeley was most unwilling to see his command so denuded and in the middle of May the Admiralty had to insist that the ships of the line and the marines be returned. He had no choice but to part with the warships, though with the marine battalion serving in the Lisbon citadel he felt that it should stay until replaced by an equivalent army formation. Wellington also pressed for the marines to remain and the Admiralty was obliged to concur.[31]

Berkeley continued to express his indignation at the removal of his more powerful warships, pointedly complaining about the number of spare sets of sails for ships of the line that the bureaucratic Admiralty machine continued sending out to Lisbon. In June 1811 such sets were surplus to his squadron's requirements 'especially at its present reduced number' and he wondered if his storehouses might be put to better use 'if their Lordships mean to keep this Squadron in its present state'. He had already twitched under an Admiralty rebuke the previous month for sending vessels home while considering them still under his orders, a usurpation of their prerogative. Protesting that any instructions he might have issued were merely provisional, he insisted that they only served to illustrate his dearth of cruisers as well as of the larger warships. Even the new troopships, so important an addition to his command, were a source of exasperation, Wellington himself complaining that these vessels tended to sail back to Britain in the course of their duties and then not return, their value making them the objects for a whole variety of troop-moving missions. The Admiralty was doing its best to give priority to the Peninsula and in November 1811 placed six of the troopships under his orders, though this was three fewer than he had originally been allocated. The Navy Board was also told that these vessels were to receive priority in all refitting work so that they might be hastened back into service as rapidly as possible. Problems continued for Berkeley, however. After the fall of Ciudad Rodrigo in January 1812 he anticipated the influx of 1600 French prisoners of war and the need to employ his two remaining troopships to ship them back to Britain. By April Wellington was asking for sufficient tonnage to move 6000 troops on 'a secret service' in June and the admiral had to request that the troopships be sent to him, he pointing out that when they were first appointed to him he sent home equivalent merchant tonnage and consequently had no other capacity available.[32] Fundamentally there were just not the resources available in either tonnage or manpower adequately to meet all the demands that were being put on a Royal Navy that was increasingly feeling the strains of a global conflict. As will be seen in a later chapter, this pressure was only to get worse from the summer of 1812 and was to cause severe friction between Wellington and the naval authorities trying to support him.

Back in Portugal the French retreat in March 1811 had seen a cautious pursuit by the Anglo-Portuguese army, the bulk of it operating north of the Tagus while a secondary force, now under Lieutenant-General Beresford, occupied positions south of the river. Both of these groups were soon very many miles away from any situation where direct naval support could be forthcoming. On 3–5 May Wellington defeated Massena's attempt to regain the strategic initiative at Fuentes d'Oñoro, while to the south the bloody battle at Albuera on the 16th saw Beresford repulsing an effort by Soult to lift the Allied siege of Badajoz. Despite these successes the situation on the Portuguese frontier was to remain stalemated for the remainder of 1811. The French were no longer able to muster sufficient numbers to mount any credible invasion of Portugal, while their continuing control of the fortresses of Cuidad Rodrigo and Badajoz provided barriers to any major advance by Wellington into Spain. Two Allied efforts to take Badajoz during the course of the year were to be thwarted by a combination of French relieving forces and grossly inadequate siege artillery.

The Navy could do little to break this deadlock and, although six 'ship-guns' were brought up from Lisbon to support the second siege of Badajoz, no requests for naval aid seem to have been made. It did, however, make a significant contribution to Allied land communications. At the end of March Wellington had ordered Beresford to march southwards to drive the French out of Estremadura and to capture Badajoz. The resulting operations were hampered by several factors, one of which was the serious problem of bridging the Guadiana south of the fortress, at Jerumenha, to allow the siege to be pursued. The army experienced delays while bridging materials and pontoons were found and it was not until early April that Beresford was able to cross the river. Unfortunately the new construction was by no means fully reliable and at the end of the month a sudden downpour of heavy rain saw the flimsy bridge washed away by a rapid rise of the river. It was evident that the crossing would have to be made more reliable if the appalling prospect of an Allied force being suddenly trapped on the wrong side of the river was to be avoided. In this situation naval personnel were once again called upon to give assistance. On 12 May a party of seamen led by Lieutenant Geddes of the *Barfleur* and Lieutenant Brown of the transport service marched from Abrantes with seven flatboats to act as pontoons for the bridge, each boat being loaded on a carriage and hauled by ten oxen. It was 84 miles to Jerumenha, though the road was a good one and the party accomplished the journey in five and half days, the main problems being the exhaustion of the oxen and the constant need to repair the carriages. These latter were built of old artillery carriage wheels and country carts strengthened by iron bars, the whole being very indifferently put together according to one observer. Shortly after their arrival fresh orders were received from Wellington. By that time the bridge over the Guadiana was more secure and the commander then wanted another one built 68 miles to the north at Villa Velha on the Tagus. Wellington wanted some of the seamen to remain for a short while at Jerumenha, but required the bulk of them to be employed at Villa Velha to construct a standing bridge and two or three flying bridges. Although the second journey would be shorter than the first, the terrain to be crossed was much more difficult. The party, with four flatboats, set out on 5 June, the initial going from Jerumenha to Nisa being comparatively easy, although even on this stretch trees and stones had to be cleared away and sometimes the carriages carrying the boats had to take to adjoining fields. Not a day passed without axles and wheels breaking and repairs being needed. However, the worst was still to come, the last twelve miles taking two days across very rugged terrain. Moving the boats down the steep slopes of mountains required the use of a seven-inch hawser for their support, while dragging them up the other side needed the efforts of 24 and sometimes 30 oxen. Another five boats were floated up the river to Villa Velha from Abrantes, though this too involved exhausting and difficult labour. The 52-mile journey took six days, each boat requiring 50 men using a seven-inch hawser to drag them through the stretches where the river narrowed, cascades of ten or twelve feet in perpendicular height and a hundred yards in length being encountered and the seamen having to work up to their waists in water. Once at Villa Velha the boats could be quickly converted into a bridge, the seamen remaining with it until they were replaced by Portuguese troops. Writing of these endeavours in August, Berkeley felt that such exertions would not be necessary again as by that time the army had arranged for its own pontoons to be in place. He smugly observed that:

> I was well aware of what an Arduous undertaking it was, but I was equally convinced that the persevering spirit and resources of British Seamen would overcome all the difficulties which appeared unsurmountable [sic], to co-operate with their Bretheren in Arms, and assist in that particular branch of duty which was a little new to our Army.

Such condescending tones may in part have been prompted by a feeling that the efforts of his men had not been sufficiently recognised by Wellington. He had earlier noted in a report to the Admiralty that his personnel had greatly assisted the army's operations, work 'in which a degree of science has been displayed which may possibly entitle them to the thanks of the Commander-in-chief, if he has any to spare, from those which are so very deservedly bestowed upon his gallant Army'. Certainly the seamen's labours were of great value to Wellington, the bridge at Villa Velha in particular being an immense asset to his north-south communications: the assorted parts of his army could march from one wing to the other twice as quickly as their more incommoded French opponents.[33]

Berkeley's peevishness was perhaps a general reflection of his irritation at the way his command was so obviously becoming a military backwater. With the removal of any direct French threat the Admiralty refused to reinforce his squadron to any great extent, nor would they even approve his scheme to establish a chain of signal posts stretching from Lisbon to the mouth of the Tagus to give early warning of the appearance of any enemy naval units. At the time he mooted the idea, in November 1811, the admiral was sufficiently alarmed about such a possibility to put the batteries at the river's mouth on a state of alert and to have furnaces for heated shot prepared. His masters in London remained unmoved, seemingly believing that their blockading squadrons off the western French arsenals were a sufficient guarantee of Portuguese security.[34]

Early in January 1812, Wellington was at last able to break the deadlock on the frontier by his seizure of Ciudad Rodrigo, a blow that had been carefully prepared and whose first stage had involved shipping the army's siege train from Lisbon to Oporto and then up to the limits of the Douro's navigation at Lamego. Thereafter the guns had to be dragged by the army overland. The capture opened up the northern road into Spain and in April it was followed up by the much more difficult, and much more bloody, storming of Badajoz. Berkeley happily reported the fortress's fall with the pious hope that the 30 cannon and 14,000 rounds of shot he had supplied from Lisbon would have been of assistance in the success. But in truth he had, for once, done comparatively little to help his colleagues. The admiral supplied the army with only 20, not 30, 18-pounder guns as a supplement to the siege train and these were Russian weapons taken from the remains of Siniavin's ships. They were in poor condition, many of the shot in the arsenal did not fit them properly and their power did not match that of the 24-pounders which Berkeley would not release. Perhaps it was his knowledge of his squadron's weakness in ships of the line, he having only two such vessels, that made him reluctant to weaken the *Barfleur*: such ordnance would have had to have been taken from his flagship, moored more or less permanently in the Tagus. Any guns so supplied would have been beyond any recall for weeks. Certainly his unwillingness stands as a singular instance of his making anything less than a maximum effort to further the Allied cause.[35]

Berkeley's tenure of the Portuguese command finally ended when he was succeeded by Vice-Admiral Martin in June 1812, and he sailed home to England in the *Barfleur* the following month. Upon his return he retired from public life and died in 1818. His name has passed into obscurity, with the notorious exception of the *Chesapeake* incident, and this is most unfair. His stalwart service in Lisbon in 1808–12 is much more worthy of notice and should entitle him to consideration as one of the more important British figures of the Peninsular War. Berkeley proved that admirals did not have to win major sea battles or oversee lengthy blockades to have a successful impact on military events.

CHAPTER 4

Convoys, Bullion and Arms

'. . . our maritime superiority gives me the power of
maintaining my army while the enemy are unable to do so'.
Wellington, 21 September 1813[1]

UNQUESTIONABLY THE MOST direct and dramatic contribution
to the Peninsular War made by naval power was the rescue of
Moore's army in 1809, and with it the promise thereafter of a
repeat performance should the situation in Portugal demand it.
Here was the most visible illustration of the importance of
British control of the seas.

Convoys

However, only marginally less important than this were the
convoys that ceaselessly plied to and from Iberian harbours in the
years after 1808. It was a crucial Allied advantage over the French
that that convoy system allowed them to move not only troops,
but all their equipment, stores and supplies with a high degree of
safety to those points considered most useful. Indeed, for island
Britain to pursue any sort of aggressive overseas strategy with
success, such security was essential. Nor did it stop there, for
alongside all the movements coming under the 'military' heading
there was also the question of trade protection. With Napoleon
using his Continental System to try and cripple Britain's
European trade, and along with it British financial muscle, the
access to any market was a matter of great importance to British
well-being. The Peninsular conflict meant that Portugal continued to be a valuable trading partner that would not be closed off
by France, while Spain, hitherto largely closed because of her
hostility, would be open for business, in her liberated areas at

least. The Royal Navy had to protect this commerce to and from the Iberian markets alongside similar duties in the Mediterranean, the Baltic, the Caribbean, and to North America and the East Indies.

For the historian this situation presents a problem. Although the protection of convoys was a vital naval responsibility and one that was carried on with an overwhelming degree of success, the whole process does include within it an element of invisibility. This period saw none of the arguments about the convoy system that so nearly wrecked Britain's strategy in the First World War, nor were there the ferocious convoy battles that were such a feature of the Second World War. However, if the drama was missing the importance was not. Any perusal of the relevant Admiralty documents pertaining to the Peninsular War immediately makes crystal clear how important convoys were and just how much time, effort and resource were devoted to the process. The despatches of the commanding admirals in Lisbon, for example, endlessly refer to convoys leaving, arriving, forming, being delayed, etc, and one list from the late summer of 1810 shows that Berkeley was employing a third of his smaller warships, frigates and below, as convoy escorts.[2]

That the Peninsular War greatly increased these responsibilities is borne out by the statistics that are available. From the summer of 1808 until the spring of 1814 one Admiralty list shows that 404 convoys sailed from Britain to an assortment of Iberian destinations, these ranging in size from small movements of just one or two ships, to huge assemblages of 90 or 100 vessels. All told it records some 13,427 ship voyages.[3] Nor does this in any sense comprise the whole picture. These numbers make no allowance for such vessels returning home from the Peninsula or proceeding to and from other non-British destinations as well as the escorts required for convoys going between Iberian ports. The net effort was a huge and complex responsibility with at least one escorting warship being required for each sailing and, in the case of important troop movements, several such warships being deemed necessary. To provide such escorts meant that there were few warship movements that did not also involve simultaneous convoy protection, as vessels sailing to join new stations or returning home for refits or assignments to other duties guarded convoys heading in the same direction. Alongside these *ad hoc* arrangements other, less fortunate, captains seemed to have found themselves more or less permanently consigned to the duty of protecting the lumbering fleets of merchantmen. Only those very small warships concerned with delivering despatches and other vessels assigned to move bullion supplies, *ie* missions where speed was considered essential, were regularly excused this tiresome duty. Senior officers who did not keep a constant eye open for the movement of convoys under all possible circumstances were likely to receive a very sharp rebuke. In March 1813, for example, Rear-Admiral Linzee, newly appointed to the command at Gibraltar, was reprimanded by his superiors for sending home the *Ajax* (74) without her convoy from Port Mahon because she was carrying despatches from Sicily as well as Lieutenant-General Bentinck's secretary. The Admiralty made it clear that in such cases the convoy's continued progress and security were the prime considerations. If speed were considered essential then a smaller warship should have been employed.[4]

In a purely military sense the value to the Allied cause of this ability to move men and equipment safely by sea was truly immense. This can be observed most obviously in the steady build-up of British forces in Spain and Portugal as the war progressed. Prior to the introduction of the specialist armed troopships in 1810, all of these movements were handled by conventional convoys and even after the troopships' appearance many soldiers and all of their heavy equipment was still shipped in the usual way. However, within the confines of the theatre itself the ability to employ coastal convoys could give the Allies a degree of flexibility and mobility often denied their French opponents. Many instances of this could be cited and some are already evident in previous chapters, but perhaps the circumstances at Cadiz and the peregrinations of Wellington's battering train will illustrate the point sufficiently.

The great Spanish naval arsenal was placed under siege by the French in February 1810 and in the same month, eager to help preserve its future, Wellington asked for convoys to move three British infantry battalions and another of Portuguese soldiers from Lisbon to the fortress. These formations were followed two months later by vessels carrying a squadron of light dragoons and their horses, camp equipage for 5000 men and 400,000lbs of salt provisions. Berkeley met all of these demands and further supplies of provisions – meat, biscuits, spirits, oats and hay – were moved to Cadiz from Britain, five victuallers leaving Plymouth in June.[5] Once the initial crisis at Cadiz had passed, and with the fortress now looking in no immediate danger, it became equally important for Wellington to see his frontline units returned to more pressing service in Portugal, being replaced in the south of Spain by less experienced formations. Consequently, in August 1810, Berkeley received an application for a convoy to move about 2000 troops and 160 horses back to Lisbon, though as it happened Lieutenant-General Graham, the Anglo-Portuguese commander at Cadiz, had anticipated Wellington's wishes and already sent the units on their way. The convoy moving them reached the Tagus early in September and a week later Wellington was requesting that three more battalions be similarly transferred to Portugal. Once again the process was smoothly managed, the net effect of this minor example of sea power in action being that Cadiz had been reinforced in its hour of maximum peril, but without depriving the main Allied army in the Peninsula of five battalions of infantry and some cavalry at a time when the French were closing in on Lisbon.[6]

Wellington's heavy siege artillery provides a similar story. In March 1811 this was loaded aboard eleven transports moored in the Tagus and two months later was shipped north to Oporto, eventually, as noted in the previous chapter, being transferred to Mondego Bay and then up the Douro as far as it was navigable. Finally it was hauled laboriously overland, a movement requiring the use of 384 pairs of oxen, 1092 country carts and hundreds of men, and successfully employed at Ciudad Rodrigo in January and Badajoz in April. After this, anticipating no immediate likelihood of sieges for his own army, Wellington asked Berkeley to send the train to Gibraltar, where some of its carriages could be repaired, and from where it would go to the eastern coast in anticipation of an Allied siege of Tarragona. In the event the guns got no farther than Alicante as no assault on Tarragona materialised, Wellington then requesting in

February 1813 that they be shipped back to the west, to Corunna. By early June the train had reached that port, moving on to Santander by the end of the month just as yet more orders arrived from the army commander ordering that they be moved again to Deba, near Bilbao. Eventually the guns were unloaded early in July at Passages, a small harbour near San Sebastian. Thanks to naval mobility Wellington could have his cumbersome siege train wherever he wanted it in a comparatively short space of time, provided, of course, there was deep-water access. Two French experiences may be compared to this. When the Army of Andalusia was finally obliged to lift the siege of Cadiz in August 1812 its larger pieces of artillery could not be moved in the circumstances of the withdrawal, they having instead to be destroyed or spiked and the ammunition blown up or fired off. Even more ignominious was the fate of the Army of Portugal's battering train. Numbering no fewer than 153 heavy guns, with all their accompanying stores, this cumbersome mass had to be left in Ciudad Rodrigo when the army marched into Portugal in September 1810. Fifteen months later all these pieces were still there when the Allies stormed the fortress and were duly captured along with it.[7]

In many ways even more telling of the vital advantage provided by maritime convoys is a Victualling Office document. At the end of 1809 it was decided that, so vast were the stocks of flour and salt provisions accumulated in the depots of Lisbon via supply convoys, that supplies then loaded aboard victualling ships in Plymouth and Portsmouth would be re-assigned for the fleet's use.[8] A year later the French outside Lisbon would be starving.

While the movement of military-oriented convoys took priority, the Navy had to protect civilian trade with the Peninsula as well. By the Compulsory Convoy Act of 1798, a measure renewed in 1803, the bulk of civilian merchant traffic was permitted to sail only as part of a convoy. Non-Iberian exceptions were the large, armed East Indiamen, those vessels involved in the Irish trade and Hudson Bay Company ships, plus some fast vessels granted Admiralty licences 'to run', *ie* sail alone. The latter apart, therefore, all merchantmen trading with Spain and Portugal required the protection of a convoy. Anyone who

defied the law and risked sailing alone was liable to a fine of
£1000. Furthermore, every master whose ship was part of a
convoy had to display the relevant act making him liable to obey
all the signals directed at him by naval escorts and committing
him not to abandon the convoy without due permission.[9]
Convoys were supposed to sail each month to Spain and
Portugal, though this could alter according to circumstances
and those returning to Britain were particularly vulnerable to
delays caused by a shortage of escorts. Moreover, trade sailing
from Ireland did not even enjoy such theoretical regularity, for
as late as 1813 the chairman of the Liverpool, Portugal and
Brazil Association was to be found writing to the Admiralty
seeking convoys to sail from Cork to Portugal at regular intervals. Previous delays had been such as to hamper the domestic
shippers very seriously to the commercial benefit of their
neutral rivals. He sought a monthly convoy to Portugal to
counteract this trend, the Admiralty going so far as to agree to
one every two months or whenever twenty merchant vessels had
assembled, whichever was the sooner.[10]

The value of this Iberian trade was considerable and comprised an important breach in the Continental System. Exports
to Portugal, which had hovered around an official value of
£1,000,000 in 1804–6, had sharply fallen during the period of
disruption and occupation in 1807–8. Thereafter they recovered slowly in 1809, almost reached £1,500,000 in 1810 and in
1811–12, with the French expelled, achieved official values
respectively of £4,729,000 and £3,461,000. In these latter two
years, difficult ones for the British economy generally, the
overall official values for British exports stood at £32,400,000
and £43,242,000 respectively. The figures for Spain tell a
similar story. Prior to the uprising against Napoleon Britain's
exports there were minimal: in 1806, even including items
exported to Gibraltar where a proportion would have been
smuggled into Spain, the official total stood at under £800,000.
By 1809 this figure had rocketed to just over £6,000,000.
Thereafter, in the wake of this glut, the market fell back, but in
1812 its total official value still stood at just over £4,500,000 if
the Gibraltar figures are included. In that year the Iberian
Peninsula was taking in excess of 20 per cent of Britain's

exports. The worth of British imports from the region was considerably less, but the figures still show that it was of significance. Items from Portugal, though varying like the export trade because of military and economic circumstances, averaged just over £850,000 per annum during 1806–12 according to official values, while those from Spain averaged just over £800,000 in the same period.[11]

This trade had specific features. Most important of the imports from Portugal was port wine, shipped from Oporto despite the uncertainties associated with crossing its difficult bar and the problems caused by the prevailing northerly winds. The country also provided figs, oranges, lemons and salt, such commodities being shipped from Lisbon. Berkeley felt it necessary to remind the Admiralty at one point of the pressures all this put on his available means. The fruit ships loaded their highly perishable cargoes between May and October, there also being monthly convoys to provide for other items moving from Lisbon as well as for all the vessels shipping salt for the domestic market and the North American fisheries. At that time, April 1809, he also had to contend with the United States Embargo Act, which made it necessary for cargoes destined for Britain to be reshipped into British bottoms. Finally, of course, he had to provide escorts for all the army's needs. Imports of fruit were also important features of the commerce with Spain, such as raisins from Malaga and Alicante as well as oranges from Seville. All such trade, though, was even more at the mercy of the war than the commerce with Portugal, where the French occupation did not last as long, and was liable to frequent interruption.[12]

In terms of exports, both Iberian nations took a portion of Britain's colonial re-exports, though with each having their own colonial settlements this was never going to be large, especially in the case of Spain where the Spaniards, much to the fury of some British ministers, remained determined to try and keep control of their own markets and exclude for as long as possible the icy draught of British competition. Of great importance to all three nations, however, was the trade in fish. Both Spain and Portugal imported large quantities of this, much of it coming from the Newfoundland fisheries. The exports from there almost doubled in 1804–15 and many of the traders involved

carried on a triangular traffic, shipping out the assorted neces-
saries of life from Britain, picking up the cargoes of fish and
transporting them across the Atlantic to an assortment of
Iberian ports, and then returning home with wines and fruit.[13]
In short, the volume of shipping movements generated by
Iberian commerce was very large and so, correspondingly, were
the Navy's escort duties.

The word 'convoy' when applied to such activities tends
immediately to suggest an image of the films and pictures of the
Second World War, with organised lines of merchant vessels
being escorted by numerous rapid warships and occasionally
ships exploding when struck by torpedoes. In the Napoleonic
period the reality was very different. In theory convoys sailed in
rectangular or sometimes diamond formations, the larger col-
lections of vessels sailing in two such groups with protecting
warships between them and around them. All civilian masters
were issued at the start of the voyage with a copy of the
Admiralty's convoy signal book, instructing them in the mean-
ings of the various flags that the senior escort would fly during
the voyage to direct the convoy's progress. These included the
sort of orders that might have been expected, such as flags for
making more sail, altering course and for vessels to close up.
Other likely instructions included signals to be made at night or
in fog, guns, flares and lights being employed at such times.
This was the theory providing for the smooth movement of
trade: in practice things frequently bore little resemblance to
this ideal.[14]

Many of the problems arising in such a process stemmed
from the often very poor relations between naval officers and
their civilian brethren, men who tended to come from different
social backgrounds and possessing different outlooks and prior-
ities. For the civilian masters, usually hard-bitten men with
years of maritime experience behind them, the prospect of
being ordered around by some young, pompous naval sprig still
wet behind the ears, to the master's mind, cannot have been
agreeable. Furthermore, the merchant skipper, preoccupied
with the approval of owners concerned with profits, and very
likely having a share in the vessel and a similar concern for
financial returns, cannot have sympathised with naval men who

could delay his ship in port for weeks while the convoy was being formed. Nor was the prospect of having a portion of his crew impressed by his protectors at the end of the voyage at all conducive to harmony. On the other side of the coin the naval officer confronted by numerous bloody-minded and wilful civilian masters who seemed indifferent to measures designed for their own protection could be quickly reduced to a state of complete exasperation. Many naval captains can be found fulminating against the indiscipline of masters who at night, even in fine weather, always tried to creep to windward in the belief that this would make them safer, one ship moving to windward of the next and so on, causing much of the following day to be spent in trying to get the whole body together again. Ships would sometimes desert convoys, perhaps to gain the first market, or out of a spirit of rivalry, or simply out of fear of the press-gang. As the Napoleonic War dragged on the increasing presence of foreign vessels, with captains who could not understand English, only made the problems worse. At their worst these difficulties could have serious consequences, one admiral reporting on damages to the *Alfred* and a gun brig when two transports ran foul of them, accidents caused by the 'wilfulness, neglect or ignorance of the Masters of the Transports'. This incident cost the lives of two seamen on the gun brig and he felt that legal action ought to be taken. Beneath the bad relations described in many despatches one can also sometimes detect the whiff of social snobbery from naval officers, who were regarded as gentlemen, towards civilian captains whose place in society was often less certain.[15]

Certainly the task of escorting convoys would appear to have been the sort of duty that could try the patience of a saint and it seems to have been heartily loathed by most naval officers. Captains referred to masters 'not one of them having paid the least attention to the Signals made by me for making more Sail or Closing'. Another, taking a convoy from Newfoundland to Portugal, was delayed by fog 'as well as the inattention & perverseness of many of the Convoy'. A third, Captain King of the *Druid* (32), arrived from Lisbon complaining of the general negligence of his charges, five masters in particular having roused his ire to the point where he summoned them aboard his ship to be lectured on their shortcomings. One of the five still refused to accept his written instructions despite having them proffered to him several times in the presence of the *Druid*'s first lieutenant. In the face of this sort of obstruction some senior naval officers, not, one suspects, individuals used to being baulked, could take the sharpest of countermeasures. One young officer of the 1790s fondly recalled Vice-Admiral Cosby, 'a glorious fellow for keeping the convoy in order, and if they did not immediately obey the signal, he would fire at them without further ceremony'. Another captain in 1804 had even reached the point of formalising his intolerance, with prepared signals instructing that crewmen be impressed from disobedient convoy members or for merchant ships to be fired upon.[16] This dislike could also prompt some commanders to try and avoid the duty altogether, Berkeley complaining at one point that captains bringing convoys to Lisbon would not enter the port so as to avoid having to escort trade and/or transports back to Britain on their return voyage. The Admiralty agreed with his request that all warships going to the Tagus be instructed actually to enter the port and come under his orders. Even so, some unscrupulous officers would still risk official wrath to avoid the hated duty, Berkeley raging in 1811 that one Captain Kent of the *Wolverine* (18) had taken some transports carrying the 5th Dragoons as far as Cape Roxant and then sent them on to Lisbon without any escort at all, his orders to the admiral being delivered by an agent of transports! The furious station commander was then left without a warship to escort the transports home. In another instance Captain Braimer of the *Castilian* (18) left Cork in March 1813 along with the *Jalouse* (18) and a convoy of trade for Gibraltar. *Castilian* was at the rear of the convoy when Braimer claimed that one of her masts suddenly required urgent repairs, and by the time these had been completed the convoy had disappeared. Despite firing rockets he was able to find only one of his charges, later falling in with a pair of Swedish ships that were also sailing for the Peninsula. This trio he escorted south, arriving a day ahead of the main convoy, which in the event was delivered safely by the *Jalouse* alone. In a corner note to Braimer's rather woolly account the Admiralty expressed its clear suspicions of the

whole business, being 'by no means satisfied' with the commander's explanation.[17]

More usually naval captains did exercise their responsibilities
with greater intelligence, as witnessed by the success and security of the convoy system. Overall in 1803–15 it has been estimated that only 0.6 per cent of all the ships that sailed in
convoys were lost, compared to 6.8 per cent of stragglers.[18]
Certainly those that sailed to the Peninsula in 1807–14 avoided
the sort of occasional catastrophes that struck movements in
other regions. From the hundreds involved one may perhaps
serve as an example of this vital but routine duty and give an
illustration of the process.

Early in July 1810 the sloop *Phipps* (16), Captain Bell, was
ordered to Oporto to collect the trade there for escort back to
Britain. The sloop stood in to the awkward harbour, a pilot on
board, early in the morning of the 3rd, Bell flying the signal for
a convoy and for all masters to come aboard for their instructions. The business of readying the merchant vessels took two
days and it was not until the evening of 5 July that the convoy,
some 35 vessels plus the *Phipps* as the sole escort, crossed the
Oporto bar. The following day began with Bell instructing his
charges at 5am to make more sail, the signal being repeated at
8.30am but evidently without success as at 3.30pm and 7.30pm
Bell had to heave-to while the convoy closed up. On the 7th a
brig, the *Two Brothers*, had to be taken in tow during the
evening, though she was cast off after the *Phipps* lost her fore-
topmast studding sail boom. By the next evening Bell found it
necessary to remind the convoy to observe the *Phipps*'s motions
during the night, enforcing the signal with the firing of two
shotted guns. That the convoy still proved troublesome was
evident by the warship's log recording on the 9th that she had
to wear as several merchantmen did not obey orders to make
more sail, more shots being fired in an effort to liven them up.
Even so, by the following morning three of the convoy were no
longer in sight, the *Phipps* having to heave-to once again while
they caught up in the evening. Then the weather, previously
benign, started to take a hand, the convoy being buffeted by a
gale and at daybreak on the 11th only 25 merchantmen were still
with the sloop, one of the masters ignoring Bell's signal for sail

to be shortened while the convoy reassembled. The *Phipps* fired no fewer than twelve shots to try and enforce the order but, either because of the state of the sea, or lack of observation, or sheer wilfulness, these were ignored. Bell had 31 merchantmen in company by 4pm, but other vessels that were sailing on regardless also ignored his signal to shorten sail, emphasised by gunfire though it was. Only 21 of the convoy were present by the following dawn, but they did gradually reform during the day and there were 30 merchant vessels with the *Phipps* by the evening. The total had fallen to 26 by dawn on 13 July and thereafter numbers remained constant until the 15th. On that day, the whole by then having entered the Channel, one vessel destined for Portsmouth was given permission to leave. By 17 July the convoy was off Beachy Head and Bell gave the signal for all ships to proceed independently for their various ports. The next day the *Phipps* entered Spithead and was ready to begin the whole process all over again.[19]

The story of the *Phipps*'s convoy has been detailed in this manner because, for all its problems, it was completely unremarkable and therefore representative. Despite its summer passage its main enemy was the weather. The gale broke its homogeneity and, as was the case in the age of wooden sailing ships, the elements posed a much greater threat to all maritime operations than the enemy. Peninsular-related operations were no different. The *Phipps* and her consorts escaped lightly when compared to the havoc that could be caused. In 1804 the frigate *Apollo* (36) was taking a convoy to the West Indies when a storm caused her to lose her bearings: as a result the frigate herself and 40 other vessels were wrecked on the coast between Aveiro and Figueira. On 10 November 1813 the frigate *Hyperion* (38) together with the sloop *Muros* (18) and 37 merchant vessels carrying cargoes of fish departed Newfoundland for Portugal. Ten days later 35 of the convoy were still present when the whole were struck by a north-westerly gale and scattered. Next day Cumby, the senior escorting officer, had only 18 merchantmen in company plus the sloop. The weather continued foul until 25 November, by which time only 16 vessels remained with Cumby; by 1 December this number had fallen to 13. On that day Cumby ordered the *Muros* to proceed alone with the four merchantmen bound for Lisbon while the *Hyperion* escorted the remainder, six of which were bound for Oporto. However, with their masters assuring him that the Oporto bar was impassable in such weather, the vessels instead steered a course for Corunna. Then they were hit by an even more ferocious storm and by the time it had blown itself out, on 6 December, the *Hyperion* was alone. Two days later, with much of the frigate's deck and upper works damaged and both her chain pumps defective, Cumby set course for Portsmouth. That night *Hyperion* fell in with another convoy under the *Iris* that, out of 200 vessels, had only 24 still in company. More important and better-protected shipping movements were just as vulnerable, as was observed in Chapter 2 with the convoy moving the Spanish troops from the Baltic in the autumn of 1808. A 24-hour gale in the Bay of Biscay at the end of September reduced the number of transports with the *Racoon*, the senior escort, from 54 to 28, a total that had fallen to a mere nine the following day. By 5 October the *Racoon* had managed to gather 22 of her charges together and safely delivered them to Santander three days later: the remainder appeared safely in due course, some making for Santona farther along the coast.[20]

Compared with the elements, the enemy posed a much smaller threat. The regular French navy superficially seemed to offer a growing menace to maritime operations centred on the Peninsula, its assortment of harbours on the Atlantic coast and its main Mediterranean base at Toulon appearing ideally situated for assaulting convoys. However, in reality the French faced serious difficulties as all the ports where their warships assembled attracted British blockading squadrons and the risks of a naval battle if they ventured forth. Psychologically and professionally the Royal Navy had achieved a large measure of superiority over their French opponents in the wake of Trafalgar and a string of lesser victories, with the consequence that, however bravely they might fight, Napoleon's sailors always tried to avoid battle if possible. Even when contrary winds blew the blockading warships off-station, any escaping French vessels still faced the problems of running the gauntlet of British warships that patrolled the main shipping lanes and of avoiding the pursuing ships that would be hunting for them once their escape had been noticed. Even allowing for all this, the numerous Peninsular convoys still enjoyed a high degree of security stemming from the simple vastness of the sea. If comparisons be drawn once more with the Second World War, Napoleon's captains had none of the advantages provided by lines of patrolling U-boats sweeping the North Atlantic in search of convoys and then being directed to them by radio once a target had been spotted. All of this should explain why no Peninsular convoy of the hundreds that sailed was savaged by French warships: the obstacles were too great. Similar reasons apply to the failure of the United States to disrupt the convoy routes with its warships after 1812. While the Americans were not overawed by thoughts of fighting the Royal Navy, a feeling enhanced by several ship-to-ship US victories in the war's early stages, they nevertheless could make no serious impact on Peninsular events. Not only did the Americans have to cope with being blockaded as well as trying to find targets on the vastness of the open sea, they also suffered from having a very small navy which, though possessing a few very powerful frigates, had no ships of the line at all.

A more continuous threat to Iberian traffic came in the shape of the privateer. This term encompasses a multitude of vessels, ranging from the schooners and brigs employed for deep-water operations, vessels often primarily armed with a single long gun for long-range work, packed with men and capable of high sailing speeds, down to the rowboat crewed by a few armed men ready to snap up the unwary merchantmen sailing too close to an enemy harbour. However, this form of warfare had strict strategic limits. Such warships, sailing under a licence, or 'letter of marque', to avoid charges of piracy, were interested in only one thing: profit. Their ships rarely had the armament nor their crews the discipline to engage a regular warship of similar size with much chance of success. Nor did they have the incentive, for even if successful in such an engagement the privateer was likely to be damaged and in possession of a prize of little worth. Consequently the merchant vessel in convoy, *ie* with an escorting warship, was unlikely to be at much risk. The privateers prey tended to be the solitary merchantman, incapable of much resistance and with a valuable cargo.

When considering privateering activities launched from, or directly impacting upon, the Peninsula, their effect was minimal, particularly on the western shipping routes. There the larger ports such as Lisbon, Vigo and Corunna were only briefly under French control, while those harbours on the northern coast that were occupied for many years were difficult to use, unable to provide much in the way of support facilities, and were away from the main shipping routes for much of the war. Although Wellington fretted about the safety of his supply lines after the American declaration of war, attempting to frighten ministers in London with dire predictions about how his plans might be dislocated – 'the loss of one vessel only may create a delay and inconvenience which may be of the utmost consequence' – there is no evidence to suggest that such bleak warnings came true. At least one writer has seen in such words a degree of danger in the privateering threat that was never really there, thanks to the steady reliability provided by the convoy system. This never came near to being dislocated and neither were Wellington's operations. As will be shown in a later chapter, the problems that arose in supporting land operations stemmed from a combination of geographical circumstance, inevitable delays and personal incompetence, not from enemy action.[21]

On the eastern and southern coasts of Spain the danger from privateers was to be much greater. There the proximity of harbours in southern France provided convenient bases for commerce-raiding and to these could be added others that fell under French control in Spain itself in 1808–12. Early in the summer of 1810 Captain Bullen, commanding a small squadron off the Catalan coast, reported on privateer activity in the area, noting that 'the Coast between Tarragona and Cape Del Gat swarms with them'. The following year Cotton sadly informed the Junta of Catalonia that:

> In the Summer Time no Merchant Vessel running in the Mediterranean is safe, for French Privateers swarm from Cape Falcon to Malta which are scarcely ever seen until they are close to their Prey, for they keep under the land in little Creeks, & often have Men looking out on the Hills, so that they do not go out until the vessel is seen. There are some however that Cruise.

Particularly energetic was one Giuseppe Bavastro, a Genoese freebooter whose earlier successes had already led to him being decorated by Napoleon in 1804. He led a squadron of privateers operating on the coast of Spain and was well known to his British opponents, Bullen referring to the 'notorious Bavastro of Barcelona' who was cruising off Alicante and had seized two Spanish merchant vessels. When one of Bavastro's ships was captured in June 1810 it was discovered that she had taken twelve prizes since April. Even more of an attraction were the waters around Gibraltar. There the narrowing at the entrance to the Mediterranean provided a concentration of shipping, convoys also being vulnerable to the sudden squalls for which the area was notorious and which could scatter vessels all over the sea, leaving them exposed to attack. With the French invasion of southern Spain in 1810, small harbours like Rota, Chipiona and Conil de la Frontera near to Cadiz all became centres for small privateers, they also making use of the Guadalquivir river as a base.[22]

Particularly vulnerable to assault was the Spanish coasting trade as it did not enjoy the security afforded by the convoy system that guarded British commerce. One French privateer from Marseilles, for example, took no fewer than thirteen Spanish coasters in June–July 1812, most of them sailing between Port Mahon and the mainland. With little naval power of their own the Spaniards had to rely on their ally for protection, for example General Palacio, the commander in Valencia, seeking British action both to preserve trade and communications with the Balearics and to protect vessels he had sent to procure provisions from North Africa. The Spaniards engaged in such traffic could also face attack from their own side, Codrington passing on many complaints he had received about the way in which some Spanish privateers did little other than plunder those inhabitants who took advantage of any French absence to carry on a little trade. Such vulnerability had serious implications above and beyond the fact of further weakening Spanish financial and commercial strength because the coasting trade was vital in maintaining food supplies to the various coastal garrisons and, most crucial of all, to Cadiz. When assessing the importance of holding Tarifa at the end of 1811 Commodore Penrose, then naval commander at Gibraltar, observed that in

French hands it would become an excellent privateering base, ideally situated both to attack convoys passing through the Straits and also the 'immense' Spanish coasting traffic. There were also concerns, it might be added, about Spanish instincts if put into the way of temptation, Penrose being worried that the fall of Tarifa might also occasion the loss of Algerciras, so encouraging the inhabitants of the latter place back into their 'old habits of Privateering, much to the detriment of British trade'.[23]

Encounters between British warships and privateers on the Mediterranean side of the Peninsula were fairly frequent, often the superior sailing qualities of the privateers enabling them to bolt successfully to the nearest harbour. Sometimes, though, escape was thwarted, as when the brig *Fearless* (12) snapped up a lightly-armed felucca with a crew of eight in the waters off Cadiz in 1812: the enemy vessel had carried away her yard and was unable to flee. In the same area earlier in the same year another felucca was driven ashore by the sloop *Onyx* (10) near Conil, the rough seas preventing her capture but seeing her completely wrecked.[24] Such successes in open waters, though, were comparatively rare and, although serving to make the privateers' lives more difficult and dangerous, could not make any serious inroads into the overall numbers involved. A much higher proportion of anti-privateer attacks were therefore directed at the one place in which they could not run away: in harbour. Such actions, however, could also prompt battles of an infinitely bloodier nature.

One of the sharpest of these took place in April 1812 when Captain Usher of the small frigate *Hyacinth* (20) learned that Bavastro's flotilla, numbering some twenty vessels, was about to sail from Malaga. With a force drawn from his own ship and from a sloop, brig and gunboat in company, Usher determined to try and forestall the move by a pre-emptive night attack on the mole where the enemy vessels were moored. The gunboat, three cutters and a jolly boat led by Captain Lilburn of the sloop *Goshawk* (16) assaulted the privateers, while two other groups, supervised by Usher himself, tried to neutralise two protecting batteries. One of these, containing no fewer than fifteen 24-pounder guns, was seized and its pieces turned on the castle on the other side of the harbour. However, the defenders were

undaunted and maintained a heavy fire from infantry positioned on the mole itself, the British being clearly visible in the
moonlight. In the face of such resistance, and with a falling-off
of the wind, the attackers were able to capture only two of the
privateer vessels, the whole action costing them 15 dead
(including Lilburn) and 53 wounded, many of them severely.[25]

Similar attacks, though on a smaller scale, were aimed at other
harbours when the opportunity presented itself. In May 1811
Captain Price of the sloop *Sabine* (16) sent his boats to assault
five small warships in the roads of Chipiona. These were protected by a battery and some soldiers, each vessel being armed
with two small cannon and manned by a crew of 25, individuals transferred from Antwerp specifically for the service. Three
of the vessels were captured for the loss of only one man
wounded, Price rounding off this nice little success the following day when, in company with the brig *Papillon* (14), he captured another privateer along with her prize. A month later
Captain Shepheard of the sloop *Columbine* (18) sent a party into
the Guadalquivir in pursuit of some privateers said to be
lurking there. Although successfully taking a settee mounting
two 8-inch howitzers and with a crew of 42, the attackers were
repulsed when also trying to capture a felucca, being driven off
for the loss of one man killed and five others severely wounded.
Even more costly was an attempt to take an armed schooner at
San Lucar in July, the attackers, men from the sloop *Rambler*
(14) and some of the Cadiz gunboats, initially boarding an
American vessel in error and then being impeded by the onset
of a strong south-westerly breeze. Finally confronted by a
barrage of musketry and cannon fire from the fully-alerted
French on shore, the enterprise had to be abandoned, the
British losing three dead and eleven wounded, nine seriously.[26]

These operations, along with others not detailed of a similar
nature, served to illustrate the truth of the matter that, however
much courage and initiative was displayed, only the actual occupation of the harbours could substantially reduce the dangers
posed by the daring, well-handled privateer. Lasting security in
the south was not secured until the French evacuated Andalusia
in the summer of 1812. Other privateer bases were eliminated
on the eastern coast as, in co-operation with Spanish land units,

naval forces cleared a variety of ports and harbours in the wake of the general French withdrawal. In May 1812, for example, Captain Adam escorted 300 Spanish soldiers in an operation to recapture Almeria, in the process destroying a 3-gun felucca with a crew of 45 and retaking a Spanish brig belonging to Cadiz. Later that month, further to the south at Almunecar, Usher's *Hyacinth* destroyed another privateer, while by August operations had advanced beyond Alicante, with the sloop *Termagant* (18) destroying a battery at Benidorm and seizing two Genoese privateers sheltering under its guns.[27]

By these means the privateer threat was restricted if never completely removed. The most important security device remained the convoy system which so effectively limited the availability of targets and provided a regular naval presence that would make the private raider look elsewhere for easier prey. As the conflict dragged on, moreover, the French had the additional problem of an increasing shortage of experienced manpower as the system of exchanging prisoners of war had, thanks to Napoleon's own actions, almost completely broken down. By the end of the war there were 11,841 men captured from privateers in British prisons and with the demands of the regular French navy also to be met, seamen were in short supply and the viability of privateering consequently declined.[28] As far as the Peninsula was concerned, privateering was at its most intense off the eastern and southern coasts where they could take advantage of the largely defenceless Spanish coasting trade and the occasional solitary merchantman. A problem though such attacks were, they never achieved a serious military or commercial impact.

Bullion

While the movement of troops and their equipment as well as the protection of trade may be regarded as the more obvious of naval responsibilities, a less apparent, but no less vital, duty was the transporting of specie. In Spain and Portugal the British were obliged to conduct their operations on the friendly soil of allied nations. In these circumstances it was not possible for them to campaign on the basis of compulsory requisitions, 'living off the land', which formed the basis of most French warfare. When

Wellington's men wanted something they were obliged to pay for it. This, it should be stressed, was nothing unique to operating in the Peninsula. The British army planned that wherever it fought in the world it would be supplied from depots and with transport that was procured locally: its own transport provisions were woeful. In this respect it was fortunate to fight its most protracted campaign of the period in a region where the war had dislocated the usual means whereby hundreds of Spanish muleteers earned their living. With their normal commercial activities gone, these individuals were ready and able, for pay, to serve the British and were priceless assets in keeping Wellington's formations supplied. To keep them functioning, and to procure those supplies that could be had locally, Wellington ideally required hard cash. Specie was also needed to pay his own troops, so preserving morale and limiting tendencies to scavenge and loot, as well as to fund Britain's Peninsular allies.

Bullion was therefore a key resource in Wellington's war and a casual glance through his correspondence would at times prompt one to imagine that he thought of little else. The impression could also be given that little effort was made to meet his needs in this respect. A year after his second appearance in Portugal he reminded Lord Liverpool that:

> We are still much distressed for money, and I shall not be able to pay the troops on the 24th of this month [April]. We owe for everything we have had lately from the country, as well as for the means of transport employed in moving our supplies from our own magazines.

By July of the following year, 1811, pay for the British troops was two months in arrears, and the muleteers, 'upon whose services the army depend almost as much as the soldiers', were six months in arrears. A month later Wellington was starting to sound paranoid about the whole question:

> I am not in general very suspicious, but I begin to suspect the Government of treachery. Nothing can be so fatal to the cause as to distress us for money, and yet all the measures of the Government appear to have that sole object in view.

Comments of this nature are to be found being penned as late as December 1813, *viz*: 'It is in vain to expect to be able to continue to carry on our operations through the winter, unless we should be supplied with money from England . . .'[29]

Considered through rather more dispassionate eyes, the provision of precious metal to the Peninsula was rather different from the penny-pinching impression given by Wellington's correspondence, though its importance is undeniable. 'During the early days of the Spanish uprising in 1808,' according to the leading expert on the subject, 'London had flooded the Peninsula with more than £2,500,000 in silver.'[30] This outpouring of treasure in the hopes of a quick victory, combined with pressures from elsewhere, meant that by 1810 the Cabinet was facing growing difficulties in procuring and providing specie, leading to the sort of complaints from their Peninsular commander that have been quoted above. Although much of the war's financing was having increasingly to be done by paper money in the shape of Treasury Bills, the discount on which was almost to reach 25 per cent by 1811, the Cabinet was every bit as aware as Wellington of the need to provide as much specie as possible. In 1810, for example, £5,382,166 was sent to the Peninsula in Treasury Bills, but so was an additional £679,069 in hard cash.[31] It was in this respect that the Royal Navy was once again to assume a crucial role, for the movement of this vast wealth was overwhelmingly a responsibility laid at the door of the Admiralty.

As with the convoy system, the shipment of bullion was almost concealed by its mundane regularity. From the start of the war specie transfers were to be an adjunct of the conflict. Captain Tremlett of the frigate *Alcmene* (38) being ordered as early as 5 July 1808 to take 839,806 dollars on board his ship for delivery to Corunna and the newly rebellious Junta of Galicia. Four days later another frigate, the *Dryad* (36), Captain Drummond, was instructed to undertake a similar mission, this time delivering 500,000 dollars to Gijon and the Junta of the Asturias, the ship then proceeding on to Corunna to hand over a further 160,000 for the Galicians. On 15 July yet another frigate, the *Solebay*, was ordered to Gijon, this time with 500,000 dollars for the rebels in Leon. As the Cabinet poured its treasure into the Iberian revolts during the summer and autumn such deliveries were to be maintained. The sloop

Forrester (18) escorted seven merchant vessels to Corunna in August and carried 500,000 dollars as well, while in the same month the sloop *Comet* (18) took another 500,000 to Gijon. Busiest of all was Captain Hallowell in the *Tigre*. He was told to ship 500,000 dollars to Corunna at the end of October 1808 while also being charged with the delivery of specie to the business communities of Oporto, Cadiz and Gibraltar *en route* to joining the Mediterranean Fleet.[32]

The movement of specie on such a scale was to be a comparatively brief phenomenon as both Britain's bullion reserves and her enthusiasm for her new, but truculent, allies diminished. However, once the long-term military commitment to Portugal had been settled with Wellesley's return to Lisbon in the spring of 1809, the task of moving hard currency to fund the campaign was also to be ever-present. In future warships were to continue to be employed in moving a whole variety of coin and bullion to Portugal as ministers in London tapped all sources to try and keep Wellington funded: deliveries in June and August 1809 included shipments of 300,000 dollars, 209,909 ounces of silver in bars and 17,948 ounces of gold in coins. Great use was also made of Cadiz, a city with strong links to the bullion-producing centres of the New World as well as a commercial centre out of French control and the seat of the Spanish government. It, along with Gibraltar, was soon to become a vital link in the chain of Wellington's specie supplies and the transport of bullion from there to Lisbon became a regular process. In August 1811 Wellington's brother Henry, serving as British ambassador to Cadiz, could write to him that he might expect to receive 400,000 to 500,000 dollars each month from the port, a rate which by then had been established for many months.

In June 1810 Wellington had already pressed Berkeley for weekly or fortnightly sailings between Lisbon and Cadiz and Gibraltar to keep the specie flowing. He ventured the view that this movement should be the sole responsibility of the Portuguese squadron and Berkeley had eagerly agreed, despite this seeming on the surface to be a suggestion that interfered with his command prerogatives. The admiral's willingness was mercenary: captains and flag officers engaged in bullion movements could claim a small but lucrative percentage of the total for themselves as freight money. Wellington, always on the lookout for any impediment to his financial supplies, was nervous that if captains did not receive the anticipated rewards from the duty then they might not pay appropriate attention to it. He wanted the privilege of specie shipments confined to the Portuguese command to help preserve morale:

> As the Officers and men of this squadron perform all the duties of the army, it is but fair that they should enjoy any benefit to be derived from the service.

During 1810 Berkeley and Rear-Admiral Pickmore, then commanding at Cadiz, got into a squabble over the spoils of the task, Henry Wellesley supporting Pickmore's view of the matter and considering that any financial rewards should be shared between the two. Relations between the two admirals were also strained when Berkeley rebuked Pickmore for sending two separate sloops to Lisbon with specie at a time when the Cadiz station was plagued by enemy privateers. A furious Pickmore protested to the Admiralty that he had only taken the step when one sloop had been delayed and after being told that the specie was urgently required. What was especially galling was that Pickmore came under Cotton's orders as Cadiz was, then, part of the Mediterranean command and was not under Berkeley's jurisdiction, whatever the rights and wrongs of the case. The Admiralty agreed with Pickmore, though it was the Portuguese squadron's vessels that in future were given the benefits of moving bullion to Lisbon.[33]

The importance of this traffic meant that it drew naval vessels away from just domestic and Iberian waters and to the harbours of Spain's crumbling New World empire. For decades Spain had famously relied on the fabled wealth of its American silver mines to support its finances, but, just as the French occupation completely disrupted domestic arrangements, so too it weakened an already-failing hold on its transatlantic colonies. Revolts broke out in Mexico and Chile in 1810 and the Spanish hold on Venezuela and the huge southern region of La Plata was weakening as well. This had great implications for the prosecution of the Peninsular War, not merely because it tended to draw Spanish military resources away from Europe, but also because of the threat it posed to bullion imports. During 1801–4 the annual importation of dollars into Spain stood at over 39,000,000: for the years 1810–12 combined the overall total was a mere 17,400,000.[34]

One of the first British gestures to their new ally only a few days after the surrender of Rosily's squadron concerned the maintenance of specie supplies, Collingwood agreeing to a request for a ship of the line and a frigate to sail unhindered from Cadiz with quicksilver for the Caribbean mines.[35] The Supreme Junta and later the Regency employed Spanish warships when they could for bullion movements to Europe, but with most of the Spanish navy either decayed or eventually laid up in the Balearics and the West Indies, the Spaniards frequently lacked their own warships. It was natural to seek British aid in such circumstances, particularly as the British were the ones who had repeatedly pressed for the Spanish marine to be put out of French reach. There was a moral burden pressing upon the situation as well as the demands of simple self-interest urging that any Spanish shortage be rectified by the Royal Navy. In 1810 the *Bulwark* (74), Captain Fleming, was sent to Vera Cruz and returned at the end of the year with 400,000 dollars. In September the *Implacable* sailed to the Caribbean as an escort for two 120-gun Spanish vessels being transferred to Havana, her captain, Cockburn, having orders then to proceed to Vera Cruz where, it was hoped, he might be able to collect up another 5,000,000 dollars. This anticipation was to be disappointed, Cockburn being able to procure only some 1,520,000 dollars and returning with it to Cadiz in February 1811, the trip to the West Indies having cost *Implacable* 49 of her crew when scurvy broke out on the outward voyage.[36] In their dealings with Spanish officialdom in the Caribbean, however, both Fleming and Cockburn displayed a degree of tact and diplomacy that was appreciated and which to some extent alleviated continuing Spanish suspicions regarding what Britain's precise intentions were towards their unsettled colonies. As far as Cockburn was concerned, Henry Wellesley requested in April 1811 that he be sent back to London to inform ministers about the exact state of the Mexican money markets.

I was extremely anxious that His Majesty's Government should be apprized of the Causes which have impeded our procuring Specie . . . and the Measures which it will be necessary to take to ensure success in the future.

Cockburn, he considered, was better informed on this subject than any man at Cadiz or, probably, in England. Not only did Cockburn return home in due course to pursue this task, but such was his standing that he was made one of three commissioners appointed to try and mediate between Spain and her rebellious New World subjects, an effort that ultimately proved fruitless.[37] The similarly high opinions earned by Fleming, however, were to be cause of some difficulty for Keats, his immediate superior at Cadiz.

At the end of January 1811 Bardaxi, the Spanish Foreign Minister, approached Henry Wellesley with a request for a British warship to be sent to Lima where a large amount of money, public and private, was awaiting collection. The Spanish had no warship of their own available and, because of his known attachment to the Spanish cause, Bardaxi particularly asked that Fleming and the *Bulwark* be given the duty. This put Keats in an awkward position as the Admiralty had ordered the *Bulwark* home, a predicament made all the more acute when Wellesley pointed out the moral responsibility that Britain had towards her ally and the vital need of transporting the specie, said to amount to 5,000,000 dollars, to the Peninsula. For the next eight weeks letters passed back and forth as the two civilians tried to persuade the reluctant admiral to send Fleming. Keats' position became all the more delicate when he received an Admiralty instruction of 27 February reiterating the order for the *Bulwark*'s return and stating that a warship of her size should not be tied up on such a mission, a vessel of 64 guns or a frigate being viewed as quite sufficient. Unfortunately Keats was also by then aware that the previous Spanish practice had always been to send a ship of the line when collecting treasure from harbours around Cape Horn and were of the opinion that the local business community in Peru would accept nothing less. Moreover, Wellesley was intending to seek a licence of exportation and this could mean that the total sum to be carried could amount from 9,500,000 to 10,000,000 dollars. Keats lamented to the Admiralty Secretary:

> Nothing, Sir, can be more unpleasant to me than the situation in which at this moment I find myself. Feeling that by a Departure from their Lordships' Instructions, I subject myself to their Disapprobation and by a rigid adherence to them, to an Imperfect and unsatisfactory accomplishment of the Service in Question.

Eventually Keats yielded to Wellesley's pressure and decided to send the respected Captain Fleming to Lima, though by way of some sort of compromise he was to go in the *Alfred*, a vessel that was short of her full complement and so would be less of a loss to the service during the many months that the voyage would take. Ultimately the Admiralty gave its approval of this decision, excusing its original stance on the grounds that it was unaware of the very large amount of treasure that was to be shipped.[38]

As the struggle in Spain and Portugal continued to drag on, the movement of bullion on a massive scale would be maintained. One list recorded the delivery of twenty-seven separate shipments of specie to Lisbon between 19 November 1812 and 15 July 1813, these ranging in size from 200,000 dollars, worth £45,000, to gold coin and dollars valued at over £250,000. The whole amounted to a value in excess of £990,000 and all, or certainly most, will have been transported in naval vessels.[39] As late as 9 April 1814, three days after Napoleon's abdication, Bathurst could be found writing from the War Office that a frigate would soon be sailing from Holland to Bordeaux with £220,000 in French gold for Wellington's army.[40] For all the specie shortages that he endured, it was a vital asset for Wellington that he was able to keep his men more or less regularly paid, and certainly with a reliability that was never matched by his French opponents. As with so much else, this was an asset for which he could thank the Royal Navy.

Military Supplies

By the time of the Peninsular War Britain was in a position through her growing industrial power to assume the mantle of the arsenal for all those powers willing to challenge Napoleon and was constantly prepared to arm and equip the Emperor's enemies. Nowhere was this more strikingly apparent than in Spain and Portugal, where a blend of economic dislocation and comparative industrial weakness rendered both nations quite unable to provide adequately for their own fighting men. Many of the convoys to the region carried such supplies and in the first twelve months of the conflict the newly-raised Spanish armies were sent, among much else, 155 pieces of artillery and over 200,000 muskets. By 1811 one account showed that since the start of the war the Iberian powers had been sent 348 cannon, over 336,000 muskets and in excess of 60,000,000 cartridges.[41]

Upon delivery this equipment came under the control of the local British representatives. In Portugal, of course, Wellington was the ultimate arbiter of its distribution. Elsewhere Henry Wellesley controlled items sent to Cadiz and at other points usually, though not exclusively, middle-ranking British army officers were appointed as military agents. A particular port, such as Valencia or Tarragona, would serve as a depot for the Spanish units serving in the region and the British agent would have the task of trying to meet the endless demands for supplies as formations were formed and reformed. It should be mentioned in passing that the extent of these supplies was by no means confined to weaponry. Items provided by one depot included greatcoats, shirts, suits of clothing, gaiters, stockings, forage caps, haversacks, shoes, caps, brushes, combs and even blacking, in short everything that troops could require to render them effective.[42] The naval role in this was initially one of safe delivery, though in the light of the fluctuating military fortunes on land this could be a hazardous process at times. The fall of Tarragona in the summer of 1811 cost the Catalans the secure harbour to which supplies had previously been delivered. The junta desperately appealed to the commander of the Mediterranean Fleet in the wake of the disaster, acknowledging the loss of the 'Asylum to which the Generosity of the English Nation had directed considerable supplies . . .', and pleading for fresh stores to be provided at other harbours along the coast. That was a lot easier said that done in the light of the vulnerability to French attack of the smaller coastal ports and a scheme to fortify Palamos as a replacement for Tarragona came

to nothing. Such was the chaos in Catalonia that even when supplies were landed at temporarily secure places there were still
problems: one transport delivering a large supply of powder
along with some clothing and muskets was stuck at Arens de
Mar when it was discovered that the Spaniards had no mules to
move the supplies inland.[43] Because such ports were so insecure
supplies could not be landed to await future movement because
of the risk of enemy attack. Even stronger positions could see
warships obliged to perform rescue missions to keep items
intended for the Spaniards out of French hands, as when the
York (74) found herself off Valencia at the end of 1811 when the
city was about to fall to Marshal Suchet. Tapper, the British
consul and also agent there, had kept his supplies aboard a
transport for safety's sake. Unfortunately this floating depot
had lost her rudder and was temporarily immobilised. Thanks
to the efforts of the *York*'s crew 495 barrels of gunpowder plus
musket ammunition and a large quantity of medicines were
transferred from the transport. Eventually, just before the city
fell, the sloop *Minstrel* (18) managed to bring out the stranded
vessel as well.[44]

Whatever the obstacles attendant on providing support
through what might be termed regular channels of supply, these
were as nothing compared to those associated with trying to
provide a similar service to the multitude of guerrilla groups.
This was never going to be easy given that the guerrillas spent
their time behind French lines, but on some stretches of coastline sufficient contacts were a possibility where geography did
not make the process too dangerous. In southern Spain the
French occupation was for a comparatively short period and
anyway the plains of Andalusia did not lend themselves to
popular resistance. To the south-east the Sierra Nevada offered
shelter for irregulars, but they were able to draw supplies from
Murcia and the depots in the great harbours of Cartagena and
Alicante. To the north-east, in Catalonia, resistance to the
invader was continuous but there the barrier in the way of naval
supply was that the foothills of the Pyrenees, the natural area for
guerrilla activity, was a region away from the coast: any bands in
the coastal plain were usually vulnerable to French attack. As a
result direct ship-borne assistance to the Catalan irregulars

could only be occasional when circumstances happened to favour it, as in 1812 when Codrington was able to send a group situated temporarily at Mataro some biscuit and 11,500 cartridges. A similar opportunity came the following year when Adam supplied a band led by Frayle with 1000 muskets and 120,000 cartridges, though it should be remembered that by the spring of 1813 the French were suffering growing shortages of manpower and were less able to interrupt such supply operations in this area.[45] In truth the only region where any form of regular supply to local resistance groups was viable was in the north and north-west. Here the rugged, tree-lined slopes of the Cantabrian mountains swept right down to the coast, allowing the guerrillas both to operate in their natural environment among the valleys and rough country, terrain in which they could avoid French detachments when necessary, while also permitting some access to the small harbours and coves dotted along the shore. At such points naval communications were a possibility.

Co-operating with poorly-organised local forces of uncertain discipline and reliability could, though, be both awkward and hazardous when there were no secure harbours available. An early illustration of this came in the spring of 1809. At the end of March, having learned of the widespread popular resistance breaking out all over Galicia, the Admiralty ordered Captain Schomberg of the frigate *Loire* (38) to receive 3–4000 muskets and a proportionate amount of ammunition aboard his ship. Once loaded the *Loire* was to proceed to Galicia with all speed and Schomberg was to distribute the arms as he saw fit to any inhabitants showing a disposition to fight the French. On reaching the coast Schomberg fell in with another frigate, the *Endymion*, Captain Capel, that had already been approached for support by some Spaniards from the town of Corcubion. Capel had issued them with 150 muskets from his own vessel and to these *Loire*'s more extensive cargo was added before she returned to Britain. This largesse, however, was put to little use. Both untrained and overly optimistic, the Spaniards neither properly distributed their new weapons nor maintained an effective watch on the approaches to the town. As a result the place was suddenly and easily seized by two French columns, Capel only managing to rescue 800 muskets and 200 kegs of powder from the debacle. These were sent to Vigo for safer keeping, but failure almost turned into downright catastrophe when Capel was persuaded to move the *Endymion* directly into Corcubion's small harbour in an effort both to protect the place and to restore some of the battered Spanish morale. Once in the wind veered and began to blow a southerly gale, trapping the frigate in harbour. At that moment the French returned. Only by the greatest good fortune did the warship escape the trap, the wind changing direction just before the French assault. As it was, the Spaniards again failed to mount a proper lookout and the first Capel knew of their attack was when artillery fire started landing around his ship. In the opinion of the *Endymion*'s officers the frigate was only then able to escape because the French bungled the assault and attacked too quickly, allowing the frigate to get out of the harbour before all the troops were in position to sweep her decks with fire. Capel took the leading members of Corcubion's junta and their families to safety at Vigo, observing with disgust that in the area there was 'not a Spaniard in arms to be seen in any direction'.[46]

Hard lessons of this sort proved that resistance and the efforts to supply it would have to be much more organised and professional if disasters were to be avoided in future. Thereafter the Admiralty was not to be found doling out arms to its captains along with vague instructions to issue them to the most likely-looking group of Spaniards that could be discovered. Arms shipments would be directed either towards secure depots for organised future distribution, or towards established guerrilla bands. For the Spaniards, popular resistance would centre on a plethora of groups operating in terrain where they could, if necessary, avoid French forces rather than being tied to vulnerable towns.

By the summer of 1809 guerrilla activity had become rife throughout much of northern Spain and with the evacuation of Galicia by Ney's corps the opportunity appeared of using the convenience offered by Corunna as a base for expanding naval operations along the coast. The Admiralty issued orders for the formation of a squadron for this purpose in August, telling Gambier that the Victualling Board had been instructed to form a depot at Corunna for its support.[47] The activities of this force will be considered in detail in Chapter 6, but respecting the particular question of supplying the Spaniards it should be noted that from that time Corunna became increasingly important as an arms depot as well. From there British military agents provided enormous quantities of assorted stores for the regular formations comprising the Armies of Galicia and the Asturias, as well as for the guerrillas in the interior.

The magazine itself could be easily stocked via the convoy system, a return for 1812, for example, showing that between April and September alone 25,000 muskets, 2000 carbines and 3000 pistols were sent there. The real problem started when it came to distributing them to the guerrillas. Those bands operating in some sort of proximity to north-western Spain that could manage overland access could be accommodated, the depot issuing 3200 muskets and 400 carbines to eight different bands in the January–July period of 1812, but for those farther away who relied on seaborne deliveries the situation was very different.[48] For one thing it was very hard to assess with accuracy what the fighters most needed, simple communication with them being tenuous at best. Then came the problem of co-ordinating how supplies were to be delivered at a set point on the coast, at a set time, and in circumstances which, hopefully, would be free from enemy interference, allowing supplies to be both landed and transported inland in safety.

The best illustration of how hard it could be to accomplish such supply missions comes from the experiences of Captain Christian of the *Iris* during the summer of 1811. On 19 May the Admiralty, responding to a request from the Secretary of War the previous day, instructed Gambier to send a warship to the northern coast of Spain to obtain information from the guerrillas as to the state of affairs in the region. The vessel was also to take out 500 sabres, 500 pistols and some ammunition from Britain, collecting a further 2000 muskets from the Corunna depot upon her arrival: all of this was to be distributed to the guerrillas. Christian was also to take on board one Captain Johnson, an aide-de-camp to Major-General Walker, then the military agent at Corunna, and the two were to arrange further shipments to the groups. The *Iris* and cargo sailed from Corunna on 6 June, Christian hoping to provide arms for all the primary guerrilla chiefs known to be active on the coast, *viz* Mina, Longa, Porlier and Campillo. Three days after sailing the *Iris* encountered the *Rhin* (38) and discovered that the frigate had just made contact with Campillo's band via a harbour near Santona. Campillo came aboard the *Iris* on the 14th but as his men had been actively co-operating with the *Rhin* the local French garrisons were very much on the alert. A heavy surf meant that the frigate could land only 200 muskets and a little ammunition and more was planned to be got ashore that evening. However, French activity suddenly obliged Campillo to retreat and, with efforts to restore communications unavailing, Christian sailed farther to the east in the hope of getting in touch with Mina. Again the state of the surf proved too much of a barrier and returning once more to the vicinity of Santona Christian found out on the 16th that Campillo's band had been chased into the mountains and for the immediate future would be beyond receiving supplies.

The *Iris* now sailed eastwards once more, Christian landing a Spanish officer at the small harbour of Andarrua in the hope that contact might be established with Mina, though for some days operations had to be suspended because of bad weather. The frigate's efforts resumed on 10 July off Montrico when an application for arms was received from El Pastor's 1000-strong group, they being provided with 100 muskets, 30 pistols, 50 sabres and 2000 rounds of ammunition. This was not a large supply by any means, but it was all the Spaniards could carry and Christian noted that the band was mauled by the French soon after. Four days later contact was established with the officer previously landed to get in touch with Mina and Christian learned that, with the inducement of British supplies in the offing, Mina and Longa had agreed to co-ordinate their efforts, a rarity among the guerrilla commanders. Mina's men would try to keep the French occupied while Longa's would secure a coastal point where the supplies might be landed. This sounded promising but unfortunately the French seemed to be equally aware of the plan and threw out several columns that kept the guerrillas divided and fully engaged. A frustrated Christian sailed away down the coast in an attempt to convince the enemy that the attempt had been abandoned, but on his return discovered that the ruse had failed and the guerrillas were still fully occupied. With his provisions now starting to run low the *Iris*'s captain was becoming very concerned, as he made clear to his commander: 'You will feel Sir that our situation from want of success became every day more anxious . . .' Finally, on 7 August, contact was established with Mina at Montrico and all haste was made to provide him with arms and ammunition, the frigate's boats together with some local fishing vessels being pressed into service for the task. Even so Mina's men still had to fend off fresh enemy attacks while the unloading took place. A week later Christian also managed to get in touch with Longa's group and similarly supply them, *Iris* thereafter being free to return to Plymouth.[49]

This mission, which tied up a frigate for three months, reveals several interesting factors. It was evident that as late as the summer of 1811 the British authorities still had little idea of the state of affairs behind French lines, at last as far as meeting the guerrillas' needs was concerned. Attempts to meet such requirements faced the acute problem of effective ship-to-shore communications, Christian discovering that the French were prepared to strain every sinew in an attempt to thwart such missions and would implement immediate military action as soon as signalling was observed between warships and the land. The vigour of their action indicates the danger the French perceived in the guerrillas receiving supplies. To try and ease the problem Christian returned to the coast with three Spanish sergeants in the hope that they might be employed to facilitate future communications: such individuals could hope to be landed in secret and establish links with the groups without alarming the French. The mission further revealed that the main shortage experienced by the guerrillas tended to be ammunition rather than arms, their peripatetic existence preventing the formation of depots where it could be manufactured and stored. Christian also reported his concern for future co-operation if British officers adopted a high-handed attitude in any dealings with the proud and independent chiefs. The French were already doing all they could to try and subvert their allegiance by means of proclamations and other inducements and the British should, in his opinion, be aware of Spanish susceptibilities.

Overall, naval power was central in the continual movement of vital supplies to Britain's Peninsular allies, equipment that Spain and Portugal would have been very hard pressed to provide for themselves. When it came to the specific equipping of those irregular bands beyond magazines placed in fortified strongpoints, then supplies could be provided only intermittently for the reasons just described. Only when the guerrillas were working closely and securely alongside naval vessels, and had secured some degree of local superiority over the French, could any reliable system of supply be established. Such circumstances briefly applied off the northern coast during the summer of 1810, and for a longer period during 1812, and as both involved more extensive and direct naval operations they will be detailed in Chapter 6.

CHAPTER 5

Cadiz and the Eastern Coast, 1810–14

'Although the aspect of the Patriot Cause is very
considerably clouded by the late disaster on the Coast, I
cannot but entertain a persuasion that a powerful spirit of
Independence remains unsubdued . . .'
Vice-Admiral Pellew, 22 July 1811.[1]

THE LATTER MONTHS of 1809 were a period of failure for the Allied cause that transformed the military situation in the Peninsula. Beyond the Pyrenees Napoleon successfully concluded the war with Austria in October. Simultaneously the British attempt to strike at his power in the Low Countries was grinding its way to disaster on the pestilential island of Walcheren in the Scheldt estuary, the fever-ridden survivors of its occupation finally being evacuated by the end of December. Outside of the Peninsula, therefore, Napoleon's authority was unchallenged and he could afford to pour reinforcements into Spain in a massive effort to subdue the region, some 90,000 fresh troops being marched south for the purpose. If this prospect were not bad enough, the Allies were also rocked by a series of defeats in Spain itself. The recriminations flying in the wake of the Talavera campaign for the moment ruled out any chance of close Anglo-Spanish co-operation along the Portuguese frontier. Wellesley, soon to be raised to the peerage as Viscount Wellington, was retreating his army back into Portugal to prepare defences against another anticipated French invasion. Despite lacking British support, the Spanish government, the increasingly discredited Central Junta, desperately sought to revive its reputation by another attempt to liberate Madrid. The resulting campaign produced crushing Spanish defeats at Tamames in October and at Ocana the following month, battles that left the southern part of Spain completely exposed to French attack. Elsewhere another defeat was suffered when the fortress of Gerona was finally compelled to surrender in December, its fall freeing the French position in Catalonia and posing a grave future threat to Spanish prospects there as well.

The first threat looming from these circumstances manifested itself in January 1810 when the French invaded Andalusia. Seville, along with its huge arsenal, fell on 1 February, the Central Junta and 12,000 Spanish troops retreating to Cadiz. The leading elements of the French appeared on the city's out-skirts on the 5th, a siege then beginning that was to endure for over two and a half years, during which time naval power would be pivotal. The topography of Cadiz was to be crucial. The city stood on the westernmost tip of the Isla de Leon, an island sep-arated from the mainland by the river Santi Petri, a waterway 300–400 yards wide that flowed through salt marshes. The com-bination of the marshes, the river and the powerful redoubts and batteries thrown up by the Spaniards along the eastern side of the Isla effectively rendered any assault on the fortress from its landward approaches impossible. Throughout the siege the French never tried to cross the Santi Petri as the obstacles were just too great. The danger to the defenders came from the other direction. First, and most obviously for any city cut off from landward supply, the question of provisions was central. Here Cadiz in normal circumstances relied on seaborne supplies and this could safely continue thanks to British sea power. Despite privateering activity the city's supply lines were never placed under serious threat and, French batteries notwithstanding, it remained a very busy harbour. This was graphically illustrated on 27 March 1811 when Cadiz was struck by a tremendous south-easterly gale, the following day it being discovered that no fewer than 53 assorted merchant vessels had been wrecked and hundreds of others damaged. Given traffic on such a scale, it is not surprising that its supplies were maintained despite the fact that, according to one contemporary source, the city's popula-tion had swelled to 100,000 with all the fugitives who had fled there. One visitor at the end of 1810 noted with horror the way

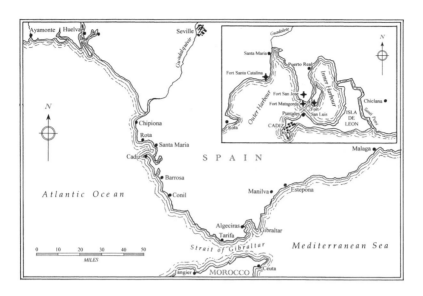

that prices for meat and wine had risen, but saw no particular shortages and wrote that there were plentiful supplies of fruit. Earlier that year a British admiral observed that bread and meat prices had actually fallen and another naval officer particularly remarked upon the relaxed attitude of the inhabitants, bearing in mind that the place was under siege. Indeed, circumstances for the besiegers seem to have been the more trying, four French deserters giving themselves up in June 1810 with complaints that they had not been paid in 22 months and were suffering from an acute shortage of bread. Nor did the French supply situation appear to improve with the passage of time, an irritated Rear-Admiral Legge writing in March 1812 that the successes enjoyed by local privateers included the capture of a brig laden with flour, a setback as he understood the enemy was enduring severe bread shortages.[2]

With its food supplies secure and its landward approaches inaccessible, the primary threat to the fortress came in the shape of a small peninsula that jutted south from the mainland, reaching, at its closest, to a point only three-quarters of a mile from the Isla de Leon and within two miles of the eastern outskirts of the city. This neck of land, known as the Trocadero, divided the bay of Cadiz into an inner (eastern) and outer (western) harbour, the former providing excellent shelter but being

useless for vessels of any size as it was completely commanded
by French artillery. On the southern part of the Trocadero and
on a low-lying mud island to the east of it stood three strongpoints, Forts San Jose, San Luis and, at the extreme tip,
Matagorda. Guns at these places could annoy parts of the Isla
de Leon and could also threaten the anchorage in the outer
harbour where the Allied fleet had to shelter.[3] If the French,
supported by these and other coastal batteries, could only come
to control the short expanse of water opposite there was the
chance of a rapid lift of troops on to the Isla followed by the
capture of Cadiz itself. The primary barrier standing in the way
of this was to be a British squadron.

From the very start of the Spanish uprising ministers in
London had been keen to establish a British force as part of the
Cadiz garrison to bolster its security, hoping for its preservation
both as the major Spanish naval base and as a strongpoint that
could facilitate any flight to the New World should Napoleon's
armies eventually triumph.[4] A blend of overconfidence and
xenophobia on the part of the Spaniards, laced, it might be
added, by a thoroughly understandable suspicion as to British
motives, prevented any British troops being accepted in 1808–9.
Only naval forces were allowed access and any support provided
by them was only grudgingly received: by the end of 1809 the
British presence at the port had shrunk to just three warships.
However, the importance of Cadiz only increased with the
passage of time and the arrival of the Spanish vessels so laboriously transferred from Ferrol. Furthermore, by the early weeks
of 1810 only Cadiz stood as a bastion in the way of a complete
French takeover of southern Spain, becoming a fortress where
in future thousands of enemy troops could be tied down in
wretched conditions in its siege lines.

During these early days sea power allowed the endangered
fortress to be very rapidly reinforced. Despite the earlier
Spanish resistance to British troops, Castlereagh had anticipated
almost a year earlier that any crisis might prompt a change of
heart and had in consequence issued instructions for units to be
transferred from Portugal should the need arise. Wellington's
rapid compliance with these orders meant that only a week after
the French appearance Brigadier-General Stewart arrived at

Cadiz with 2446 Anglo-Portuguese soldiers. Additionally, on 18 February, Purvis sent the frigate *Rota* (38) with eleven transports to collect 3000 Spanish troops from Ayamonte at the mouth of the Guadalquivir.[5] Throughout the course of the siege troops could be moved with great flexibility in and out of the fortress as circumstances dictated, the average garrison comprising around 15,000 Spanish soldiers supported by about 5000 Anglo-Portuguese. Opposing them by the summer of 1811 was Marshal Victor's I Corps, numbering about 27,000 men in the lines with a further 8000 troops either sick or in detachments.[6] Naval reinforcements were also rushed to the beleaguered fortress, the Admiralty dispatching Pickmore with six ships of the line on 16 February 1810 and by April, with Collingwood also having sent vessels from the main body of the Mediterranean Fleet, the squadron at Cadiz consisted of eleven ships of the line, two frigates and four bomb vessels.[7]

As the French approached the Spaniards, encouraged by pressure from Purvis, allowed a detachment of marines to blow up the three forts on the Trocadero as well as Fort Catalina, a mainland strongpoint a little over three miles across the bay directly opposite Cadiz. Having done so, however, there were worries as to the wisdom of the move with the French making no effort to cross the Santi Petri but instead concentrating their attentions on embarrassing the defenders by making use of those points from which artillery could directly be brought to bear upon the port and fleet. Most sensitive was Fort Matagorda, on the very tip of the Trocadero, that stood on tidal flats and was the closest to the Isla de Leon. This was guarded by either water or mud depending on the state of the tide and was a position the Allies decided to re-occupy, a garrison consisting of a company of the 94th Foot, a 26-strong detachment of British artillerymen, 25 Royal Marines and 26 seamen – all told about 150 men – being moved into the place on 22 February. The ruined fort, which was about 100 square yards in extent, was made defensible by fascines, gabions and sandbags brought over from Cadiz and eventually mounted six cannon and two mortars, these firing a good deal upon the busy French. Supporting the fort were boats and armed launches manned by seamen from the four ships of the line and the *Rota* that Purvis then had present. More substantial support was also provided by the *San Justo*, a Spanish 74 manned by 200 British seamen that was positioned near to Matagorda to fire on the batteries the French were constructing. Unfortunately the *San Justo*'s guns had been condemned in 1807 and in the heated engagements that followed two of them burst, killing two British sailors and wounding several others. The vessel was replaced by another 74, the *San Francisco de Paula*, but Purvis complained of the lethargy of Vice-Admiral Alava, the Spanish naval commander, and the downright hostility of most of the Spanish naval captains. He asked for another Spanish 74 to be positioned off Fort Catalina once it became apparent that the French were repairing the place, but his request was ignored. It was with some sense of relief that he reported in early March that Alava had been replaced by the more energetic Villavicencio.[8]

The occupation of Matagorda was to prompt an intense struggle in the weeks that followed as the French determined to drive the British out. Victor steadily constructed batteries on the Trocadero until he had 40 pieces able to pour a concentric fire into the half-ruined strongpoint. The defenders replied with their cannon and the fire from the assorted supporting craft. Alongside the gunboats, launches and the *San Francisco de Paula*, Purvis also deployed four bomb vessels, the *Thunder*, *Etna*, *Hound* and *Meteor*.[9] One of these, the *Thunder*, was to fire no fewer than 558 mortar shells during 12–22 April as the battle for Matagorda reached its height and the defenders unavailingly tried to halt the progress of the enemy batteries. It was a struggle the French were always going to win because of Victor's ability to bring up more and more artillery combined with the Allies' problem of providing adequate naval support when the tide was out. The naval units fought hard and not without cost – a gunboat crewed by men from the *Temeraire* (98) exploded on the 18th when struck in the magazine by a hot shot and 15 of her complement were killed and 11 others injured – but during the early morning of 21 April hot shot hit the *San Francisco de Paula*, setting her on fire and forcing her withdrawal. One eye-witness wrote of how the French suffered heavy losses but still forced the vessels to retire, the latter being fortunate that the state of wind and tide allowed them to do so in safety. Now, though, Matagorda was exposed to the full weight of the besiegers' artillery and soon only a few of its guns remained serviceable. On the 22nd Lieutenant-General Graham, who had assumed command of the Anglo-Portuguese troops at Cadiz, ordered Matagorda's evacuation. Almost half of its garrison had become casualties, with the naval craft also suffering nine dead and 24 wounded. The fort was then refortified and rearmed by the French, as were San Luis and San Jose to which Matagorda's previous resistance had prevented access. 'Everything,' according to Henry Wellesley, 'now depends on the activity of the navy . . .'[10]

For the moment, after Matagorda's fall, there was a relative pause in the intensity of the action around the fortress as the French concentrated on fortifying their new positions and the Allies attempting to disrupt the garrison as much as possible. Although it was apparent that the annoyance likely from long-range cannon fire would be minimal, it was also evident that constant vigilance would be necessary to preserve security. Pickmore, who succeeded Purvis as the British naval commander on 4 May, wrote that his men were responsible for guarding the outer harbour up to Matagorda, the inner harbour and the Santi Petri being patrolled by the Spaniards. The British were initially provided with gunboats by the Spaniards and drew their crews from the Cadiz squadron. Four small vessels, each manned by a lieutenant and ten men, helped to guard the Santi Petri, while two mortar boats, two howitzer boats and four or five gunboats, each crewed by a lieutenant and 30 men, patrolled the waters off Matagorda. These vessels harassed the French whenever the opportunity presented itself and were supported by the bomb vessels that constantly shelled the works on the Trocadero. *Thunder*'s log indicates that the British practice was to bombard for a period of a few hours every day, generally during the morning, weather permitting, and during 26 April–1 May she alone fired 236 shells at the enemy's works. On top of this, the British squadron also provided guard boats that closed with the shore at night to observe the French and prevent any surprise attacks on the larger warships.[11]

At first the French were able to offer little challenge to all this, though there were occasional moments of drama. On 22 May the Spanish *San Elmo* (74) was leaving Cadiz with £250,000 in specie aboard when she got under the guns of Fort Catalina and had to be worked out. A sharp artillery duel ensued before the ship could effect her escape, her guns manned by British sailors. They suffered no casualties though two of her Spanish crew were killed and eight others wounded. A week before this the *Castilla* prison hulk had broken her moorings in a gale and run aground on the French-controlled shore: according to Pickmore 3–4000 of her wretched inmates managed to escape. Cadiz was the unwelcome home of thousands of French prisoners of war, many of them survivors of Baylen, and numbers of them died every day, their bodies tossed overboard at sunset and being left to float in the bay. Every tide deposited them on the beach and the shoreline was littered with them. Pickmore complained that the Spaniards had ignored his requests to have the hulks secured by chains for greater security and, following the *Castilla*'s escape on 26 May, the *Argonauta* prison/hospital ship with 500 prisoners on board also went ashore, though this time on a mud bank a few hundred yards from the Trocadero, the stranded vessel becoming the target for hours of fire from the British gunboats. Attempts to board the *Argonauta* were unavailing as her ports were kept closed and there were no ropes over her side to climb up: the prisoners had also captured some muskets, which they fired at the attackers. The French on shore brought out boats to try and save their compatriots, though many were drowned as these craft were sunk by the gunboats and others were said to have been burned alive when the *Argonauta* caught fire. The British lost seven dead and 42 wounded in the efforts to recapture the hulk. Thereafter the remaining prison ships were moored closer to the Allied batteries and in due course the remaining unfortunates incarcerated in them were transferred to equally appalling confinement in the Canaries and the Balearics.[12]

After Purvis expressed serious concerns for the security of Cadiz in March, fears that did not materialise, a continual seaborne reinforcement of the fortress rendered such worries even less justifiable. By June the 2/30th Foot had boosted Graham's command on the Isla de Leon and the *Resistance* had escorted eleven transports to Alicante to bring back a further 3482 Spanish soldiers.[13] For the British, though, any threat to Cadiz, however secure the place seemed, produced nightmares about the future safety of the Spanish fleet. Although some of these warships had been moved to places of greater security during 1809, many others remained, their number ironically increased by the vessels from Ferrol. The appearance of the French had caught one ship, the *San Roman* (74), on shore in the inner harbour dockyard and she had had to be burned. A storm that struck the port on 6–9 March 1810 drove three more to destruction on the enemy-controlled shore, but according to a list handed to the British the Spaniards still had ten ships of the line and two others mounting 50 guns in the fortress at the end of August. Additionally there were two others, the *Fernando VII* (112) and the *San Carlos* (112), at Gibraltar. At British prompting these had been moved from Cartagena earlier in the year, that port still sheltering two 74-gun vessels and three frigates that had to be secured.[14]

Shortly before the siege began, Purvis was fretting about the generally lethargic attitude of the Spanish naval officers at Cadiz, observing that they were not actively Francophile but merely dispirited through not being paid. Many of the Spanish vessels were in a poor state of repair and lacked cables and cordage into the bargain. His view of Spanish efficiency was strongly echoed by his successor, Pickmore, who informed the Admiralty that, although the Spaniards were planning to send their warships to Minorca once that island had been adequately garrisoned, their characters were marked by 'jealousy', 'indolence' and 'want of determination'. Cotton had to exert all his authority as commander in the Mediterranean to prevent the Spaniards actually moving more warships to the fortress. Although he had met the Supreme Junta on 2 May and been told that the two First Rates at Gibraltar were to be transferred to Port Mahon, their commander on the spot, an officer named Losada, insisted that his instructions were to collect convicts from Ceuta and ship them to Cadiz. Cotton was obliged to force the Spaniards' hand by pointing out that if the ships sailed to Cadiz then they would have to rely on their own crews as no British vessel could spare the manpower for such a voyage. This effectively checkmated the plan and meant that the Spanish were unable to move their ships to any port not approved of by the British. In the event, the two vessels were still at Gibraltar in August, the plan by then having reverted to one of moving them to the Balearics.[15]

It was not that the Spaniards, despite British suspicions, were actively trying to be obstructive respecting their fleet, merely that the paralysis caused by years of maladministration, now compounded by the disastrous effects of invasion and occupation, had left the Spanish navy in an advanced state of chaos. This situation had already been observed at Ferrol and circumstances were to be little different at Cadiz and Cartagena. At the end of May 1810 Captain Adam of the *Invincible* (74) reported that he had successfully reached Port Mahon from Cartagena along with the Spanish *San Paobla* (74) and an old and rotten frigate, noting that the Spaniards had raised no difficulties about moving the ships and were also busy working on another 74, the *Guerrero*, that was still there. By August, though, the *Guerrero* had still not sailed and the *Eagle* (74), Captain Rowley, arrived at Cartagena to hasten matters along. The British also wanted to see the large quantity of naval stores held at the port moved to somewhere safer and Rowley brought a transport with him for the purpose, providing some officers and 80 seamen from the *Eagle* to assist in the necessary labour. It clearly indicates the parlous state of the Spanish navy that Nunez, the Captain-General of Cartagena, had to petition Rowley for 2000 dollars to provide for the subsistence of the *Guerrero*'s officers and the small number of seamen and marines that would crew her in any pending voyage. Nunez's department had not been paid for weeks and a similar provision had also had to be made before the *Fernando VII* and the *San Carlos* had earlier sailed to Gibraltar. Rowley provided the money via the resources under the control of Major-General Roche, the British military agent in the area. As well as this finance for her crew, the *Guerrero* also needed cordage and cables to make her seaworthy, though other frigates in the port were judged too rotten to sail and were anyway fully employed as prison hulks. When it came to the naval stores, Nunez initially proved resistant to the prospect of their removal, insisting that the large quantity of spars and timber at Cartagena be retained both for the repair of shipping and the construction of fortifications. Given the amount under consideration, Rowley estimated that the whole would fill six large transports, the British view being that it was essential to move it. Rowley sought Henry Wellesley's permission to purchase all of it for British use, also passing on a suggestion of Roche's that the Cartagena dockyard officers and artificers be taken into British pay. They had received no wages for ten months and it was thought that it would be easy to persuade them to accompany the timber to Port Mahon and maybe to get them to emigrate to Gibraltar, Malta or even Britain. Such a migration would effectively cripple Cartagena as a naval base for years, whether controlled by the French or the Spanish.

Permission for this purchase scheme was given by Wellesley and Rowley cynically noted how Nunez, previously so determined to retain the timber, agreed to its sale in a mere six hours once sufficient money was in the offing to cover his own salary arrears, those of the marine officers and all the dockyard artificers. The little squadron consisting of the *Eagle*, the *Guerrero* and the transport finally left Cartagena on 3 September, the vessels carrying a substantial number of anchors and some ordnance for Port Mahon as well as a supply of shot, powder and shell that was to be transferred to Tarragona for the Catalans. The timber itself was to prove a lingering headache. Not until March 1811 was a group of no fewer than 17 transports assembled at Cartagena for its removal. Twelve of these were loaded, but it was discovered upon draining the mast ponds that some of the spars were so long, ranging from 75 to 95 feet, that only the largest transports would be able to ship them. With the timber that could be moved was also going the first batch of the 900 dockyard workers who were to be transferred, a group of 142 carpenters and caulkers (338 people once their families had been included) who at that time had not been paid for 13 months. Not until 1812 was the removal of the Cartagena timber finally completed, the whole process being delayed at one point when Cotton vetoed the employment of much-needed warships to provide the necessary escorts and also through the problem of finding transports able to move the larger spars.[16]

Back at Cadiz the movement of the Spanish warships also progressed slowly, to the increasing concern of the Admiralty, where there were worries that the anchorage would remain cluttered with warships that the Spanish could not man and work effectively. This was a highly dangerous situation given the approach of winter and the possibility of an attack by French fireships, the Admiralty considering that the Spanish vessels would be vulnerable from September onwards and urging their commander on the spot and Henry Wellesley to stress the looming menace. This pressure finally began to bear fruit at the end of July when Villavicencio informed the British that, of the twelve largest warships in Cadiz, the *Principe de Asturias* (112) and the *Santa Anna* (112) would be transferred to Havana, while one other was moved to Vera Cruz and four others went to Minorca. Of the remainder, two would be employed as floating batteries at Cadiz and three were to be maintained in regular service. After many further delays, caused by problems with their stores and the embarkation of families wanting to leave the city, the two First Rates finally departed for Cuba on 6 September. Because of their shortage of crews they were obliged to seek an escort for the voyage, one being provided in the shape of Cockburn's *Implacable*. She provided an officer and 20 men to help crew the *Santa Anna* and the vessels set out on a voyage that would, before its eventual conclusion, witness a severe outbreak of scurvy. The four warships for Port Mahon, the *San Francisco de Paula, Glorioso*, (74), *Justo* (74) and *Neptuno* (80), departed on 6 August, accompanied by the British *Blake* (74) and *Norge*. Codrington, the senior British officer, wrote of the dreadful condition the Spanish warships were in, he being obliged to provide them with provisions, water, fuel and 230 men to help crew them. It was anticipated that the voyage would last only a week, though in the event it dragged on for 38 days due to adverse winds and the poor sailing qualities of the neglected and rotten Spanish ships. At this time the two Spanish First Rates at Gibraltar were also moved to Minorca, their going relieving Cotton of the duty of stationing one of his own ships of the line at the Rock as a guard vessel. Although these new dispositions now prompted Admiralty fears for the security of Port Mahon, ordering Cotton in a 'most secret' despatch at the end of August to burn or otherwise destroy them if the French ever managed to land on the island,

nevertheless the bulk of the Spanish fleet was now out of immediate harm's way. This went a long way to preserving British
naval supremacy whatever the outcome of the land campaigns
in the Peninsula.[17]

While these movements were taking place, activity around
Cadiz was also becoming increasingly frenetic. Having expelled
the Allies from Matagorda in April, the French then set about
building a network of batteries all along the shoreline opposite
the fortress as well as a flotilla of gunboats and small craft which
threatened an eventual amphibious assault on the Isla de Leon.
With the siege obviously settling down for a long haul, and with
its concerns about the Spanish fleet to the forefront, the
Admiralty decided on 12 July to replace Pickmore as their local
flag officer. This was a startling move as he had only held the
post a mere two months, Henry Wellesley writing to his eldest
brother that: 'I am sorry for poor Pickmore, who has really done
very well here; and his removal came upon him like a clap of
thunder, for he had no previous notice of it whatever.' Although
the Admiralty tried to reassure Pickmore that it was not
dissatisfied with him, such an abrupt removal combined with
his transfer to the comparative backwater of being port admiral
at Port Mahon hardly constituted a vote of confidence.
Pickmore's standing at the Admiralty may not have been helped
by his quarrel with Berkeley, a senior admiral with powerful
political friends, over freight money on Cadiz–Lisbon specie
movements, but his replacement was more likely due to a desire
on the Admiralty's part to see a commander with an established
reputation in what was evidently going to be a difficult position.
If so, their choice of successor, Richard Goodwin Keats, was an
excellent one. He had successfully led a squadron in the treacherous waters of the Great Belt off the coast of Denmark in
1807–9 and had played a prominent role in the rescue of the
Spanish corps that deserted from the French in 1808 (see
Chapter 2). This put him in good standing with the Spanish and
his dealings with the unstable King Gustavus IV of Sweden
suggested as well that Keats would be tactful in any future dealings with the Spanish authorities.[18]

Certainly the new admiral was energetic and the days following his arrival at Cadiz on 27 July were marked by a flurry of

despatches to London that made clear the vigour with which he pressed the Spaniards to put in hand the transfer of their war-ships and which stressed the problems he faced in defending the fortress. Interestingly, Keats remarked on the way the French were busy fitting-out small privateers in the local harbours and how three merchant vessels had already been seized and taken into San Lucar. He asked for small cruisers to help keep them in check and the Admiralty immediately promised him frigates and small warships: when Pickmore had made the same request in May for exactly the same reason, his plea had been ignored, suggesting that Keats's opinions were more highly regarded.[19]

Keats's main worry, after the question of the Spanish war-ships, was the French effort to control the shoreline opposite Cadiz and to construct a gunboat flotilla. By August there were rumours that the enemy had moved a force of seamen said to number between 800 and 2000 men to the nearby harbours of San Lucar and Santa Maria, Keats talking in terms of large British warships, possibly three 64s, having to remain at Cadiz through the winter. He further speculated that a thousand seamen would be needed to man the British gunboats in con-junction with the Spaniards, the admiral also being of the view that half the gunboats at Gibraltar might be needed to reinforce Cadiz's defences.[20]

Throughout the summer of 1810, Cadiz and the small har-bours along the coast were to witness what amounted to a mini-ature naval race as both sides sought to assemble flotillas of small armed craft. The French worked tirelessly at San Lucar, Rota, Santa Maria and in the lower reaches of the Guadiana to build vessels and convert others seized locally. Keats observed that by the end of August they had 20 gunboats in the last two places, with some smaller ones at Rota. Although the threat was not yet serious, he believed that it could easily become so, par-ticularly if the French could block lateral communications across the Isla de Leon at Puntales, its narrowest point. He worried about the Spanish capacity to provide the defenders with enough gunboats to meet the danger, though some outside assistance came in the shape of 90 Portuguese shipwrights and caulkers in August, followed the next month by 80 similarly-skilled Spaniards from Ferrol and Corunna and a further 20

British shipwrights brought out from Plymouth in the *Cossack*. Added to these there were also the carpenters and others provided by the British squadron. By the middle of September Keats was offering to equip a gunboat every day if the Spaniards could provide him with the necessary craft. His resources were also boosted in the middle of October when the Admiralty gave him permission to take 30 men from each ship of the line sailing to the Mediterranean and when orders were sent to Penrose at Gibraltar to send all the gunboats there to Cadiz.[21]

Thanks to these exertions, by the end of October Keats had at his disposal a flotilla comprising 16 gun- and mortar boats employing 512 officers and men, with an additional six flatboats suitable for mortars soon to be added. These opposed a French force of 36 such craft at San Lucar and the other harbours, but Keats reckoned that in any emergency he could double the size of his force by the use of Spanish vessels and armed boats drawn from the British squadron, the Allies also enjoying the support of the British bomb vessels. Certainly the craft available were of a very disparate nature, Keats writing that he commanded three different types of mortar vessel, British and Spanish, a mass of men-of-war launches, and four different classes of gunboat, plus those that were under construction at Cadiz itself. The British mortar vessels he regarded as largely useless, their single armament, a light 8-inch mortar, having an inadequate range and in one of them he had had the piece replaced by a massive 68-pounder carronade, a weapon that had twice the range. The Spanish-built mortar vessels were much better, being armed with 13-inch or 10-inch mortars, the craft weighing about 90 or 50 tons respectively, and being propelled by sails or oars. The men-of-war launches were fitted with movable frames and beds formed from bags of oakum, being armed with Congreve's marine mortar. However, such craft would not withstand the rigours of prolonged service and had to be reserved for a crisis. The British-built gunboats varied in length from 48ft to 54ft and were armed with a 24-pounder cannon or carronade, but it was necessary for him to sanction some local alterations for the sake of the comfort and health of their crews. The demands during prolonged period of service, as was the case in Cadiz Bay, placed great strains on the men concerned and it was discovered that once manned, stored and provisioned even the larger gunboats would ride very low in the water and were unsafe in the winter.[22]

To such discomforts the crews of this mosquito fleet also found themselves exposed to greater dangers as the summer turned to autumn and the military activity around the fortress increased in tempo. During September vigorous, though unavailing, efforts were made to prevent the French constructing their batteries along the shoreline, gunboat attacks being directed on them on the 12th, 15th, 17th and 19th. At 10.30pm on 2 October a heavy bombardment was begun on Fort Catalina, gunboats, mortar vessels and bombs maintaining a heavy fire for 90 minutes, this then being added to by the use of Congreve rockets though, as usual, their value was very limited. Parts of the fort were observed to be ablaze, though the French continued to fire back at their assailants, the two sides keeping up a desultory bombardment during the following day. Two other batteries, near Matagorda were also bombarded on 5 October. On 1 November the French were finally ready themselves to concentrate their new flotilla at Cadiz. Seven vessels moved successfully along the coast to Santa Maria, though an eighth got stranded on the bar outside and was burned by the British gunboats and launches. Twelve other French boats initially sought safety in Rota and the following afternoon also moved towards Santa Maria under some cover provided by hazy weather. Keats had had to move his flotilla to a less-exposed anchorage after a north-easterly wind had blown up in the night and so, when the enemy movement was observed, the French enjoyed the benefit of a head start and a strong breeze. The British gunboats, launches and bombs were unable to intercept them and had to face heavy fire from Fort Catalina and mobile batteries along the shore, the French boats having reached the safety of Santa Maria by 5pm and the British assault being called off. Though Keats later learned that these engagements had cost the enemy 20 dead and 62 wounded, he was disgusted by the sudden alarm that had been generated in Cadiz and by the Spaniards' failure to reinforce him with more than three of their own gunboats to meet the emergency.[23]

On 14 November the French tried to complete the process of concentrating their flotilla by moving boats from Santa Maria to the canal that stretched across the Trocadero, a point from which any landing on the Isla de Leon could most easily have been managed. Keats learned of the move at midnight and ordered all his gunboats and launches to engage, a step that could have brought on a general engagement between the two flotillas had not the French instead chosen to retreat back into Santa Maria. On the 23rd the British mortar and howitzer boats bombarded the harbour and flotilla while other British and Spanish gunboats and the bombs engaged Fort Catalina. One British gunboat alone fired off 70 rounds in an assault in which hundreds of shells were fired at the French boats and construction facilities. The action was maintained all day long at a cost to the Allies of three officers killed and eight seamen wounded.

The tireless French responded by spending the days after the action digging a canal to link the Guadalette and San Pedro rivers to enable them to move their boats to the Matagorda peninsula out of attack range. Heavy rains in early December allowed their lighter craft to use a branch of the San Pedro to reach Port Real, their ultimate destination, the heavier vessels being moved overland across the neck of the peninsula on rollers. Such movements were beyond attack and Keats noted that the French only moved two or three boats at a time, so avoiding any target that might prompt the Allies to risk engaging the numerous defensive batteries. The admiral was also concerned by the way the enemy only worked at night, to prevent any close observation being maintained, and worried at the way they seemed to be linking some of their boats in pairs and fixing wooden rackings around them. This seemed intended to give protection from musket fire, or to allow the conveyance of more troops, or possibly allowing their use as bridges. The constant employment was also starting to tell on some of the British vessels. By mid-December Keats was writing that one of his bomb vessels had suffered a burst mortar, the explosion seriously wounding two of her seamen and destroying her mainmast: he had had to send this vessel, the *Hound*, to Gibraltar for repairs. Another, the *Etna*, had had her mortar disabled and required a replacement, and several of his smaller craft were showing signs of wear and tear. At least the enemy was also having problems as intelligence reports suggested that several boats in the French flotilla had suffered damage, either from artillery fire or through the strains of being dragged overland.

The final gathering of the French flotilla suggested that the moment of crisis was at hand, the Allied boats doing all they could to harass the enemy and some at least of the inhabitants of Cadiz making preparations to flee the city. On the evening of Christmas Day the British gunboats moved east in preparation for a joint attack with the Spaniards. The next day at high water, around 1pm, the Allies attacked, the Spaniards engaging Fort San Luis while the British targeted the flotilla and its protecting batteries. Fire from Puntales was aimed at the works near Matagorda and the bombs distracted Fort Catalina. A furious action ensued for 90 minutes, at the conclusion of which the Allies withdrew, leaving 12 French craft destroyed behind them.[24]

The Boxing Day action marked the culmination of the danger to the city. The difficulties of assembling their flotilla, their transparent reluctance to fight the Allied gunboats head to head, and their complete inability to stop their constant assaults along the shoreline, all made it clear just how costly and unlikely a full-scale amphibious assault on the Isla de Leon was going to be. To rub the message home, two more French gunboats were destroyed between Rota and Santa Catalina in January 1811 and it appears that around this time Victor finally abandoned any real thought of being able to mount an effective naval challenge in the waters around the fortress. Instead he now concentrated on the construction and manning of small privateers to prey on the city's supply lines. Even had his naval position around Cadiz looked more promising, however, by the early weeks of 1811 the French in the siege lines were starting to feel the effects of events elsewhere. In January, responding to orders from Paris, Soult launched an invasion of Estremadura aimed at providing support for Massena in Portugal and which would lead, in March, to the French capture of the vital border fortress of Badajoz. Assembling the troops for this, though, meant that Soult had to draw an infantry regiment and all the cavalry from Victor's I Corps in front of Cadiz. This left only 19,000 French troops to besiege a fortress held by 25,000 Allied soldiers. Such a disparity of force, combined with the Allied control of the waters around it, left the fortress besieged but secure.[25]

Rumours of the French movements reached Cadiz by mid-December and these continued into the following month. By the end of January active preparations were underway to try and strike at Victor while the French were committed to the north, though operations intended for the 28th had to be postponed because of bad weather. Eventually, even though the weather remained very unsettled, a force of 7000 Spanish and 2000 British troops was shipped along the coast at the end of February, the British element landing at Algeçiras on the 22nd and marching from there to Tarifa where the Spaniards and the expedition's heavy stores were put ashore. Such was the state of the sea that back at Cadiz Keats had no idea of what the expedition was doing until the morning of 5 March when word finally came that it was advancing along the coast. Two British warships, *Implacable* and *Standard* (64), immediately weighed to sail in support, but so dangerous was the state of the weather that their pilots refused to take them to sea. On that same day Victor struck at the British contingent of the Allied force but was repulsed in a bloody fight at Barrosa, an action that caused a good deal of mutual recrimination thereafter when the force re-entered Cadiz. Although all of this had achieved little, Keats at least had usefully seized the opportunity of Victor's predicament and a calmer sea to launch two diversionary landings on 6 March, one between Rota and Santa Catalina and the other between Santa Catalina and Santa Maria. All of *Implacable*'s marines along with 200 British seamen and 80 Spanish marines made up the landing parties, the bombs *Hound* and *Thunder* firing upon Santa Catalina while the mortar and gunboats engaged the batteries on the north and east of Cadiz Bay. Two batteries were stormed and all the guns between Rota and Santa Maria, excepting those in Fort Catalina, were spiked and their works dismantled. The French rushed up reinforcements but the attackers, with some difficulty, were re-embarked in time. One gunboat was sunk in the action and the British suffered five dead and 11 wounded: 31 French soldiers were captured.[26]

The Barrosa campaign yet again illustrated the problems of effective Anglo-Spanish co-operation and was perhaps a serious missed opportunity as after the battle the French, had the Allies advanced on them again, would probably have retreated to Seville. However, whatever its shortcomings, it was another indication of the increasingly hollow nature of the French threat to Cadiz. With its security more assured Keats felt able to report at the end of March that his gunboat flotilla required no further augmentation. In an effort to try and preserve morale among the crews he therefore planned to rotate the seamen serving in them as far as possible, intending to send home men originally from the *Atlas* and *Colossus*: neither of these vessels was present at Cadiz and the behaviour of these seamen had recently been particularly unsatisfactory. More significantly for the general prosecution of the war, on 18 March 7000 Spanish troops under Zayas were released from garrison duties on the Isla de Leon and shipped to Huelva. From there they marched north, joined Beresford's Anglo-Portuguese army before Badajoz and played a vital role in the battle of Albuera on 16 May.[27]

From early 1811 the siege at Cadiz stagnated. Rear-Admiral Legge, who succeeded Keats during the course of the year, wrote early in 1812 that Soult had recently put in an appearance in the lines and that the French were still busy in their efforts to maintain their flotilla and build batteries that could annoy Allied shipping. Significantly, though, he also considered that they lacked the manpower to pose a serious threat and were primarily trying to distract Allied forces. In some respects this was just as well. In the waters off Cadiz, as everywhere else, the Royal Navy was feeling the effects of an increasing shortage of manpower, with the gunboat flotilla being 500 men below its establishment and of the four ships of the line three, the *Alfred* (a reduced 74), *St Albans* (64) and *Stately* (64), were short of their full complements. Each of these ships provided crews for four to six boats armed with carronades as well as their own boats and launches for any alarm, on top of which each also provided 30 or more men as part of the gunboat flotilla. Legge worried that in any emergency the ships would simply not have enough men to sail in safety themselves, though it was a fear the manpower-starved Admiralty could do little to obviate.

Illustrative of this was Legge's disgust when 15 men were sent out to him from Plymouth to reinforce the gunboats: 14 of them were pressed foreigners and the other was an Irishman. He complained that the Admiralty seemed unaware of just how close the flotilla served to the enemy and how easy it was in consequence to desert. The previous year gunboat No 15 had been seized by her crew while the commanding midshipman was absent and 16 out of her 18-strong complement had deserted, four of them being foreigners. For individual seamen who wished to desert the shore was temptingly close.[28]

Fortunately the decline in French power in Andalusia spared the Cadiz squadron any embarrassment from this weakness, Soult being more than occupied in simply trying to control those parts of the region theoretically under French occupation. Here again the flexibility of naval power proved an enormous thorn in the French side. In June 1811, with the French distracted in the wake of Massena's failure in Portugal, Blake led a force in the region between southern Portugal and Spain that offered a threat to Seville. He was too weak to achieve much, though it was a danger the harassed Soult could not afford to ignore and early in July two French divisions were dispatched to try and destroy the Spaniards. This Blake managed to avoid by means of a very rapid retreat to the coast at Ayamonte. There the bulk of his command was embarked and 7000 troops were taken back to the safety of Cadiz. Six weeks later the remainder of the force, under Ballasteros, which had initially withdrawn northwards to avoid the French, was embarked at the mouth of the Guadiana: these too were safely shipped back to the fortress.[29]

Shortly after this Ballasteros led another force, about 7000 strong, from Cadiz, this time moving along the coast to Algeçiras to threaten the enemy's control of southern Andalusia. Soult was compelled to respond by moving troops from the north and from the Cadiz siege lines to meet the danger, a 10,000-strong force obliging Ballasteros to seek shelter under the guns of Gibraltar in October. When a shortage of provisions obliged a French retreat the following month, the Spaniards were able to savage their rearguards as they withdrew. These operations prompted Soult into a more vigorous attempt to remove the danger posed by Ballasteros, who had

been reinforced by a 3000-strong Anglo-Spanish force stationed in the small coastal fortress of Tarifa. From there this
unit had harassed the French before Cadiz as well as providing
Ballasteros with support.

Towards the end of November Soult sent 15,000 men against
the Allied positions. Initially Ballasteros's command near San
Roque seemed to be the main target, all available naval means
at Gibraltar being mobilised to assist the Spaniards, Penrose
sending his remaining gunboats, the sloop *Termagant*, the
mortar vessel *Rebuff* and the cutter *Dash* to bolster the Spanish
left, while the frigate *L'Aigle* (36) backed up their right. It
quickly became apparent, though, that the bulk of the French
force was being directed at Tarifa. On 1 December Penrose provided a gunboat and tonnage to move 1400 reinforcements to
the fortress, also providing sufficient transports to embark the
whole garrison if an evacuation became necessary. Tarifa also
received substantial naval support from Cadiz, Legge sending
the *Stately*, *Druid*, three mortar vessels and three gunboats.
Vessels from Gibraltar also set about bombarding enemy troops
occupying Algeçiras and shipped 800 Spanish troops eastwards along the coast to the mountains around Manilva to
operate as a diversion on the French rear. All of this took place
to the accompaniment of dreadful weather, gales and constant
rain making movement difficult and conditions miserable. The
French finally launched an assault on Tarifa on 31 December
and it was smartly repulsed. A few days later they abandoned
the whole enterprise and retreated, the pouring rain even preventing them from burning their abandoned wagons.[30]

Whatever plans Soult may have harboured for another
attempt at subduing the southern part of Andalusia during
1812 were to be frustrated by the steady deterioration in the
whole French position in Spain. At Cadiz Legge would express
some alarm in July at the size of the French gunboat flotilla, by
then numbering 33 such vessels and some other craft, and
would be disconcerted by a renewal of the French bombardment of the city. Such fears prompted him to ignore an
Admiralty order to send the *Standard* home. Nevertheless, the
enemy still did not have the manpower available to consider an
assault and the hollow nature of the siege was finally proved on

25 August when the French retreated altogether from the fortress, abandoning their lines, blowing up some of their works and rendering all their guns unserviceable. Two days later an Anglo-Spanish force, previously shipped along the coast to Huelva, moved north and liberated Seville.[31] A siege that had been maintained in some shape or form for 933 days was over, its ultimate failure being a striking instance of the way naval power could profoundly influence a land campaign and, in the case of Cadiz, completely dislocate French plans for the conquest of southern Spain.

*   *   *

While the Allies had been able to block French progress around Cadiz, the same could not be said elsewhere in Spain. In Catalonia the final surrender of Gerona in December 1809 freed French communications in the northern part of the province and opened up the possibility of substantial future progress. The continuing millstone around the neck of Napoleon's strategy, however, was the provisioning of Barcelona and its garrison. Although in January 1811 a squadron of three frigates escorted a convoy laden with grain to the Catalan capital, the vulnerability of this supply method was clearly shown on the return trip when, although the frigates reached Toulon safely, most of the merchant vessels were captured by the British. That the convoy got to Barcelona at all was viewed as a sufficient achievement by the French for the escort commander to be rewarded with the Legion d'Honneur. With this means of supply being so tenuous it was necessary to devote considerable time and effort to the movement of food overland. In March 1810 Marshal Augereau, then commanding in Catalonia, laboriously moved a train of no less than a thousand wagons to replenish the city's depots. During the following summer Marshal Macdonald, the successor to the indolent and incompetent Augereau, was obliged to escort three more such convoys in June, July and August, with yet another being hauled through the guerrilla-infested Catalonian hinterland in November. Such activities tied up a large proportion of the available French forces for most of 1810, much to Napoleon's annoyance. With these events occurring well inland there was little immediate scope for naval participation in a direct sense and for most of 1810 a small squadron of two frigates and two sloops under Captain Bullen was sufficient to blockade Barcelona and maintain communications with the Spaniards via Tarragona.[32]

Such comparative French quiescence could not last indefinitely, the looming menace being made clear in May and June when the energetic Suchet captured Lerida and Maquinenza, two fortresses blocking the main lateral road linking Catalonia with Aragon. The danger was sufficiently apparent in London for the Admiralty to draw Cotton's attention very particularly to the coasts of Catalonia and Valencia, urging him to try and prevent communications between French-controlled ports, to give all possible assistance to the Spaniards – especially at Tarragona – and to harass the enemy as much as possible. For the moment, though, Cotton, who had already turned down a Catalan request for more naval support in July, seems to have believed that there was adequate strength off the coast for the tasks in hand.[33] Larger warships were to be found occasionally off eastern Spain, but not on any regular basis. In October 1810 Codrington's *Blake* shipped Doyle, the British military agent in Catalonia, and some Spanish soldiers from Tarragona to Peniscola and while thereafter sailing on to Gibraltar discovered the useful information that all of the Valencian coast could be easily approached. Despite being previously informed that those waters were too dangerous even for the employment of a frigate during the autumn and winter, Codrington came to the opposite conclusion: 'Never was there a coast which had so few difficulties in approaching it . . .' Such knowledge would soon be invaluable. Cotton did order the *Invincible* to patrol the southern coast of Catalonia early in February 1811, but, even though Captain Adam was informed that the sloop *Minstrel* would aid him in the duty, it was quite obviously only intended as a temporary assignment as the following month both warships were to be found back in Cartagena helping to move its naval stores and dockyard artificers.[34]

If the French were unable to make much headway in Catalonia in 1810, they could at least tighten their grip along the northern parts of the coast that were under their sway. Such a reinforcement of control at least offered the chance of their being able to use some coastal convoys in the continuing battle to keep Barcelona fed, these being able to move slowly to the city under the protection of a series of fortified harbours and batteries. Attacking such convoys could be a very dangerous undertaking and there was to be a sharp illustration of this at the end of the year. By December the traffic had become sufficiently important for two 74s, the *Kent* and *Ajax*, to be sent from the main body of the Mediterranean fleet to try and interdict it. These were off northern Catalonia with the *Minstrel* and *Sparrowhawk* when Rogers, captain of the *Kent* and the senior officer, learned that there were twelve enemy vessels at Palamos *en route* for Barcelona. Rogers knew that the town and adjacent area had been reinforced and that in Palamos itself the enemy had sited two mortars and two heavy guns in a position above the mole beyond the range of British fire. He wrote on the 12th that he had decided that any attack on the convoy would be too risky and that he planned to send the *Ajax* to Tarragona in the hope of acquiring 3–400 Spanish troops to make an assault viable. No sooner had this decision been taken than the frigate *Cambrian* (40), Captain Fane, hove into view. With her arrival Rogers changed his mind and decided to attack the convoy at once, a decision in which he may well have been influenced by Fane himself, an aggressive commander who had enjoyed some success a few months before in some boat attacks on the French near Tortosa. Certainly Fane volunteered to lead the assault force of 350 marines and 250 seamen drawn from the squadron, these also being supported by two pieces of artillery. On the afternoon of 13 December the force landed on a beach near the town, the operation, conducted under the cover of the sloops' guns, being managed successfully and without loss. Palamos was occupied with little resistance, its garrison of 250 Frenchmen retiring to a nearby hill. The convoy, in the event consisting of eight merchant vessels and three small armed escorts, was destroyed, its ships being either seized or burned. As well as this the defending batteries were eliminated and a magazine blown up. To this point the attackers had suffered only four or five casualties, but then things started to go horribly wrong. Part of the British force had occupied a hill overlooking the town to protect the main body and as these men started to pull back they were suddenly attacked by the reinforced French. In disorder they fell back into Palamos rather than retiring to the beach, the pursuing French then re-entering the town and bringing a heavy fire of musketry to bear from behind walls and inside houses. Great efforts were made by the ships' boats to evacuate the landing party, but in the resulting chaos British casualties were heavy, 33 men being killed, 89 wounded and another 87 captured. Fane, who was supervising the convoy's destruction from the mole, was among those taken prisoner. In his report Rogers cravenly tried to throw all the blame for the disaster on him, smugly considering that 'the force I employed was fully adequate to the service and I confided the execution of it to an officer of reputation therefore I cannot reproach myself. . .'.[35] It was unquestionably a botched operation that highlighted all the risks involved in landings made in the vicinity of strong enemy garrisons and illustrates, as did other smaller-scale landings around this time, that such attacks on harbours were becoming increasingly hazardous in the light of French defences. It is significant that Barcelona's supply problems were considerably eased as the war progressed, the French not only employing land and coastal convoys but also offering inducements to the Spaniards themselves to bring in grain. The British entertained grave suspicions that local fishing boats were being used to break the blockade, one of them indeed even being discovered smuggling in a mortar! One naval officer passed on a report from Barcelona's American consul stating that the French were also circumventing the British blockade by offering to allow the export of colonial produce, chiefly sugar and cocoa, provided that two quintals of wheat or flour were brought in for each quintal of colonial goods that went out. Many of the city's business community had taken up the offer and deliveries of American flour from Gibraltar were even attempted. The winter gales made maintaining the blockade difficult anyway, but the French seemed from the autumn of 1811 to experience fewer problems and were obtaining illicit supplies from the Balearics, Malta and similar places. Codrington reported in July of that year that, although usually stationing two warships off the city, he still could not prevent some supplies getting in. He had urged the Catalans to prohibit the movement of grain in the sort of small vessels that could easily slip in and out of the place, but his suggestion had not even received a reply. It was observed that, while Barcelona's poor starved for want of bread, the rich were making money supplying the French with corn and other provisions. At one point in the summer of 1811, Captain Buck of the *Termagant* even had to endure the spectacle of numerous carts and individuals hauling sacks of grain from Spanish-controlled Mataro along the coast road to Barcelona, this taking place with the permission of the local Spanish commander.[36]

Part of this tendency to co-operate with their occupiers was undoubtedly due to a decline in Spanish morale in the wake of French successes. In December 1810, after months of preparation and covered by part of Macdonald's Catalonian command, Suchet's Army of Aragon laid siege to Tortosa, a city that stood athwart the main road linking Catalonia to Valencia. It fell in January and thereafter Suchet began preparing to attack Tarragona. This presaged a crisis for the Catalans as they relied almost completely on naval communications for contact with the outside world and on Tarragona for the security of those communications: there was no other substantial fortified harbour on that part of the coast.

French progress did seem to have received a check on 10 April 1811 when, in a daring *coup de main*, a group of guerrillas managed to seize the fortress of Figueras and quickly garrisoned the place with 2000 men before the French could react. In the manner of Gerona in 1809, Figueras blocked the main road linking Barcelona to France and its loss temporarily threw the French in northern Catalonia into chaos as Macdonald stripped his garrisons to form a covering force while awaiting reinforcements from France. Unfortunately for the Allies, Suchet refused to send any of his troops north to meet the emergency, so maintaining the looming threat to Tarragona, but the French were nevertheless momentarily vulnerable and Cotton was as alive to this as anyone else. Being ten miles inland from the coast, Figueras could not benefit from direct naval support, but operations did appear viable against the coastal strongpoints in its vicinity with the hope of increasing the discomfiture of the

French. With this in mind on 18 April Cotton committed the *Blake* to full-time coastal duties, telling Codrington that he was to command all the warships then serving off northern Catalonia, *viz* the frigates *Cambrian* and *Volontaire* (40) and the sloops *Termagant* and *Sparrowhawk*, and was to employ them in aiding the Spaniards and harassing the French, hopes also being entertained that the Italian and German regiments under French command were in a state of mutiny (this was to prove optimistic). Four days later, after having received official confirmation of Figueras's capture, Cotton reinforced the squadron still further by the addition of the frigate *Undaunted* (38) and the sloop *Blossom*. The warships off Catalonia had already been busy, *Cambrian* and *Volontaire* sending parties ashore on 12 and 14 April to destroy batteries at Palamos and Sant Felieu and taking a settee laden with grain for Barcelona. Shortly after, a much larger convoy of 19 vessels was captured at Cadagues and by the 19th the only points on the whole stretch of coast still in French hands were Rosas and the Medas Islands.[37]

The *Blake* reached Palamos on the 20th, Codrington issuing orders to maintain the blockade of Barcelona and to impose one on Rosas. At the end of the month he also promised the Marquis of Campoverde, the Captain-General of Catalonia, that he would make landings at Cadagues and Rosas to distract the French while the main Catalan field force tried to throw supplies into Figueras. The Spanish part of this plan was largely frustrated, but Codrington was as good as his word when, on 3 May, all the marines from the *Blake* and the *Undaunted* were put ashore at Cadagues and the *Blake*, *Undaunted* and *Volontaire* then stood into Rosas Bay to engage Fort Trinity and a shore-line battery. The next day the landing party re-embarked in the face of an advance by a 400-strong French force from Rosas, the British vessels directing a heavy fire on the approaching French in the process.[38] However, the strategic initiative remained with the French and at the end of April Suchet began to advance upon Tarragona, his forward units reaching the outskirts of the port on 3 May. At that stage, with Campoverde's main army near Figueras, there were only 7000 troops in Tarragona itself. However, the French were being constantly harassed during their advance up the coast road by the *Cambrian*, *Termagant* and some gunboats, Suchet's battering train being able to advance only slowly and it was not until 8 May that he could commence serious operations against the place. This threat to his main base immediately obliged Campoverde to suspend other operations and on the 7th Codrington received a letter begging him to ship troops back down the coast to meet the danger. Next day *Blake* sent her boats into Mataro to help load Spanish troops into about 60 small feluccas, arriving with them and a Spanish frigate at Tarragona on 10 May, though Codrington grumbled in a letter to his wife that the reinforcements would never have sailed at all if his own energy had not overcome Spanish indolence. In the days that followed, *Blake*, *Cambrian* and *Termagant*, along with the Spanish frigate, were engaged in repeated artillery duels with the French as the warships tried to hamper the construction of Suchet's siege works, the *Blake* alone firing off 1159 roundshot on 14 May. The following day *Termagant* had to be sent to Port Mahon, the consistent firing having severely reduced her supply of powder and damaged her decks. However, despite these efforts the French continued to progress, a completed earthwork armed with heavy guns obliging the squadron to retire to a more distant part of the anchorage on the 14th; thereafter the naval fire on the besiegers was to be much less effective. At least the French were unable to block Tarragona's maritime communications and this was to be crucial in making the defence viable. The convoy from Mataro at the start of the siege had brought in 4000 reinforcements and on 22 May *Invincible* arrived from Peniscola with a further 2300 infantry and 211 artillerymen. Codrington had fallen in with Adam and four transports on their way to Cartagena and had ordered them to undertake this more important mission, later instructing them to return to Peniscola and await further orders. In the meantime the *Blake* proceeded to Alicante to take on board 80 artillerymen plus arms and a variety of other much-needed supplies: encountering the Spanish corvette *Paloma* and a transport from Cadiz loaded with powder, shot, cartridges and suchlike, Codrington sent them on to Tarragona as well. He also arranged with Charles O'Donnell, the Captain-General of Valencia, for 4000 troops to be shipped from that province to reinforce the Catalan army being assembled for the relief of the fortress. The

Blake returned there on 7 June and unloaded her stores, these being so badly needed that hand grenades went directly from the ship to be used against the French who were attacking one of the defenders' positions. Next day the *Blake* and the *Paloma* went back to Peniscola, the squadron now being reinforced by a third 74, the *Centaur*: Codrington had left word up the coast that all passing warships should join him in the event of an emergency.

Certainly Tarragona's situation was becoming increasingly serious. On 29 May Fort Olivo, a strongpoint on a hill overlooking the place, was stormed by the French, the Spaniards suffering heavy losses. This was followed on 1 June by the first assaults on the city proper, the defenders being forced to abandon Fort Francoli, an outlying position on the shoreline, on the 7th. Tarragona's only hope lay in the arrival of an outside relieving force, but Campoverde who had left the city to oversee its formation could only assemble 6000 regular troops and was with growing desperation looking for reinforcements from Valencia. Although O'Donnell had promised such aid to Codrington, the Spaniard was reluctant to see them employed. Evidently Codrington, who was becoming increasingly irritated at what he viewed as Spanish indolence and lethargy, was at the centre of a struggle to prise the Valencian troops out of their home province, the nervous O'Donnell telling him 'that he considered me as entirely answerable for the safety of the Kingdom of Valencia; and that if I should fail in redeeming my pledge [to evacuate the Valencian troops in case of need], he would resign his Command on that particular account'. Despite his moral cowardice O'Donnell did finally permit the 4000 troops to be embarked at Peniscola on 11 June, 800 being taken aboard each of the three 74s and the remainder in transports and feluccas. Unfortunately after these men had been disembarked at Tarragona the following day it was decided that they would be of more value serving in the relieving army. Accordingly they were re-embarked and transferred to Villanova de Sitges, some 30 miles up the coast, from where they marched to join Campoverde. However, the arrival and immediate departure of so timely a reinforcement had a disastrous effect on the morale of those troops remaining in Tarragona.

At least from 17 June the garrison did enjoy the support of a

very powerful naval squadron, Codrington on his own responsibility retaining all three ships of the line off the port. These
remained there for the remainder of the siege, usually also supported by a frigate, a sloop and ten Spanish gunboats.
Unfortunately there were no bomb vessels present as their
higher-trajectory fire would have been a great asset to the
defenders: the speed of events around Tarragona did not allow
time for any to be moved from Cadiz. Despite the danger posed
by the French batteries, every night the ships' boats and the
Spanish gunboats moved close inshore to pound away at the
ever-advancing siege lines. During daylight hours the British
crews were kept equally busy ferrying out of the fortress those
whom Codrington described as 'useless mouths', namely
women, children and the wounded. This process too was not
without its moments, the *Blake*'s log laconically noting on 24
June that the jolly boat brought out several women, 'one of
whom was delivered of a fine Girl alongside before she could be
got on board'. Death was the more usual experience and the
next day *Blake*'s barge was swamped by a French cannonball,
killing a woman, taking the leg off her child and injuring three
of the crew. When not engaged in such dangerous work the
sailors were still kept busy by the labour of supplying the
Spaniards with thousands of sandbags.

For all of this effort, though, Tarragona's doom seemed inexorable. On the 21st Suchet's troops stormed the lower section of
the port, the area that included the mole and which was the
primary means of maintaining communications with the ships.
Some 200 Spaniards trapped on the mole were rescued by the
squadron's boats and moved to the upper city. The next day all
five British warships moved inshore and between 12.40pm and
1.30pm bombarded the French with their full broadsides. This
may have caused some loss to the enemy, but was too risky a procedure to repeat once the lower city had been protected by new
batteries: as it was the action cost the warships two dead and
three wounded. On 26 June the armed troopship *Regulus*
arrived with a convoy bringing just over a thousand British
troops from Cadiz but, in consultation with Codrington, their
commander, Colonel Skerrett, decided that it would be futile to
try and land them in the face of a heavy surf and the general

weakness of Tarragona's position. On the 28th the final French assault was launched, the attack taking place so quickly that the squadron did not have time to send boats inshore to bombard them in their assembly trenches. Amidst scenes of fire and slaughter the French stormed into the remaining parts of the city and overwhelmed the defenders in about half an hour, the warships being able to evacuate only 5–600 of the 10,000-strong garrison, many of them fished naked from the water and supplied with clothing by the British vessels. Ironically, at this, the moment of its fall, Tarragona enjoyed the greatest concentration of naval support witnessed during the whole of the siege, Codrington's squadron, reinforced by the arrival of several convoys in the preceding days, comprising three ships of the line, five frigates (four British and one Spanish) and three sloops (two British and one Spanish).

The siege of Tarragona provides a clear illustration of both the value and the limitations of sea power in the Peninsular conflict. Control of the Mediterranean allowed the fortress to be very rapidly reinforced once Suchet's threat materialised, with additional forces being steadily fed into the place in the weeks that followed. Oman estimates that the siege cost the Spaniards 10–15,000 men in all and that the city's initial garrison comprised no more than 7000 soldiers. On top of this may be added the several hundred wounded shipped out during the fighting – there were 800 Tarragona wounded at Sitges just after the city fell – and the movement of the 4000 Valencians brought in to reinforce Campoverde's unavailing relief efforts. A series of convoys also kept a whole variety of supplies and provisions flowing into the fortress, Rear-Admiral Fremantle at Port Mahon even grumbling at one point that he had had to provide 500 bags of biscuit plus some rice, both of which he could ill-spare, to make up a Spanish deficit. The defenders' morale, as well as the interests of humanity, must also have been bolstered by the removal of many civilians as the fighting became more intense, though the fiasco of the Valencian detachment and the flying visit of Skerrett's force presumably undid much of this effect. For all of this, however, and the courage and endeavour of the sailors, the squadron was doomed to fight a losing battle. Unlike Cadiz, Tarragona did not sit on an island where naval power could keep the besiegers at a distance and most of its defensive perimeter was beyond the range of naval gunfire. Even where the French could be bombarded from the sea, any sustained duel with land batteries was likely to see the warships coming off second best: the steady advance of Suchet's works obliged Codrington's vessels to retreat from the intense fire that could be directed at them. Only in the hours of darkness could boats move close to the shore, Codrington remarking that he and his senior captains spent most nights in their gigs conducting such operations, but this could do little more than harass the enemy. A smaller squadron had made the difference when it came to preserving a land fortress at Acre in 1799, but when, as at Tarragona, the attackers were stronger and better equipped with heavy artillery, warships could not make up the difference.[39]

Tarragona's fall was a disaster for the Allies, most immediately manifested by a sharp decline in Catalan morale as members of the Army of Catalonia and of the guerrilla bands deserted to return to their homes and a majority of the senior officers decided in council that the province should be completely evacuated. Given the determination of other, more junior, officers to go on fighting it may be doubted if such a resolution could have been put into force anyway, but as it was the whole idea was scotched by Codrington, who refused point-blank to move any Catalan units out of their own area, though he did ship the Valencian contingent home in line with his promise to O'Donnell. The Spanish naval units on the coast were also badly affected, their general desire seeming to have been to flee Catalan waters. Codrington responded by sending *Invincible* and *Cossack* in pursuit of three frigates going to Majorca with the treasury archives of Catalonia along with various military supplies and personnel rescued from Tarragona. This Adam successfully accomplished, ordering the vessels to set a course for Arens de Mar, one of the few small harbours still under Spanish control. He also instructed two feluccas under a Spanish lieutenant to go there as well, but, despite providing them with stores for the voyage, they did not appear. A furious Codrington raged that 'I cannot describe to you the difficulties to which I have been put by the misconduct of all the

Spanish Ships and Vessels of War which I have had to commu-
nicate with upon this Coast. . .'. Worst of all was the future lack
of any secure Catalonian harbour as an alternative point of communication. Although the Spaniards talked hopefully of fortifying Palamos or possibly Blanes as a replacement, the truth of the
matter was that they had neither the time nor the resources for
such a project. In future naval communications would have to be
maintained via small and very insecure harbours with all the
consequent risks. In January 1812 Codrington himself was
almost captured by some French dragoons when trying to co-
ordinate operations with the guerrillas and several of his officers
were taken, only later being freed when their captors were themselves surrounded and destroyed. So bleak did the future seem
that Pellew, newly appointed to command the Mediterranean
Fleet, could write in August 1811 that the Spanish cause in
Catalonia 'is every day becoming more desperate, and I appre-
hend without some very vigorous measure for its support, in a
short time, must be irretrievably lost'.[40]

Support for the Catalans was also not helped at that moment
by a personal spat between Codrington and the British military
agent in the province. This position had previously been occupied by Major-General Doyle, with whom Codrington seems to
have established a close working relationship. However, Doyle's
successor during the summer, a Lieutenant-Colonel Green,
infuriated the sailor by moving out of Catalonia and into
Valencia during the period of crisis following Tarragona's fall.
When Green suggested that another warship would be useful
serving off Peniscola and, moreover, took the liberty of recom-
mending Pringle's *Sparrowhawk*, Codrington brutally
responded that such suggestions were none of Green's business.
'After quitting this principality in the hour of its greatest distress with such Arms and Money as you had under your charge
. . . I think you might have left the disposition of the Squadron
. . . to those whose duty it is to judge of its immediate application.' An enraged Green appealed to Pellew, stating that he had
only left Catalonia as the wrangling among the Spanish generals had led him to the view that he could be more useful elsewhere, requesting 'that I may not be again exposed to a similar
Insult. . .'. Pellew was obliged to try and smooth ruffled feath-

ers and suggested to Codrington that the military agent probably intended no offence with his naval suggestions and that he, Codrington, should amend his tone in future. Pellew also recommended to Green that in the weeks to come he remain in Catalonia and not stray into other provinces. Although Codrington seemed to feel the rebuke very sharply, and both parties promised that their quarrel would not hinder future cooperation, in private Pellew seems to have shared his opinion, writing to Henry Wellesley to seek his support in trying to make sure that Green stayed in Catalonia in future.[41]

Distractions of this sort must have tried Pellew's patience as he faced a military situation in the region which seemed to go from bad to worse. A minor Allied success was scored in September when Codrington sent the *Undaunted* and two sloops with a small Spanish force to seize the Medas Islands, some rocky outcrops within sight of the north-eastern coast of Catalonia. These were easily captured and thereafter fortified with artillery seized *in situ* and other pieces laboriously hauled ashore from the British warships. Their occupation was an irritation to the French and proved an obstacle to coastal convoys seeking to feed Barcelona, that city again suffering shortages by the autumn.[42] In general, though, the outlook was bleak. In August the French recaptured Figueras and Soult's movements in the south combined with Suchet's recent triumph seemed to threaten Valencia, Major-General Roche, the military agent for that province, telling Pellew that both Alicante and Cartagena were in danger and requesting naval support for that part of the coast. Pellew responded by sending Eyre's *Magnificent* followed by the frigate *Volontaire* to Alicante, though reflected what was perhaps a general weariness when he observed to Roche that though:

> . . . the presence of our ships has certainly the effect of raising the spirits of the Patriots . . . it has not infrequently offered to those of less energy and resolution an inducement to relax in their efforts for independence when such a resource was afforded to them in the event of a Retreat.

When a copy of this despatch later reached the Admiralty somebody scrawled the comment 'perfectly true' in the margin.[43]

The threat to Valencia eventually materialised from the north when Suchet began the invasion of that province in September. Captain Eyre could do little to block this movement, though with the support of some Spanish gunboats he was able to evacuate the 150-strong garrison of Oropesa, a small fort blocking the coast road that led to Suchet's first objective, the fortress of Saguntum. Valencia's primary shield lay in its army under the command of Blake: he and 8000 reinforcements had been moved from Cadiz by a Spanish squadron in August. In October, with 21,000 troops under his command and Saguntum besieged, Blake engaged the French but was routed in the resulting battle. Saguntum then surrendered and Suchet was free to advance on the city of Valencia itself.[44]

By December 1811 the *Magnificent*, battered by storms, struck by lightning and with her hull leaking, was having difficulties maintaining her station, not that there was a great deal the Navy could do to influence events on shore – neither Saguntum nor Valencia were directly on the coast. At the end of the year Suchet was able to surround Blake and 17,000 troops in Valencia itself, the city being indefensible and the whole force being compelled to surrender. Offshore, just prior to the final Spanish collapse, the British had been joined by the *York* and her captain, Barton, became the senior officer present. Unfortunately he seems to have been a most uninspiring commander for a moment of crisis. Landing on Christmas Day to meet Blake, he ran into French fire and quickly returned to his ship. Enemy advances prevented any further efforts to establish communication and although Barton directed three Spanish gunboats and a mortar vessel inshore to engage the French, as soon as they came under fire they too quickly took to their heels and Barton did nothing to make them return to their duty. He did order the *Papillon* to close with the shore and engage the enemy as well, but she could have little impact: shoals prevented the larger warships from moving within range. Barton was able to rescue various supplies, including 495 barrels of gunpowder held by Consul Tapper, who acted as military agent in the city, and moved them to Alicante. The following month he sailed back up the coast to Denia to recover an anchor and destroy the guns at the castle there, in the event managing neither task and the harbour became a useful base for French privateers. Fortunately at the end of January the more energetic Adam returned to the station, reporting from Alicante that he had sent the *York* and an assortment of merchant vessels to Gibraltar and was about to sail himself for Cartagena to try and procure some gunboats for Alicante's future protection. The Spaniards at the latter place were doing all they could to fortify it, fearing that it would be Suchet's next target, but Adam considered that it would take years to ready its defences adequately. The governor was pleading for a battalion of British troops to bolster its garrison and Adam hoped that at least a British warship might be able to be constantly stationed there.[45]

The defeats at Tarragona and Valencia brought Allied fortunes in eastern Spain to their nadir, though the French tide of conquest had in fact reached its high-water mark. Strategically Napoleon was becoming overstretched as he drew troops away from Marmont's Army of Portugal to support the invasion of Valencia while simultaneously moving thousands of veteran soldiers out of Spain altogether as he assembled forces for his pending invasion of Russia. In eastern Spain Suchet could make no further progress after the fall of Valencia, other than taking the small but powerful fortress of Peniscola, as his command was fully occupied in just holding the territory it had captured. In the south Soult confronted similar difficulties and was stalemated before Cadiz, while to the west in January the weakened Marmont was unable to prevent Wellington's sudden capture of the border fortress of Ciudad Rodrigo.

If the French success in Valencia had been bought at the price of dangerous weakness elsewhere, it also had direct consequences for the eastern theatre. Immediately after Blake's surrender the Spaniards began looking to Britain for more direct assistance in the shape of British troops, the xenophobia witnessed in 1808 now giving way in the face of military disaster as it had already had to do at Cadiz. In January 1812 Henry Wellesley was asked by Bardaxi if part of the British force there might be moved to help secure Cartagena, the ambassador agreeing to the request providing the troops were stationed near the harbour and that the Spaniards undertook to move or destroy the remaining naval stores in the arsenal. By March a small contingent comprising one British infantry battalion and five companies of De Watteville's regiment, a unit made up of enemy deserters, had been transferred to the port, these being followed by five 24-pounder cannon to reinforce Cartagena's defences. The British commander, Major-General Ross, also proposed moving six mortars from Port Mahon and planned to employ Cartagena's own foundry for the production of ammunition, relying on coal for its fires being shipped in from Gibraltar. Adam also took Ross on an inspection trip up the coast to Alicante, the soldier confirming that it would require a very large garrison to make it secure. However, they did discover that although the Spaniards had garrisoned the small coastal castle of Aguilas with 100 men, they lacked the means to provision even so small a body. Adam was able to step into the breach and provide them with sufficient pork and pease for six weeks and intended to provide bread as well once a supply arrived from Gibraltar. He particularly wanted to see the place under Allied control as it was the only spot on the coast where good water was easily available for shipping.[46]

Of much more significance than this, however, was the question of a more substantial body of British troops being committed to eastern Spain. In the wake of Tarragona's fall Codrington had reported to Pellew on a conversation he had had with some Catalans during which they assured him 'that if a few English Troops with an extra proportion of English officers were sent to their assistance . . . the whole population of the Country [would] flock to their Standard'. Pellew needed little convincing of the importance of such a move, believing himself that a mere 5000 British soldiers off Catalonia rendered mobile by troopships would rouse the Catalans to renewed efforts. Certainly he felt that something had to be done or the Allied cause in the region would be 'irretrievably lost'. This opinion he repeated the following year when reviewing the situation in the area for the Admiralty's benefit. At that time, February 1812, he considered Catalan resistance to be feeble, lacking in system and suffering from divided leadership. His hopes that Blake might use his forces in offensive operations had come to nothing and offers of naval co-operation had been met with 'coolness and disregard'. However, Pellew still believed in the Catalan cause and felt that British troops would by their presence arouse them to action, a view he pressed again in March. That the commanding admiral in the Mediterranean should be urging such a strategy upon ministers in London, though, was ironic. There was a substantial body of British-controlled troops stationed on Sicily to preserve that Bourbon enclave from attack from southern Italy and as early as the autumn of 1808 the Cabinet had wanted to see them employed in eastern Spain. Similar pressure for such a policy was repeated in the years that followed but a combination of the French threat to Sicily, political uncertainties on the island itself, and a reluctance by successive British commanders to serve in Spain – where they would be under Wellington's orders – all served to paralyse the strategy. By early 1812 the commitment of part of the Sicilian garrison seemed even less likely given the ambitions of Lieutenant-General Lord Bentinck, then commander on the island, to pursue a campaign on the Italian mainland. This flew completely in the face of the Cabinet's wishes, to the fury of at least one minister, and it was only with the greatest reluctance that Bentinck could be persuaded away from Italy and towards Spain. Finally, after four years of delay, a British force would be sent to eastern Spain in the summer of 1812.[47]

Such developments had obvious naval implications. In February Rear-Admiral Hallowell was instructed by Pellew to conduct a reconnaissance along the coasts of Catalonia and Valencia, he reporting the following month that although there was considerable jealousy among the various Spanish generals, the arrival of a British force would nevertheless galvanise resistance. Hallowell recommended that such a force ought to land either at Palamos, where there was a mole and shelter for smaller vessels, or, his own preference, Blanes, where the fleet could obtain water and the occupation of which would force the French to use the mountain roads to supply Barcelona. However, and crucially as matters turned out, he also stressed that any landing force would have to support itself for a time without Spanish aid and would, in view of the denuded condition of the countryside, have to rely on outside sources of provisions. Pellew himself acknowledged Admiralty orders the following month to co-operate fully with any expedition from Sicily and he optimistically anticipated that perhaps in excess of 20,000 British and Spanish troops might be landed in Catalonia to campaign alongside the forces already there. Bentinck, however, would not be implementing any troop withdrawals from Sicily until June because of the continuing unsettled state of affairs there.[48]

Any hopes among the naval commanders that the long-awaited expedition would radically transform the Allied position were to be quickly dashed. Bentinck himself did not command it, delegating the task to Lieutenant-General Maitland, who left Sicily towards the end of June with 7000 troops loaded in 65 transports. Not until 31 July did this force, sailing via the Balearics where an additional 4000 Spanish soldiers were collected, reach the Catalonian coast at Palamos. Now the nervous Maitland, fearful of French strength in the area and to Pellew's intense disappointment, refused to disembark and advance on Tarragona, or indeed to land in Catalonia at all. Pellew tried to convince him of the vital importance of such a landing and promised to bring the fleet from Toulon to the coast as a diversion at the first opportunity (this the admiral did in September), but Maitland refused to be swayed. Instead the expedition sailed south to land at Alicante. At least from a naval viewpoint that port provided a secure base, Hallowell reassuring Maitland that it provided a safe anchorage for shipping during possible autumn gales would be quite suitable for any future evacuation if such a move were necessary.[49]

If the final appearance of the expedition proved to be something of a damp squib tactically, Maitland remaining more or less inert at Alicante for the remainder of the year, it did at least have some strategic impact, tying the French down in eastern Spain and keeping them nervous about the possibility of sudden future strikes up the coast. Suchet was fully aware of the fleet of transports at Maitland's disposal and of the potential mobility they provided, naval power not merely bringing them to Spain but extending their threat once they had arrived. As historians of the Peninsular War have pointed out, while Wellington was able to crush Marmont's Army of Portugal in July, enter Madrid in August, and advance briefly into Spain thereafter, no French reinforcements were forthcoming from eastern Spain to help their hard-pressed colleagues.[50]

The Navy had brought the expedition to Alicante and thereafter played the major role in maintaining it there as well as continuing to harass the enemy within the limits of its capacity. The denuded condition of eastern Spain threw great reliance on provisions brought in by sea and Hallowell wrote in August and September on the arrangements he had made, sending three transports to Palermo for flour and barley, two to Majorca for wood, and three others to Oran for bullocks. He also anticipated the pending appearance of the ships bringing salt-fish from North America and had further sent a vessel to Gibraltar to collect money for the expedition's use. Nor had the movement of troops been completed, a detachment being sent from Alicante to reinforce that already at Cartagena and two additional groups, almost 7000 men in all, being shipped from Sicily to reinforce Maitland. Finally Hallowell also planned to provide a thousand seamen and 200 marines for the defence of Alicante should it come under siege, it also being able to enjoy supporting fire from his flagship, the *Malta* (80), as well as the *Fame* and a dozen mortar, howitzer and gunboats.[51] During the second half of August the *Fame*, *Termagant* and the sloop *Philomel* (18) sailed up the coast to the north of Alicante destroying evacuated French batteries and fortifications, guns and strongpoints being eliminated at Vila Joiosa, Benidorm, Altea and Calpe; two Genoese privateers were also captured in this operation. Bathurst, the *Fame*'s captain, then sailed around Cape St Martin and exchanged fire with a French fort at Denia, afterwards anchoring in Xabia Bay in response to a plea from the local inhabitants who, having aided the Allied cause since the appearance of the British warships on their section of the coast, were fearful of French reprisals. Seamen and marines were put ashore and there was a brief skirmish with the French before Bathurst evacuated most of the inhabitants to Alicante, leaving Xabia and the surrounding countryside to be thoroughly plundered. In October *Fame* and the sloop *Cephalus* (18) returned to Denia with 600 troops from Alicante in an attempt to take the fort, though this failed and they were obliged to withdraw on the appearance of a French relieving column. Hallowell's squadron did manage a minor success, however, when the *Minstrel*, patrolling off Valencia at the end of September, captured four vessels moving cargoes of shells to Peniscola.[52]

To the north, off Catalonia, the Navy continued busy in its efforts to foster local resistance even without the stimulus of British troops. Between the end of May and the beginning of November 1812 the *Blake* and a transport, the *Brailsford*, delivered over 4500 muskets together with pistols and bayonets and over 300,000 cartridges to the Catalans, landing the supplies at small harbours like Arens de Mar and Villa Nova de Sitjes. This helped keep resistance alive, but it was centred inland away from the coastline where direct naval support was available. The only major exception to this came on 27 September when Codrington and Eroles, one of the most enterprising of the Spanish commanders, co-ordinated a night attack on some shipping in the harbour at Tarragona. At 1am boats from the *Blake* and the frigate *Franchise* (36) were sent on a cutting-out expedition, Eroles having in the meantime assembled a small force of his men between the docks and the garrison in the city. When the British opened fire the French were taken completely by surprise and, thinking it was just a seaborne attack, rushed a party of 200 grenadiers down to the harbour to help fend it off. This force was then ambushed by Eroles's men and obliged to retire. In the action the Spaniards lost three dead and eight wounded, the British escaping without loss: all the shipping in the harbour, amounting to eleven small vessels, was captured. So impressed were the British by their ally's performance that the officers and men unanimously volunteered that any prize money resulting from their capture should go to the Spaniards.[53]

Barcelona continued under blockade, though it was a testament to its limited effectiveness during the winter that early in February 1813 Codrington reported that a large land convoy of colonial produce had been assembled in the city ready for transportation to France. Learning of its movement he took the *Blake*, the frigate *Castor* (32) and the sloop *Goshawk* to Mataro where the coast road was within range of the ships' guns. On the 3rd, supported by some armed boats, fire was opened up on the French who had, in Codrington's estimation, assembled no less than 5000 troops as an escort. Next day the ships moved to Arens de Mar, still pounding away at the enemy before the

French finally admitted defeat and took to the difficult mountain roads and the tender mercies of the guerrillas. Effectively this action marked Codrington's Peninsular swansong as he had already been given permission to take the *Blake* back to Britain.[54] But however satisfying it was to harry the enemy in such a fashion, it had no impact on the general military stalemate that had settled over the region. With Soult evacuating Andalusia in August there were fears that he might move his forces into eastern Spain, a threat that hamstrung Maitland during the late summer and early autumn. In the event Soult moved instead to re-occupy Madrid in November 1812 and to menace that part of Wellington's army engaged in the fruitless siege of Burgos. The manoeuvre finally obliged Wellington's shambolic winter retreat back into Portugal and thereafter the armies settled down to await the spring.

In Portugal Wellington concentrated his attentions on preparing his army for the pending summer campaign, a process involving naval support as he requested that his heavy artillery, shipped to Alicante during the summer of 1812 in anticipation of sieges on the eastern coast, be moved back west to Corunna. This was achieved and alongside it 2000 Spanish troops at Corunna were transferred by sea to the east coast, arriving in May 1813. These reinforcements, along with four more regiments from Andalusia and two others from Galicia, meant that the new commander of the Anglo-Spanish army at Alicante, Lieutenant-General Murray, would be able to field a heterogeneous force of some 21,000 men.[55] Wellington intended that Murray would ship the bulk of his command up the coast to seize Tarragona, an operation that would fully engage the French in the region while simultaneously stimulating local resistance in the manner urged by the naval commanders for months.

Murray's force, finally comprising 17,059 troops together with 1453 horses and 152 mules, left Alicante on 31 May, reaching Salou Bay, to the south-west of Tarragona, on 2 June. The troops were disembarked the next day and began constructing batteries and trenches for a formal siege, Hallowell, the senior naval officer present, directing three bombs and two gunboats into Tarragona's roadstead during the hours of darkness to bombard the garrison and inhibit any attempts at disrupting the attackers' works. While these labours progressed Murray asked Pellew to demonstrate with the main body of the fleet off the northern part of the coast to try and prevent the French sending forces to succour the fortress. He also asked for naval support for an assault on the fort at Col de Balaguer, a position that blocked the southern road from Tortosa. If it were captured it would prevent the French moving cannon directly to Tarragona from the south, they instead having to make any such movement via Lerida. Hallowell immediately obliged by sending Adam's *Invincible* along with the *Thames* (32), the bomb vessel *Volcano*, the troopship *Brune* and eight gunboats manned by British seamen. These carried a detachment of 1300 troops under Colonel Prevost that was landed on 3 June. By noon the following day four cannon had been got ashore and, crewed by the seamen, served to check the fort's fire while five heavier pieces were landed and hauled into positions opposite the fort's eastern face. Immense effort was needed to construct the batteries and to bring up their ammunition, the whole business being made all the more wearisome by the outbreak of a massive thunderstorm. Not until the afternoon of 6 June were the heavy guns and a pair of mortars established in their positions, a general fire then being opened on the fort where a lucky shot exploded a magazine and did much to undermine the defenders' morale. Next day the French surrendered and Adam could write effusively of the high level of inter-service co-operation that had been displayed during the brief but gruelling operation that had cost him one seaman killed and seven wounded, six of them severely.[56]

Ultimately, though, this success was to be in vain as Murray, fearing the arrival at any moment of a powerful French relieving force, decided to abandon the siege of Tarragona altogether on the 12th. During that day and night and most of the morning of 13 June the whole force was ferried back on board the transports, such being the haste at which it was conducted that 18 pieces of artillery had to be abandoned. The aggressive Hallowell was incandescent with rage at this timidity, observing when Murray proposed a fresh landing at Col de Balaguer that:

. . . knowing as I do, by experience, the indecisiveness of the General's Character, I do not augur any favourable result from his intended operation. We have already been disgraced more than any British Army ever was, & I fear every movement made by the present Commander will add to the disaster.

Elsewhere he referred to Murray's 'retiring precipitately' from Tarragona and of the whole operation being a 'disastrous measure'. Indeed such was the admiral's annoyance that he most particularly sent one of his captains to Wellington's head-quarters so that he might be sure to receive the Navy's interpretations of the late fiasco.

To rub salt into naval wounds, on the same day that the evacuation was completed, the frigate *Thames* engaged some French troops moving up the coast road from Tortosa and during the action some of her marines' ammunition caught fire. The resulting explosion wounded 31 men, 23 of them severely. The elements also seemed to conspire against the retreating British when a gale struck the transports and drove ten of them ashore near the mouth of the Ebro. The *Fame*, the primary escorting warship present, got five of them back afloat, but when Adam's *Invincible* appeared on 22 June a gunboat and five transports, carrying ordnance, horses and a detachment from the 10th Foot, were still aground. The two vessels carrying horses were both saved, but all the others were lost. *Invincible* remained until the 29th, employing five local fishing boats to save most of the ordnance stores and the detachment of troops. Two seamen were drowned when the transports beached and later a French privateer from Tortosa slipped down river and captured a master and three seamen from one of the vessels and a midshipman and two seamen from one of the warships.[57]

While Murray had been losing his nerve, Pellew had taken the bulk of his fleet to Rosas Bay on 9 June to try and create a diversion. On the 16th, two hours after receiving the 'very mortifying intelligence' that the siege of Tarragona had been abandoned, he was joined by the *America* (74) which had on board the elusive Bentinck, finally coming to take command on the eastern coast. Both officers immediately proceeded south, but Bentinck did not feel it wise to overrule the preparations for Murray's withdrawal as by that time the disorganised and dispirited troops were in no condition to face any sudden French assault. In consequence the whole expedition returned to Alicante, Pellew leaving Hallowell to take charge of naval matters there while he returned to the blockade of Toulon.

Bentinck's appearance was not to galvanise events. In July Suchet evacuated most of Valencia, leaving garrisons only at Tortosa and one or two other strongpoints, and Bentinck followed him by land into Catalonia with most of his command at the end of the month. Only one detachment, along with the battering train, was left aboard the transports and these were moved up the coast once again in case the opportunity arose to seize Tarragona by means of a sudden landing. *Invincible* along with a Spanish frigate, the *Paulina*, and two gunboats harried the French as they retired along the coast road, Adam claiming that their fire caused the enemy much damage and disrupted their march, but nothing decisive was accomplished. Tarragona could not be taken and so the troops were disembarked at Col de Balaguer to join the main body. Bentinck blockaded Tarragona during August but was too wary of French counter-measures to land his artillery for a formal siege. When Suchet assembled a relieving force the Allies retreated to Col de Balaguer, a position from which they could at least draw supplies from the fleet. Early in September Bentinck advanced once more having heard rumours that Catalonia was about to be evacuated. Tarragona was finally captured, though the Allies then had to set about repairing its defences as these had been levelled prior to the French retreat. The Allied army continued its advance as far as Villafranca, some 15 miles farther up the coast, though the anticipated French evacuation did not materialise and, worse still, on the 13th Bentinck's advanced guard was mauled at Ordal. By the end of the month riots in Sicily had compelled him to leave Spain for good and his departure marked the end of any major Allied operations on the eastern coast for the remainder of the conflict.[58]

Until Napoleon's first abdication in April 1814 naval duties off Catalonia were confined to the routine of convoy protection and trying to maintain the blockade of Barcelona. Adam, that stalwart of east coast waters, returned to Britain in the *Invincible* in October 1813 and command off Catalonia eventually passed early in 1814 to Bathurst of the *Fame*. A particular feature of operations in these waters being the way that certain officers, such as Codrington and Adam, served off the eastern coast for many years, gaining a detailed knowledge of the local conditions and of the Spaniards with whom they had to deal. This can only have added to the general standard of naval efficiency and effectiveness, though in the latter stages of the war only the continuing activities of French privateers provided any opportunities for action. Many of these nautical pests operated out of Barcelona and some enjoyed quite a measure of success. In January 1814 men from the frigate *Castor* seized *L'Heureux*, a privateer mounting a single 12-pounder carronade and having a crew of about 25: this vessel alone had made five captures since the middle of December. Another, also taken by the *Castor*, had recently captured a transport off Mataro and the brig *Badger* (10) took *L'Aventure* of 2 guns and 28 men in October 1813 just as she was about to seize a merchantman from a convoy. All three of these prizes were vessels operating from Barcelona.[59] Both at sea and on land the Catalonian theatre of the Peninsular War ended with a whimper rather than a bang.

The war in southern and eastern Spain after 1810 illustrated both the potential and the limitations of sea power on a land campaign. The semi-insular situation of Cadiz, with its landward side being too difficult to approach, meant that a vigorous naval presence was able to protect the fortress from capture. Where a coastal strongpoint was accessible from the land, however, as at Tarragona, it was always vulnerable if the French could marshal sufficient forces. For all that, though, constant coastal operations served to render enemy progress more difficult, more costly, and more time-consuming. Once French manpower had been reduced by demands from other areas and was less concentrated following the invasion of Valencia, coastal mobility gave the Allies opportunities for counterstrokes, though in the event these promised more than they delivered and the whole campaign stagnated.

CHAPTER 6

The Northern Coast, 1810–14

'. . . the security of the navigation of the northern and
western coasts of the Peninsula is very important for our
hospitals, our provisions, our stores, our money, the stores
and clothing for the Spanish and Portuguese army, etc, etc,
the whole of which must be occasionally transported by sea'.
Wellington, 4 October 1812.[1]

AS WAS NOTED AT THE END of Chapter 2, by the summer of
1809 the Admiralty had become aware of the possibilities for
making effective attacks on the French along the northern coast
of Spain. In August of that year, with the enemy having evacuated north-western Galicia, it was decided that a squadron of
frigates and small warships would be permanently stationed on
the coast, with the Victualling Board establishing a depot at
Corunna for its support. By October this force comprised five
frigates and a sloop and was commanded by Captain Mends of
the *Arethusa*. Initially the squadron concerned itself with
attacking the French maritime supply route along the coast, this
being maintained primarily by small luggers and chasse marées
that tried to move provisions between Bayonne and Santander.[2]
Some minor assistance was also given to the Spaniards, who
spent the first six months of 1810 fighting a fluctuating campaign against the French in the Asturias, during the course of
which the provincial capital of Oviedo changed hands no less
than four times. Naval help for such an inland campaign was
inevitably limited, though Parker's *Amazon* landed some of her
crew at Gijon just prior to its fall in February to spike its
defending batteries and bring off stores and ammunition.[3]
    Useful as such operations were, the full potential of the
Allies' naval advantage did not really become apparent until the

192

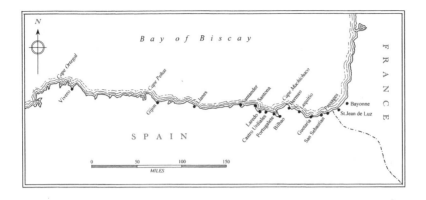

summer. At the end of June, after consultations with the Junta of the Asturias, Mends agreed to take a group of guerrillas on board the squadron with the intention of assaulting French positions along the coast in order to create a diversion for Spanish forces inland. On the 24th Porlier, a nephew of de la Romana and one of the most enterprising of the guerrilla commanders, and 500 of his men were embarked, being landed again near Santona on 5 July. With the support of seamen and marines from the frigate *Narcissus* (32), that place was quickly occupied without resistance, the garrison having withdrawn. All of Santona's defending batteries were destroyed and two days later, with covering fire provided from some boats' carronades, a 700–800-strong French relieving force was driven off, Aylmer, the captain of the *Narcissus*, claiming that all told the enemy had lost about 150 men. On 8 July the force was re-embarked, the Spaniards having suffered only seven wounded and the British none at all. A delighted Mends reported that landing parties had destroyed every French battery between Santander and San Sebastian except those at Castro Urdiales, about a hundred pieces of artillery having been eliminated. In future the French would have to try and employ their coastal shipping to bring up fresh pieces, the terrain being too mountainous for overland movement, while in the event of gales his warships could seek shelter in protected bays without fear of bombardment from enemy cannon. A final satisfaction was that, while these operations had cost the French in all about 200 men, Porlier had been able to gain 300 recruits for his command.[4]

Most of the British squadron remained for the time being at Santona, apart from two of the frigates that returned to Corunna on 21 July with Porlier's men. Mends enthusiastically supported the inhabitants' determination to resist future French attacks and on their behalf pressed the junta for more arms and ammunition. He believed that reinforcements should be committed to the coast, given the region's general state of commotion, the high level of the guerrillas' morale and the evident weakness of the French. Certainly the success of the July expedition seemed to have made a great impact, not only prompting the Spaniards to speak of future efforts of a similar nature but also in August the Admiralty sent Captain Popham to Corunna to confer with the Junta of Galicia on the best way of either expelling the French from the region altogether or at least of tying them down. In his resulting report Popham poured cold water on any notion that Santona might be permanently held, but at the same time stressed how intercepted despatches made clear just how rattled the French were and that they remained vulnerable to seaborne attack.[5]

During September the Spaniards planned to reinforce their garrison in Santona with 2000 men led by Colonel Renovales, an officer who had won a good reputation fighting the French in Aragon, though assembling this detachment took time and Mends fretted at having to keep his ships inactive at Corunna, their provisions running down and the autumn gales looming. Not until 14 October was the squadron finally able to depart, reinforced by some Spanish warships from Ferrol and carrying 1200 Spanish troops – 'mere country boys' according to Mends – as well as 10,000 muskets for the guerrillas. Some success was initially enjoyed on the 17th when a landing co-ordinated with an attack by Porlier's men seized weakly-defended Gijon: some French vessels there were captured, though the garrison escaped. Thereafter everything went wrong. Two gales struck the squadron and twice prevented it from reaching Santona, that port soon being recaptured by the French. Having had to abandon this part of its mission, the squadron then returned to the west and entered Vivero, a small harbour to the east of Cape Ortegal where Renovales wanted the troops to be landed to save them a long march from Corunna to their future area of

employment in the Asturias. Now failure turned into catastrophe. Although Vivero was open to the wind on only three
points of the compass, yet another gale, blowing directly from
one of these three, the north-north-east, struck the anchored
vessels on 2 November. Around midnight a Spanish 40-gun
frigate, the *Magdalena*, parted her cable and crashed into the
Narcissus, the latter losing her masts and bowsprit. Both warships seemed doomed, though suddenly the cable that bound
them together snapped and allowed the British ship to escape.
The *Magdalena* was not so fortunate, smashing on shore and
breaking up, taking to destruction her crew along with about
100 artillerymen and 30 shipwrights who were also aboard.
Soon after this a Spanish brig was also hurled ashore. All told,
out of the 600 or so men involved, only 14 were saved.
According to Mends both wrecked vessels were the victims of
poor management, the *Magdalena* having lost two of her
anchors in the gales off Santona, a third being secured only by
a worn cable that had not been freshened, a fourth being lost
because it had not been properly stowed, and a fifth had been
left behind in Corunna. The loss of the two vessels provides a
sharp insight into the wretched state of Spain's navy at this
time, the whole institution palpably suffering from years of
neglect, disruption and defeat.

Meanwhile Mends had to send the shattered *Narcissus* back
to England, jury-rigged and with the *Amazon* as escort. The
final woe for the expedition came when the remaining vessels
completed their voyage back to Corunna in December and were
hit by yet another vicious gale during the night of the 9–10th.
Battered for twelve hours, the *Arethusa*'s forecastle and quarter-
deck guns had to be thrown overboard and in Corunna itself the
Surveillante (38) was nearly wrecked. Reviewing the failure
Mends considered that: 'The Expedition was too long in preparing, too much talked of, and undertaken at too late a season
of the year to insure success.'[6]

This marked the end of naval operations off the northern
coast for the remainder of the winter, during which period of
grace the tireless French set about rebuilding their assorted
strongpoints. However, during the early months of 1811 their
forces in the northern part of Spain did not amount to many

more than 30,000 men (they would be massively reinforced during the course of the year) and these were fully stretched in trying to control the assorted bands of guerrillas. In a captured despatch Rouget, the French commander of the Santander province, grumbled in March about how vulnerable to guerrilla attack his area was, predicting that it would be lost upon the first appearance of a British warship.[7] The following month the first spell of fine weather allowed Collier, the new senior captain, to reconnoitre the coast in the *Surveillante*. He captured a lugger off Bilbao, a rowing-boat off Santona and another lugger off San Martin d'Arena; landing parties also destroyed two batteries and a guardhouse. This was an encouraging start and by the summer his squadron, now comprising four frigates and two small brigs, were busy harassing the enemy. Captain Tobin's frigate, the *Princess Charlotte* (38), was particularly active in the waters off Bilbao where various small vessels were captured and burned and four signal posts were destroyed, the latter cutting French communications between Santona and San Sebastian.[8]

However, Rouget's fears of a complete French collapse did not materialise. In part this was due to the limited force committed to the region by the Allies, no doubt to some extent influenced by the disaster at Vivero, and also to the vigorous French efforts to repair the damage done to their strongpoints the previous year. Although their exposed positions along the coast remained very vulnerable to naval attack, as Tobin's activities in June illustrated, they busily applied themselves to their defences, lavishing particular attention on Santander and Santona, the two main harbours on the central stretch of the coast. They made extensive use of hundreds of small local fishing boats, vessels weighing several tons each, manned by 14–20 men and capable of moving by both oars and sail. These could be used as gunboats and transports and their sheer numbers made them hard to control. Tobin observed that even using the *Princess Charlotte*'s launches for inshore patrols could not prevent the enemy getting supplies into Santona and Santander. The French were also able to employ Spanish vessels granted licences to ship iron from Bilbao to Corunna to smuggle heavy items such as shot, shell and even cannon. By August Santona was guarded by over a hundred pieces of artillery shipped to it by such means. Finally there was the question of manpower as the French Army of the North was hugely rein-forced, reaching a strength of over 88,000 soldiers by the middle of July. Such a force was still inadequate to suppress the guerrillas, contain the regular Spanish forces to the west and secure the coast, but it did mean that the French were far too strong for their position to be significantly undermined.[9]

Collier, for one, remained optimistic that despite the obsta-cles, much might still be achieved given an appropriate amount of energy and vigour. However, his efforts to obtain troops from Valverde, the Governor of Corunna, for coastal attacks were quite unavailing and he believed that in general the Spanish guerrilla chiefs were much more energetic than their regular counterparts. Collier suggested that perhaps part of the problem lay in the lack of any obvious authority enjoyed by the senior naval officer on the coast and that that individual (himself!) should have the benefit of a distinguishing pennant, *ie* be made a commodore. This helpful suggestion was turned down by the Admiralty.[10]

If the guerrillas were the most credible threat, though, the problem remained one of effectively co-operating with such will o'the wisps. Collier spent part of August trying to get in touch with Porlier, finally discovering off Llanes on the 12th that the Spaniard was planning to attack Santander. With the *Surveillante*, the *Iris* and the brig *Lyra* (10), Collier hurried to the port and try and lend assistance. Delayed by light winds and westerly currents the ships did not reach Santander until 15 August, only to discover that a small guerrilla force had attacked the previous day and been repulsed. However, there was word that Porlier intended another attack on the 16th and to support this Collier sent marines ashore on the night of the 15–16th to seize Fort San Martin, a post overlooking a fortified convent that was a major French strongpoint. San Martin was taken but then a French column obliged the British to take to their boats to escape, a marine being killed in the process. Unfortunately the anticipated guerrilla assault then did not take place, a frustrated Collier believing that Santander and its whole garrison might have been taken. It is hard to blame Porlier for any missed oppor-tunity; his attack on the 14th had cost him over 500 casualties and the whole business merely serves to illustrate how difficult it was to co-ordinate land and sea operations in the region. At least when Collier did finally meet the guerrilla chief on 18 August he was able to hand over a supply of arms and ammunition brought from Corunna, the guerrillas being especially delighted with his provision of a carronade and two 8-pounder guns.[11]

For the remainder of the summer the squadron maintained its efforts to supply the guerrillas, interdict French coastal traffic and attack any exposed enemy positions. On 22 August, with the French abandoning some points to concentrate their troops to engage the guerrillas, Tobin landed parties to dismantle their batteries at Bermeo and did the same at Plencia on the 28th. *Surveillante* and *Lyra* also landed men to attack batteries near Santander, Collier reporting that his vessels were deliberately hovering around the coast to try and keep the French in a perpetual state of alarm and hamper their attempts to concentrate against the guerrillas.[12]

By the end of September 1811 Collier had returned to Corunna, the squadron already starting to feel the effects of the approaching winter: the *Unicorn* had been obliged to abandon her station between Santona and Bilbao after being struck by northerly gales. There was still time, however, for the *Surveillante* to convey Porlier and Longa to Gijon early in October and to land 2000 muskets, half a million cartridges and an assortment of shoes, sabres and suchlike for their groups. Later in the same month further supplies were landed at Anchove for El Pastor and, with 200 of his guerrillas loaded in fishing boats, *Surveillante* and *Iris* sailed along the coast and once again attacked Bermeo. Collier was intent on seizing a convoy, though in the event this had already sailed and the Allies had to satisfy themselves with destroying all the works repaired since Tobin's raid in August: the 120-strong garrison fled at their approach. With the weather now worsening very rapidly *Surveillante* was back in Corunna by November, she having at one point been driven by gales as far north as Quiberon Bay before resuming her station. On land the fluctuating military fortunes had once again led to the loss of Gijon on 7 November, though Collier could at least report that no British vessels had been taken when it fell.

Meanwhile the *Iris* had remained behind to support the guerrillas as long as possible, seizing two small launches and cooperating with El Pastor's group in successful assaults on Matrico and Deba. The true nature of this aspect of the war in Spain was also made startlingly clear when Mina's group appeared at one point and insisted that the British take control of 600 French prisoners in their charge. Captain Christian was very reluctant to do this as he was short of both water and provisions, but was informed that if he did not take them they would be slaughtered to prevent their liberation by a French column that was in hot pursuit. Under this pressure, Christian took 400 of the unfortunates aboard the *Iris*, the remainder being placed in small boats towed by the frigate (the latter were landed at a small harbour along the coast shortly afterwards when a gale seemed likely). Inevitably it was just at this awkward moment that word arrived from El Pastor that he needed help from the *Iris* to attack Santona. With the frigate cluttered with prisoners, many of them dying, and very difficult to manoeuvre, all Christian could provide was his launch armed with a carronade, which achieved nothing. The *Iris* then sailed for Corunna with her unwanted human cargo, they arriving 'in a most wretched and destitute state', many of them 'literally naked' and having to be clothed from British stores. Effectively this ended naval operations off the northern coast for 1811 as the weather closed in: a homeward-bound convoy escorted by the *Lyra* was twice forced back into Corunna in November–December by vicious gales.[13] Less dramatically than in 1810 the year had continued to illustrate the exposed condition of the French in northern Spain, a weakness that would finally be dramatically exploited in 1812.

The early months of the new year witnessed several profound changes in the strategic situation in the Peninsula which in turn had a profound influence upon naval operations. With the French concentrating their limited offensive means for the invasion of Valencia, their temporary weakness in the west allowed Wellington brilliantly to seize the initiative by the capture of the border fortress of Ciudad Rodrigo on 19 January. This opened up the main northern road of invasion from Portugal to central Spain and was a success followed up by an even more important capture when, on 6 April, the fortress of Badajoz fell after a bloody assault. Its capture both opened up the main southern road from Portugal into Spain for Allied operations while simultaneously guarding Portugal from an invasion from that direction. Wellington could now plan a future invasion of French-occupied Spain and, more particularly, an attack on Marmont's Army of Portugal, a force weakened by the removal of formations sent to cover Suchet's activities. Indeed the whole French position in Spain was being undermined by Napoleon's gathering of troops for his projected invasion of Russia, some 27,000 of his best soldiers being withdrawn for the purpose. As part of his general plan of operations for the coming year, Wellington was eager to see British troops committed to eastern Spain to tie down Suchet, the operations stemming from this having been considered in the previous chapter. However, it was similarly desirable that the French Army of the North be kept similarly occupied so that its commander, Caffarelli, would also be unable to send reinforcements to Marmont. If this were to be achieved and the guerrillas galvanised to maximum effect it would be necessary for the Royal Navy to make a major effort.[14]

The first indication that such an effort would be made came on 19 May 1812 when the Admiralty told Admiral Keith, commanding the Channel Fleet, that they were putting the *Venerable* (74) and the armed transport *Diadem*, as well as a battalion of marines, under his orders for service off northern Spain – the *Magnificent* would also soon be attached to this force. These would all be added to the squadron already present in those waters, *viz* four frigates and two brigs, and other warships could also be sent at Keith's discretion. The whole would be commanded by *Venerable*'s captain, Sir Home Riggs Popham, his objective being to give all possible assistance to the Spaniards short of actually endangering his own vessels. The Admiralty was particularly keen that no word of these intentions leak out to the French so that any attacks might be delivered with maximum surprise.[15]

Popham's appointment for this task was quite contentious. A clever man who had revised the system of naval signalling, his greedy and ambitious nature had got him into severe trouble in 1806 when, without any authorisation, he had led a force from

the Cape of Good Hope to attack Buenos Aires. This had ultimately failed, leading to British humiliation and Popham's
court-martial. From this he had managed to emerge relatively
unscathed professionally, probably due to a combination of
political influence (he was an MP) and a popular perception of
him as a hero who had tried to secure Spanish America for
Britain. He had been annoyed not to receive the command off
northern Spain following his report on the situation there in
1810, but, in appointing him in 1812, whatever misgivings they
may have felt, the Admiralty was ensuring that their consider-
ably-reinforced squadron would at least have a commander who
was energetic, imaginative and determined.[16]

Popham arrived at Corunna on 9 June, spending five days
there while co-ordinating plans with the Spaniards and loading
supplies for the guerrillas. He also issued a memorandum for all
his captains making clear the arrangements he required for the
forthcoming campaign. Each vessel was to keep her boats in a
constant state of readiness for any landing, those from each ship
being regarded as a single division with its own identifying flag
under the command of a lieutenant. All warships were to
submit returns listing the boats, sailors and marines they had
available, with their crews organised into 30-strong companies
for duties ashore. Each ship of the line would provide two such
companies and each frigate one, the smaller warships not being
called upon to provide men at all except in an emergency,
though their boats would still be employed. All sailors who
went ashore were to carry on their sleeves a piece of canvas indicating their ships and number in their company: any who failed
to do so would be punished. As a rule only one day's supply of
wine and three days' supply of provisions would be landed.[17]

Initial hopes of operations with Porlier's guerrillas were
ruled out when it was learned that they were fighting inland;
however, with the wind westerly, Popham instead sailed
towards Bermeo and Lequitio to establish contact with El
Pastor. The latter's men appeared near Lequitio on the afternoon of 19 June and the next day, despite a strong surf, a heavy
24-pounder gun was landed and, thanks to the efforts of 100
seamen, 400 guerrillas and 20 oxen, dragged half-a-mile up a
hill and opened fire on a fort that covered the town. A second

battery was also positioned on an island offshore. The fort was eventually stormed and the gun on land then advanced to a second French strongpoint, a fortified convent. Then the remaining 290 defenders chose to surrender, the victors blowing up all the captured fortifications.

This was a heartening start and in the days that followed the French positions between Lequitio and the estuary of the Bilbao river were ravaged, a succession of batteries, strongpoints, magazines and guardhouses being seized and destroyed, Popham reporting on 25 June that these assaults had seen the destruction of 34 enemy guns. After this the squadron sailed east and made a thrust at Guetaria, a powerfully situated harbour near to San Sebastian, but support from the guerrillas failed to materialise and the appearance of a French column obliged a rapid return to the ships. Returning to the west, the squadron then established contact with Longa's group on 6 July at Castro Urdiales. The British marines and two guns were landed, fire soon being opened upon the defending castle. However, once again the appearance of a relieving column obliged the marines to be rapidly re-embarked and the guns abandoned. During the following day Longa's men were able to drive the French off while the warships bombarded the town, Castro and its 150-man garrison finally capitulating on the 8th. Popham decided to leave the marine battalion to hold the place for the moment as its harbour was suitable for the anchoring of vessels of up to 400 tons.[18]

Now another strike was aimed at Guetaria, though once again a French column came to its relief and forced the guerrillas to retire, the British this time losing two more guns and 32 men taken prisoner as they hurried back to their vessels. Having learned on 20 July that Porlier's band was back in the coastal region and was intending to attack Santander, Popham now sailed west to try and provide support. Intercepted despatches suggested that the 1600 troops stationed at Santander would soon abandon the place and join up with the garrison at Santona, a move Popham was keen to prevent. By the 26th the squadron had established a battery of four cannon and a mortar on the Isla de Mouro to bombard the castle of Aro, a strongpoint guarding the entrance to Santander's bay. The next day, with 4000 guerrillas blocking the landward side, Popham boldly ordered the brigs *Lyra* and *Insolent* (14) to lead the frigates *Surveillante*, *Medusa* (32) and *Rhin* into the harbour despite the enemy guns, a manoeuvre successfully accomplished without loss. The French now evacuated the castle, though an Allied attempt to expel them from the town itself was sharply rebuffed with the loss of 27 dead and 31 wounded, Captains Lake (*Magnificent*) and Collier being among the latter. During the night of 2–3 August the French evacuated Santander, linking up with a rescuing force led by Caffarelli himself.[19]

This success marked the apogee of the naval campaign off the coast. By the end of July Popham had heard of Wellington's crushing victory over the Army of Portugal at Salamanca on the 22nd and knew from intercepted despatches that Caffarelli had been quite unable to send reinforcements to help. Indeed some units that had been sent southwards had had to be recalled in light of the mayhem being stirred up in the Biscayan region. This had been the primary task of the reinforced squadron, to tie the French down, and it had been triumphantly accomplished, with the taking of Santander as a valuable bonus. Popham noted that the sea on that coast was persistently heavy and that his ships 'materially suffer by it'. Now, though, the Allies held a port that could safely hold two or three ships of the line, six frigates and almost any number of smaller warships. It was also rendered even more useful by the movement of provisions from Corunna, converting Santander into a forward victualling depot. Communications with the guerrilla groups operating farther inland could also be improved from Santander and at least one of their leaders, a man by the name of Saldaña, promised to send intelligence to the port every Tuesday and Saturday.[20]

Popham's next target was Bilbao, which the French were rumoured to be on the point of evacuating. While Spanish units moved on the city from its landward side, the *Rhin*, *Iris*, *Surveillante*, *Diadem* and the brig *Growler* (12) moved 3500 guerrillas to Lequitio as a further support, the squadron then sailing on to Bilbao itself to discover on 12 August that its garrison had been withdrawn to become part of the force trying to fend off the guerrillas. Popham landed two companies of marines to destroy 16 guns in its defensive batteries and the following day the French retreated to Durango. By that time, with the Biscayan capital now in Allied hands and the whole region in turmoil, the overall French position looked bleak. Along the coast only the fortresses of San Sebastian, Guetaria and Santona remained under their control and Popham was urging Mendizabal, the Spanish commander in the area, to allocate him forces to take Guetaria. This had only a small harbour but it was exceptionally defensible as it stood at the end of an isthmus, some naval officers, like Collier, regarding it as a potential northern Gibraltar if only it could be captured. Possessing a mole for the protection of any vessel lying at anchor and being situated close to the great road connecting Bayonne to central Spain, the primary French communications artery to the south, both Melville at the Admiralty and Wellington himself were keen to see Guetaria taken.[21]

Unfortunately Mendizabal, dismissed by one British captain as 'an old woman', did not seem to share this view and in the wake of Bilbao's capture did not supply Popham with the necessary land forces to cover any siege. Popham began to unload the necessary guns to besiege Guetaria at the end of August, though he was covered only by weak guerrilla units: at this moment Caffarelli, who had concentrated all the troops he could, struck back, retaking Bilbao and mauling the Spaniards in the process. Popham was now obliged to abandon the attempt. Such was the keenness at the Admiralty to see Guetaria's capture that a second battalion of marines was even sent to northern Spain, though even this did not assist Popham in his efforts to prod decisive support from Mendizabal. During the first half of September there was an increasingly acrimonious correspondence between the two about the whole project, the Spaniard even having the gall to suggest that it was Popham who was dragging his feet! Although highly dubious about the backing he might expect from Mendizabal, Popham did undertake another effort. On 18 September a marine battalion, some guerrillas and several guns were landed at Guetaria, but Mendizabal's main covering force never came closer than 15 miles, leaving the besiegers to be protected by a mere 2300 men from the groups of El Pastor and Campillo. The inevitable happened on the 23rd when Popham learned that a French relieving force was approaching, the guerrillas heading for the hills while the British re-embarked, the siege being abandoned once again.[22]

However frustrating such manoeuvres were, they did at least continue to keep the Army of the North fully occupied along the coast and formed just one part of the strategic conundrum that looked increasingly difficult for the French to solve. After his victory at Salamanca, Wellington had initially concentrated his attentions on the liberation of Madrid, a task completed on 12 August. With his colleagues' situation deteriorating Soult was now finally compelled to evacuate southern Spain, his Army of Andalusia completing its northward withdrawal and being in contact with the armies of Suchet and King Joseph in Valencia by the end of September. This movement would eventually concentrate 80,000 French soldiers to the south-east of Wellington's position, but in the interim he believed that there was sufficient time to deliver another blow to the battered Army of Portugal, then licking its wounds behind the Douro. Accordingly, part of the Anglo-Portuguese army began slowly advancing northwards during the early part of September. The French simply retired before this movement, a retreat that was eventually covered by the fortress of Burgos, a citadel Wellington's men laid siege to on 19 September.[23]

Unfortunately, in a piece of poor military planning, Wellington allowed his forces to reach the fortress with only three pieces of heavy artillery suitable for battering its walls, this despite large concentrations of such guns at Madrid, Ciudad Rodrigo and Almeida. Anticipating that some of these would be required did not take any great degree of military prescience as, embarrassingly for the army commander's reputation, even Popham had been making enquiries of the Spaniards two months previously about the defensive capacity of Burgos, being informed that it would require six or eight heavy guns to reduce its walls. As it was, Wellington's unfortunate soldiers were destined to batter away at its defences in a series of futile attacks that lasted until 21 October and cost over 2000 casualties.[24]

The September attempt on Guetaria was in part an effort by Popham to effect a diversion in support of the operations before Burgos, but this was not to be the limit of naval involvement in the siege. Within a week of its commencement Wellington was requesting that 40 barrels of powder, each weighing 900lbs, and 100–150,000lbs of biscuit to be brought to him from Santander. The supplies were duly dispatched despite problems procuring mules and reached Wellington's forces a week later after a journey of over 70 miles along dreadful mountain roads. Further requests for powder were made on the 5th and 12th, Wellington also asking Popham to supply 200 quintals to a guerrilla planning to use it to block French supply routes. Popham strained every sinew to meet these demands despite concerns about his own flow of supplies being maintained to Santander, part of the problem being that Corunna remained the main depot with stores then having to be shipped along the coast to the more exposed harbour to the east. By early November the sailors had received yet another demand for powder, this time for 200 barrels, but could only supply half of it. Given the army's woeful dearth of heavy artillery Popham also volunteered to provide ships' cannon. At first Wellington declined, a refusal that meant that when he did finally have to accept the offer the pair of 24-pounder guns got no farther than Reynosa, just over half way to Burgos, when the siege was abandoned.[25]

The army's retreat from the fortress proved to be a nightmare as its logistical arrangements collapsed and the troops were lashed by drenching winter rains. Fortunately the French were unable to seize any significant strategic advantage from the situation, but even so almost 5000 men were lost to starvation, capture or desertion and by the end of November Wellington found himself back at Ciudad Rodrigo with Madrid having been abandoned. True to character, he blamed everyone else for the disaster, writing a graceless letter to Lord Liverpool in which he dismissed Popham's efforts to supply him at Burgos. Popham was 'a gentleman who picques himself upon his over-coming all difficulties', Wellington wrote, going on to deprecate the powder and ammunition hauled from Santander and whining that the two guns provided had caused his army much inconvenience through his having to provide oxen to assist in their movement. Presumably the futile loss of hundreds of his soldiers in the trenches before Burgos was less of a problem.[26]

For the Navy the central remaining question in the wake of

Wellington's retreat was how long to continue operations off the coast. For all of his expressed contempt, the army's commander was keen enough to see Popham's squadron remain *in situ* throughout the coming season as this would, he believed, 'render me the important service of preventing the enemy from taking the whole Army of the North across the Ebro'. As early as 10 September Melville had written from the Admiralty that a strong squadron would not be maintained there during the winter, though that the Admiralty was also aware of Wellington's needs was evident as late as 27 October when orders were issued for Popham to remain, he being exhorted to use what facilities Santander had to offer to preserve his warships. During much of October and November Popham laboured to get Mendizabal and the other Spanish officials to provide the means for an attack on Santona, the one other good harbour on the coast and where the garrison was supposed to be disease-ridden and demoralised. All his efforts proved fruitless, however, Mendizabal being fully preoccupied with civil controversies with the Biscayans and with reorganising his forces after all the exertions of the summer and autumn. An exasperated Popham concluded that the Spanish commander's 'military functions appear to be completely dormant' and by 9 December the Admiralty had had enough. For all Popham's hopes that Santona might still be taken, they decided that the project was no longer viable and that the *Venerable*, the marines and the troopships were to return home. With Santander in Allied hands the smaller vessels, *viz* three frigates and three smaller warships, for the moment commanded by Captain Bouverie of the *Medusa*, were to remain on the station for the winter, their primary duties being the blockade of Santona and the maintenance of contacts with the Spaniards.[27]

The presence of these vessels and the flow of supplies through Santander and Castro Urdiales played their part in keeping northern Spain in a state of ferment during the early weeks of 1813. Napoleon was keen to see the region pacified before the main campaigning season started in the late spring, but, despite replacing Caffarelli with the more energetic Clausel and reinforcing him into the bargain, the Emperor's instructions could not be implemented to any significant extent in the winter conditions and against determined guerrilla resistance. Clausel did, however, determine upon the recapture of Castro Urdiales, the only fortified harbour actually controlled by the Allies. He approached the place at the end of March but considered it too strong to assault without the support of a siege train and a month passed before a suitable force could be assembled for a formal siege. The supporting British warships at the time consisted of the brigs *Royalist* (18), *Sparrow* (16) and *Lyra*, they being able to prevent the enemy from moving any artillery by water from Bilbao to the east (it had to be hauled overland instead), but could not stop some heavy pieces being shipped from the other direction, from Santona. By 7 May the French were busily engaged in constructing a battery to the west of Castro Urdiales and the warships responded by landing a 24-pounder carronade on a small offshore island just opposite. Fire from this, and from the Spanish inside Castro, wrecked the French works, but unfortunately they were also building a battery to the south-west of the town, a position the Allied guns could not reach. By the 10th another battery sited to the south-east was also operational and two others were being constructed as well. Despite the gallantry of the thousand-strong Spanish garrison and the efforts of the British, who landed a second carronade on the island and placed a third in the town's castle, by noon on the 11th the French artillery had blown a massive gap in the walls. At 9pm the assault was launched and there was house-to-house fighting before the garrison, having thrown its guns into the sea and exploded its magazines, was evacuated to the waiting ships; however, in the final confusion the castle itself was not blown up. The Spaniards were moved to Bermeo from where they marched to join up with Longa. The siege cost the British ten wounded and the Spanish and the French perhaps a couple of hundred casualties each. More importantly it had occupied 11,000 French soldiers for sixteen days, yet again showing how naval power could significantly boost the powers of resistance of a coastal fortress and provide the defenders with an escape route.[28]

Despite the previous autumn's defeat at Burgos, the strategic initiative in 1813 very much remained with Wellington. However terrible the Anglo-Portuguese retreat had been, it was nothing compared to the cataclysm of the French retreat from Moscow, a disaster that cost Napoleon tens of thousands of troops and left him facing the prospect of fighting a huge campaign in Germany in 1813 to fend off the new coalition forming against him. For this he had to call upon all of his resources, the armies in Spain being no exception. Four regiments of the Young Guard were transferred north and scores of experienced officers and NCOs taken from the Peninsular regiments to put backbone into the new formations being raised in France. Nor could the armies south of the Pyrenees anticipate any reinforcements in the immediate future. Wellington was fully aware of the opportunity and planned to make full use of it by concentrating his forces on his left, marching north to cross the Douro within Portugal and then sweeping round to attack the French in northern Spain. Such a movement would probably take the French by surprise as it would avoid the main roads and would oblige a march through some of the Peninsula's most desolate areas. That Wellington could contemplate such a bold strategy was primarily because sea power's flexibility allied to the capture of Santander the previous year meant that he could draw supplies from the northern coast rather than having to rely on tenuous lines of communication back to the depots in Portugal. Early in February 1813 he was requesting that all the heavy ordnance shipped to Alicante in 1812 be returned to Corunna and was urging that naval forces be committed once more to distract the French along the coast, being particularly keen to see the capture of the important port of Santona. At the end of April, just a few days before the campaign opened, he reminded Martin that he would be relying on supplies brought in via the northern harbours. Thereafter, on the surface, all seemed to go smoothly. The Admiralty, it will be remembered, had maintained a force of smaller warships on the coast through the winter and on 21 May they informed Keith that a squadron, now once again under the command of Collier, lame after his wounds of the summer, would operate in northern Spanish waters.[29] As the year progressed, though, it became increasingly marked by a bitter wrangle between Wellington and the Admiralty over the whole question of the scale and nature of the naval support being provided, a row which, for the first time in the Peninsular conflict, threatened the hitherto harmonious relations between the two services.

The root of the problem went back to the previous summer and the outbreak of war with the United States. Wellington immediately began to worry that his communications through Portuguese waters and the mouth of the Channel would be interrupted by American privateers. This concern prompted him to start making unwelcome suggestions respecting the stationing of British cruisers and to demand reinforcements for the Lisbon command. To judge by his later comments, this interference received a very dusty response from the Admiralty. 'In our country,' Wellington sourly observed, 'it is better to suffer any inconvenience, than to suggest a measure as a remedy which is to be carried into execution by another department.' Nevertheless his fretting continued and in October 1812, while acknowledging to Lord Bathurst, then Secretary of State for War, that only one packet vessel had been lost (in 1810) since he went to Portugal, he still feared for his future communications. However: 'I'll not write another line on the subject.'[30]

This self-denying ordinance lasted until the following spring when he told Bathurst that there had been privateer activity off the Portuguese coast and that several vessels had been taken or destroyed off Oporto.

> I cannot express how much we shall be distressed if the navigation of the coast should not be secure from Corunna, at least, to Cadiz. We have money, provisions, clothing, military stores and equipments on all parts of the coast almost every day in the year, and the loss of one vessel only may create a delay and inconvenience which may be of the utmost consequence.

It should be observed first of all that no statement makes clearer the vital·importance of sea power in the prosecution of the Peninsular War. Equally it is hard not to regard it as an attempt by a successful military commander to try and frighten a civilian minister over possible future disasters unless he gets his own way. Wellington was unable to cite any direct examples of this 'inconvenience' and if the loss of a single vessel could dislocate his plans then he had much more to fear from shipwreck and fire than Yankee privateers. His real motive was simply to get more warships committed to Iberian waters, writing also to Martin in Lisbon to urge the admiral to press for reinforcements from the

Admiralty. On 6 May Wellington pushed matters further when he wrote directly to Collier asking that a frigate be permanently stationed off Cape Finisterre – a pet notion he had asked for the previous year – and also to Bathurst to request that Martin's command be extended to include northern Spain in the belief that it would simplify future operations. By June he was becoming more excited: 'For the first time I believe that it has happened to any British army, that its communication by sea is insecure . . .' Ludicrous though this assertion was, it clearly indicates how Wellington was becoming obsessed with getting more warships committed to guarding his communications.[31]

This attitude was a classic example of the military commander whose eyes are fixed solely on his own area of responsibility to the exclusion of everything else, a blinkered view that in his case seems to have been compounded by a complete ignorance of the difficulties being faced by the Admiralty, problems that Melville patiently tried to explain to him at the end of July. At that time the Navy was having to find warships for the American war which would require 19,000 men: 7000 of these had been found by reductions in the North Sea Fleet, but providing the remainder was leaving the Channel and Mediterranean Fleets very stretched. Even with such efforts the scale of force being committed to North America was inadequate. Nevertheless the First Lord insisted that the needs of the Lisbon station had been fully met, its responsibilities even being reduced by the creation of a separate Azores command with its own warships so that Martin's captains would not be called westwards in pursuit of American privateers. Furthermore strict orders had been issued to the Lisbon squadron's captains to remain within their station's boundaries, *ie* available to support the army, as three of them had, seemingly with Martin's connivance, been discovered hunting prizes way out of their normal cruising grounds. One of these had been dismissed from his ship and the others were under investigation. Trying to keep a tight rein on such vessels was part of the reason why the Admiralty did not want the station extended to the north, and it had of course already been extended south to include Cadiz the previous summer. Melville pointed out to Wellington that his talk of vessels being captured off the Portuguese coast was a matter of ships being taken when they sailed alone, not when they were part of the convoy system. Previous Boards of the Admiralty over a period of twenty years had been unable to prevent such losses along the British coast, let alone that of Portugal. 'Ten times the amount of Admiral Martin's force could not give that entire protection against an active and enterprising enemy. . .'.[32]

This should have been the end of the matter. It must be acknowledged that in July 1813 Collier's squadron off the northern coast comprised only the *Surveillante* and five smaller warships, with Keith unfortunately fuelling Wellington's suspicions by admitting that this was not as strong as he would like but that he would badger the Admiralty for more vessels. However, it should also be borne in mind that the northern coast west of Guetaria, excepting the strongpoint of Santona, was now controlled by the Allies and that there were many other vessels engaged in protecting the vital convoys, Wellington's primary concern. During May and June the general's planned sweeping movement, unhindered by any naval losses, successfully went ahead and culminated in the triumphant battle at Vittoria on 21 June. Thereafter things started to go wrong. The pursuit of the routed French was ill-managed and their capacity for reorganising and recovering their fortunes sadly underestimated. By the middle of July Wellington's army was again facing the prospect of difficult sieges, progress being blocked by Pamplona, a fortress Wellington determined to starve into submission, and San Sebastian, which he wanted to storm in order to clear the coastal road to France.[33]

Until the Allies reached the coastal region naval power could have little direct impact on events. There was the final satisfaction of occupying Guetaria on 1 July after its garrison had retired, though this was marred when a magazine containing 200 barrels of gunpowder suddenly exploded, killing 20 Spaniards and wrecking all the fishing boats moored to the mole. The day before this the harbour of Passages, a couple of miles to the east of San Sebastian, had also been liberated by the guerrillas and was thereafter to become the focal point for naval activity for many weeks. Situated so close to the great fortress about to be besieged, Passages was a harbour of great value but of a singular nature. According to one observer:

As you approach it, you run along a bold rocky shore, in which no opening appears to exist, nor is it till the very mouth of the creek has been reached, that a stranger is inclined to suspect the existence of a harbour. The entrance, scarcely more than fifty yards wide, runs up between overhanging cliffs, and has the appearance rather of an artificial cut, than of nature's forming.

Although the actual basin was quite spacious and could accommodate many ships, it speaks volumes for the generally inadequate state of the harbours along this coast that the Allies were obliged to rely on such a haven as the army's main forward supply depot.

Passages's great initial asset was its simple proximity to San Sebastian, that fortress being blockaded from its landward side by the end of June with the *Surveillante* and some smaller warships appearing to seaward shortly after. The naval task was twofold: to blockade the fortress from the sea and to provide artillery support preparatory to any assault. The latter process had already got off to an excellent start when the convoy delivering the army's battering train arrived at Santander from Corunna on the very day, 29 June, that an officer appeared from Wellington's headquarters sent to enquire after it. Immediately after this, 28 heavy pieces of ordnance were shipped to Passages and unloaded ready to commence the bombardment. In addition to this, Collier provided six of *Surveillante*'s 24-pounders manned by 60 men drawn from her and the *Lyra*: during the operations that followed in the first siege they would suffer four killed and 20 wounded.[34]

Unfortunately the squadron was much less successful when it came to sealing off San Sebastian from seaward communication. This was chiefly due to its proximity to the French-controlled harbour of St Jean de Luz, a mere 20 miles or so along the coast, from which small coasting vessels could quickly run supplies and some reinforcements into the fortress. The French had also aided their cause by organising matters in a typically efficient Napoleonic fashion: a senior naval officer with the rank of capitaine de frégate was stationed at St Jean de Luz to coordinate the supply run and had at his disposal a number of trincadores. These were small, fast gunboats, capable of being propelled by oar or sail depending on the wind, and were the sort of craft that were very difficult for the British to combat, well able to capture a warship's boat sent to patrol close inshore while being sufficiently manoeuvrable to avoid the warship herself. Several trincadores were also stationed at Santona and launched bold attacks on merchant vessels sailing unprotected along the coast, Collier receiving a request early in July from the Biscayan deputies seeking naval protection: one Spanish brig had been taken outside Bilbao and another pursued right into the harbour entrance. With the larger British warships now having to operate right at the head of the Bay of Biscay, its most dangerous part, and it being an area of deep water with a rocky bottom, ie where anchoring for security was difficult, Collier's position was an uncomfortable one, especially when the enemy could sneak along the coast on a dark night.[35]

Not surprisingly this prompted another flurry of complaints from Wellington. In June 1813 he was complaining that convoys from Lisbon to Santander were delayed in their movements for want of escorts and by 2 July this had turned into open sarcasm: 'Surely the British navy cannot be so hard run as not to be able to keep up the communication with Lisbon for this army!' Just over a week later the problems off San Sebastian were adding to his feeling of neglect. 'Your Lordship,' he complained to Bathurst, 'will have seen that the blockade of the coast is merely nominal. The enemy have reinforced by sea the only two posts they have on the north coast of Spain [his emphasis].' At this time the Portuguese squadron that he considered so inadequate consisted of no fewer than nineteen frigates and smaller warships.

On 25 July an assault on San Sebastian was repulsed, the Allied army suffering almost 600 casualties. Simultaneously Wellington received word that the main French army, rapidly reorganised after Vittoria by Soult, had counter-attacked around Maya and Roncesvalles and that a serious crisis was starting to manifest itself around his right flank. This prompted several days of hard fighting until the French were driven back, but in the interim the siege of San Sebastian had to be abandoned. Insult was added to injury when the withdrawing besiegers lost 200 men of the rearguard to a French sally. However at least the artillery train was safely reloaded aboard ships at Passages and under the Navy's supervision moved to safety.[36]

As at Burgos the previous year, failure put Wellington in a foul mood in which scapegoats were busily sought in self-justification. As early as 22 July he was to be found writing that if the Admiralty did not secure the coastal communications and the convenient use of harbours 'they will be responsible for any failure that may occur'. As well as the usual complaints about the shortage of warships and the delays in moving convoys, he also grumbled about the inadequate unloading facilities at Passages, where the boats employed in unloading the transports were quickly destroyed by the weight they had to bear and where the work was done by local women who were unequal to the task. All of this came to a head in a despatch to Bathurst on 19 August. Not only, it seemed, had Keith been willing to send a ship of the line to support the siege but had not received Admiralty permission, but also:

> The supplies of all kinds from Lisbon and other parts of Portugal and from Corunna, are delayed for want of convoy; the maritime blockade of San Sebastian is not kept at all; the enemy have a constant communication with San Sebastian from St Jean de Luz and Bayonne; and they have introduced, besides supplies of different kinds, reinforcements to the garrison of artillery men and *sapeurs*, and some officers belonging to the medical department.

He also protested about the state of affairs at Passages and added that were the naval forces off San Sebastian more substantial he could contemplate a simultaneous assault on the fortress from both its seaward and landward sides.[37]

These charges were flatly rejected by the Admiralty. They had never had any plans to employ ships of the line off what was, for nine months of the year, a lee shore that lacked secure harbours. Keith would be permitted to provide one or even two such vessels if their presence would be temporarily valuable, but they stressed that this was for him to decide. As it happened Keith had already, on 15 August, instructed the *Ajax* to make a fleeting appearance off the fortress to try and overawe its defenders before sailing back to join its squadron in the Basque Roads. Respecting convoy delays from Lisbon and other ports, the Admiralty denied that this had happened, though they pointed out – and this was perhaps at the root of Wellington's dissatisfaction – that single merchant vessels or even every two or three of them could not necessarily receive immediate protection. There were so many transports involved in moving the enormous amount of supplies involved that only when eight or ten had assembled could they be provided with escorts. Once such an assemblage had taken place they were moved, ten different warships having taken convoys to Passages between 30 July and 9 August alone. It is hard to escape the conclusion that Wellington could not, or would not, grasp the reality of his supply situation. The depots in Portugal from which his army had operated for so long had taken months and months to become stocked from the numerous convoys directed to them and he appears to have had no comprehension of the time required to achieve this happy state. Stocking the new northern depots in 1813 had to be done from scratch, via harbours whose facilities were nowhere near as good as those provided by Lisbon, with a large army present and demanding immediate supply, and the process inevitably seemed slow and cumbersome.

The Admiralty Lords acknowledged that San Sebastian was not being completely blockaded and that French coastal traffic in the area was not being interdicted, but, quoting Collier, they doubted if supplies beyond 'a few eggs and fowls' were being taken in. Given that the fortress was only an hour's favourable sailing away from an enemy harbour this was unavoidable. However, they denied that Collier's squadron was too weak for its duties, acidly wondering why, if the army officers before San Sebastian were concerned to have the transports at Passages unloaded as a matter of priority, they employed seamen in the siege lines rather than at the harbour. Because Passages had only three wharves the Admiralty felt that a backlog in unloading was inevitable and, although admitting to initial delays, they believed that by the end of August, with the process under naval supervision, it was progressing smoothly. The employment of local women in the harbour was because that was the local Spanish practice and they were, by all accounts, more suited to it than the men. Finally, respecting the idea of a seaborne assault, the Admiralty felt that this would be far too dangerous: even demonstrating close in to the fortress risked dangers from red-hot shot.

Accompanying this rebuttal was a despatch from Melville himself, the First Lord this time making his resentment of Wellington's charges more evident:

> I will [Melville reassured him] take your opinion in preference to any other person's as to the most effectual mode of beating a French army, but I have no confidence in your seamanship or nautical skill. Neither will I defer to the opinions on such matters of the gentlemen under your command who are employed in the siege of St Sebastian, and which happen to be at variance with those of every naval officer in His Majesty's service.

His exasperation was expressed even more clearly in a despatch to Keith where Melville observed that army officers 'seem to consider a large ship within a few hundred yards of the shore off San Sebastian as safe in its position and as immovable by the winds and waves as one of the Pyrenean mountains'. Whatever his annoyance, though, Melville could not but be aware of the serious breakdown in relations that this acrimonious correspondence indicated. It was in an effort to calm matters and to discover precisely the nature of the support that Wellington required, particularly as there had been talk of a naval presence being wanted through the coming winter, that it was decided to sent a special naval representative, one might almost say an emissary, to the general's headquarters. The officer selected was Rear-Admiral Sir Thomas Byam Martin, then second-in-command at Plymouth and an individual Melville held in high esteem.[38]

While these despatches had been going back and forth, in Spain Wellington had been able to check Soult's offensive and by early August the French had retreated, allowing Allied thoughts to return once more to San Sebastian. On the 6th Collier was reporting that the siege was to be resumed as soon as possible and was preparing to remove bread and shot from his vessels to help meet any need: the following day he confirmed that 600 shot had been unloaded from the recently-joined frigate *Revolutionaire* (38). However, no resumption of siege operations could begin until the battering train had returned to Passages, the army also wanting extra heavy artillery to be sent out from Britain as well as an accumulation of a large stock of ammunition. These had all appeared by 23 August, but were then subject to the usual delays while being unloaded at the hugely clogged harbour at Passages.

In the meantime attention was directed to the island of Santa Clara, a rocky outcrop standing 500 yards offshore of the fortress and whose occupation it was decided would both facilitate the pending bombardment as well as help the blockade. Given Wellington's constant complaints about the boats the French slipped in and out of San Sebastian, it may be wondered why the island's capture did not form part of the first siege. However, during the night of 26–27 August boats from the squadron, towing others drawn from the transports, carried about 150 soldiers and 40 marines to effect an assault. Spearheaded by the marines, and despite the barriers of a rocky shore and a heavy surf, the attackers stormed ashore through a blast of grapeshot that wounded almost half the men in the leading boat. However, once the British were established on the island the French garrison of 85 men surrendered very quickly. Afterwards a battery of five 24-pounder guns and an 8-inch howitzer manned by the squadron was situated to add its fire to that which was already doing much damage to San Sebastian's walls.

By 30 August a breach of sufficient magnitude had been made for an assault to be planned for the following day, Collier's men now being called upon to support the main attack by providing a feint involving men drawn from both the squadron and the 85th Foot. For this one division of boats carrying 100 men were to assemble to the west alongside the *Despatch* and *Beagle*, while a second, or eastern, group carrying 200 men would form up between Passages and San Sebastian itself. At the appropriate moment these would push forward to as to threaten an amphibious assault on the fortress's rocky northern face. Covering fire would be provided by the sloops and brigs as well as two newly-arrived gunboats. Collier planned to supervise the whole operation from his gig and exhorted his officers to move their boats slowly so as to prevent any early appreciation by the enemy that the whole thing was a diversion, though there was a proviso for it to turn into a proper landing if the main assault on San Sebastian's southern side went very well. This was all arranged, it might be noted, despite the Admiralty's fears that any sort of approach to the place was too dangerous.

In the event the main attack did succeed, though only at a heavy cost to the attackers, Collier reporting that the feint managed to tie down at least part of the garrison at the cost of only three or four wounded. On 8 September the remnants of the garrison, who had retreated into the citadel at the time of the attack, finally capitulated and the fortress came completely under Wellington's control.[39]

This success seems to have done little to improve the general's humour respecting the Navy in the following days and it was at this time that Byam Martin met Wellington on 13 September. The army commander, 'with some warmth', again recited his litany of grievances about naval shortcomings, now reinforced by details of San Sebastian's communications with France procured in the wake of its capture. Wellington continued to insist that the division of responsibilities between the Channel and Lisbon commands was materially hindering convoy movements, though he confessed astonishment when Byam Martin pointed out that during August no fewer than 22 different warships, over and above those in Collier's squadron, had escorted convoys to Passages, the admiral providing a list of their names as proof. However, in an effort to appease Wellington, Byam Martin did offer several concessions at the meeting and during the days that followed. Four warships were to be taken from the Lisbon station and four more from the Channel Fleet with the exclusive duty of escorting convoys from Lisbon northwards along the coast. Very quickly, though, he found himself having to clarify this by stating that four plus four did come to eight: such was Wellington's paranoia over naval matters that within a few days of the meeting he got it into his head that only a total of four warships was to be so employed. Furthermore, with Wellington having now given assurances that Passages was safe from French attack, Byam Martin was prepared to order the *Surveillante* into that harbour for shelter and a necessary refit. Wellington had wanted such a step both as a means of adding to Passages's security and as a means of keeping Collier, one naval officer who seems to have gained his trust, on station and present to supervise the unloading of the transports. The admiral also ordered Collier to keep four warships patrolling between the Gironde and St Jean de

Luz in an effort to restrict enemy coastal activity, the placing of a light on Cape Higuera being agreed to facilitate navigation, and to send the frigate *Magicienne* (36) on a three-month cruise between Capes Ortegal and Finisterre in pursuit of a privateer that had been causing Wellington concern. Finally it was also agreed to implement Wellington's wish for all the armed troopships to be transferred to the western coast. By early September, furthermore, Collier's squadron had been reinforced to a strength of four frigates and a dozen brigs, cutters and schooners, only one of which was with a convoy and so unavailable for direct army support. There were also five gunboats present and at the end of the month the Admiralty agreed to provide four flatboats and the bomb vessel *Vesuvius*, though the latter would first have to be manned.[40]

After the fall of San Sebastian the squadron chiefly concerned itself during the winter with maintaining the army's flow of supplies. Given the complete unsuitability of the region's harbours for large-scale traffic and the deteriorating state of the weather, this was no easy task. Towards the end of September Collier submitted a return which showed that 52 transports and troopships had been cleared from Passages during the preceding month and that there were still present in the harbour a further 49 transports. In addition there was also present an unspecified number of Spanish and Portuguese vessels and, even as he wrote, he noted the arrival of another 30-strong convoy. In some desperation Collier suggested that a relieving depot be established at Guetaria or San Sebastian. This intense pressure had been somewhat relieved by the end of October as the system became more regulated, army officers having been appointed to Passages and Santander to co-ordinate with Collier and the transport agent at Santander respecting which stores were needed immediately and when convoys were to be moved between the two. There were still 48 transports present at Passages, but 16 others in San Sebastian's harbour indicated that some use was being made of it as well. It had also been agreed between Wellington and Collier that San Sebastian's easier access made it a more suitable harbour for the receipt of packet boats. The problems in Passages were also somewhat alleviated when a large church was taken over to receive at least some of the huge quantities of supplies being landed.[41]

The weather was a menace that was much harder to cope with. On 11 October a gale with a heavy swell got up and wrecked two transports trying to enter Passages, Collier soon being very concerned to report doubts about the harbour's safety during such gales. One of these prompted an extraordinary ground swell that at high tide swept the vessels from their anchors and hawsers. One transport broke up and threatened the *Surveillante* in the process, the cutter *Landrail* (4) and the schooner *Arrow* (12) drove on board each other, and some Portuguese transports lying higher up the harbour parted their cables and crashed into some British transports, doing much damage. On 1 November a transport carrying a cargo of oats was forced to anchor in the harbour mouth and was immediately run into by another vessel, causing her to go on to the rocks and break up. Two others that had also anchored, refusing good advice to put to sea again, almost suffered the same fate. Just over a fortnight later storms were still pounding the coast and two convoys were driven back into the harbour, things not improving as the year turned. During the night of 16 January 1814, the packet *Queen Charlotte*, anchored off San Sebastian, had two of her cables snapped by a northerly gale and was immediately dashed on to the rocks, 16 of her crew being drowned. Collier believed that San Sebastian was only really secure as a harbour during the summer. A week later he had to report that the *Arrow* had parted from her convoy during a gale that sprung her foremast, she being further damaged when she touched a rock on entering Passages. On the same night two transports broke adrift from the mole in the small forward harbour of Socoa, four men being drowned while trying to escape in a boat, and two other vessels were driven ashore north of the Adour river.[42]

In the teeth of much sustained foul weather the direct military support that could be provided to the army was inevitably limited in its scope. One abiding naval responsibility was maintaining the blockade of Santona, the last remaining French outpost on the northern coast. This could be fully effective only as long as the weather allowed the blockading warships to keep their station, any absence allowing the trincadores based there to sally forth and cause trouble. A further problem was that many of the civilian masters do not seem to have been aware that Santona was still an enemy port and blithely sailed into the place. In October Wellington complained that two such vessels carrying his stores had done exactly this, he finding it 'extraordinary that a vessel in the public service should run into any port excepting that to which she is bound. . .'. Vice-Admiral Martin in Lisbon seems to have been remiss in this respect, the Admiralty finding it necessary to remind him to update all civilian masters respecting the French fortress. However, there are grounds for believing that much of the problem may have had a more subtle cause. Santona stood on a headland and, from the sea, looked very similar to Santander, especially when the massive volume of traffic meant that many masters were sailing the coast for the first time. One naval captain blockading Santona wrote that hardly a convoy passed the place but that some straggler did not try to enter it. When he could he anchored his vessel at the port's entrance to stop such mistakes, but he believed the harbour of Laredo, just across the bay, ought to be seized so that gunboats could be stationed there to stand sentinel. This project was to cause yet more friction with Wellington as by the end of 1813 he was again complaining of French naval activity from Santona and pointedly venting the opinion that it would have surrendered already had the blockade been properly maintained. Collier evidently responded to the charge by observing the failure to occupy Laredo and, when Wellington tried to claim that he knew of no despatches pointing to that harbour's importance, the sailor referred him to one of September and two more in October that had made this perfectly clear. Wellington then promised to ensure that Laredo was occupied, though in the event Santona was still able to hang on for some time before its final capitulation in March 1814.[43]

One small naval success did at least happily take place under the gaze of many watching troops on 13 October when the British schooner *Telegraph* (12) engaged the French brig *Filibustier* (16). The latter had been sheltering in St Jean de Luz while awaiting a chance to deliver supplies and some reinforcements to Santona, the approach of the Allied army obliging her to put to sea. A sudden calm forcing the French vessel to anchor in the mouth of the Adour, she was discovered there and engaged by the *Telegraph* in a lively action that continued for three-quarters of an hour. With other British warships then appearing the French set fire to their ship and made for the shore, British efforts to save the *Filibustier* proving unavailing and the vessel eventually blew up. The following month the squadron was also able to provide some limited fire support during the battle of the Nivelle on 10 November. The *Vesuvius* and three small warships engaged the French batteries at St Jean de Luz, suffering a single seaman injured in the action. The weather prevented any of the frigates taking part but even so Wellington acknowledged the help provided. However, his general attitude regarding naval matters remained carping and petulant, dismissing a request from Collier to help secure advancement for some of his officers with a brusque 'I assure you that I have no interest with the Board of Admiralty'. At the end of the year he would write the astonishing 'nor have I, or shall I, venture to give any opinion on any naval concern what-soever'. For the previous eighteen months he had been doing little else when it came to naval matters and a mere nine days earlier he had badgered Bathurst on the old topic of his sup-posed want of naval support. He now considered that the Admiralty was doctoring the figures to give a misleading impression of how extensive their commitment was by includ-ing in their lists warships assigned to convoy protection: this after all his statements about how vital convoys were! He also grumbled once more about the way the French were able to maintain their traffic along the coast, now between Bordeaux and Bayonne. It is hard to avoid the conclusion that Wellington was and remained, despite numerous explanations, woefully ignorant of what was nautically viable. As late as 1 February 1814 he could be found submitting a memorandum to the Under-secretary of State for War that included the statement: 'The assistance I require from the navy is so little of a military nature that it can scarcely be called *co-operation* [his emphasis].' He blithely defined this minimum as consisting of secure navi-gation along the whole coast from Gibraltar to St Jean de Luz; regular movements of money from Lisbon and Cadiz; a weekly convoy from Lisbon; two convoys a week from Corunna; two convoys a week from Santander; and a gunboat force in the Adour. This was 'all'. Not only did these duties tie up a considerable number of warships as convoys and specie were moved up the coast, but it also meant others sailing back to the various ports to maintain the service. Nor was this process ever seriously incommoded, other than by foul weather and the occasional bureaucratic delay in the moving and unloading of the mountains of stores involved. Considering the nature of the coast and the season in which it was called upon to operate there, the Navy gave Wellington a level of assistance that was both tireless and crucial in enabling the army to function, an effort he was both too ignorant and too mean-spirited to acknowledge.[44]

It must also be made clear that the services listed in his memorandum were by no means the end of Wellington's requirements. A week later, as part of a plan to drive the French away from the fortress of Bayonne, he was requesting that the Navy construct a bridge over the lower reaches of the Adour river, at a point where it was some 520 yards wide. If successful such a construction would allow the army to turn the French right flank as well as allowing the lower waters of the Adour to be used as a haven for transport vessels. This was no easy task to accomplish and it was to be the first challenge facing the new squadron commander, Rear-Admiral Penrose. The reasons for Collier's removal at the end of January from a station he knew so well are unclear. His experience of the region went back over three years of very active service, he had performed his duties professionally and well, and he had even managed to maintain more-or-less harmonious relations with Wellington during the general's war of words with the Admiralty. Even so he may still have been a victim of the animosity that had been stirred up and was possibly viewed in London as someone who had become too close to Wellington. At the end of November 1813 Keith had been ordered to reprimand Collier for having, without permission, shown Wellington an extract from a despatch containing suggestions for new convoy arrangements. These ran contrary to the opinions of Keith, Byam Martin and the Admiralty Board itself and had caused 'much inconvenience'. Perhaps Collier was a marked man in the wake of this, though in fairness it should also be observed that his replacement was an officer of known tact and diplomacy (he would later conduct negotiations with the Dey of Algiers for the release of Christian slaves) and that, newly-promoted to flag rank, he may have been viewed as someone more capable of the delicate task of maintaining cordial relations with Wellington.

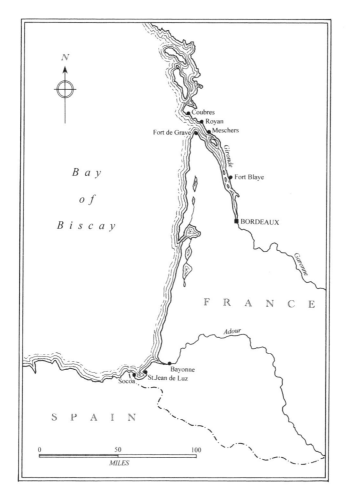

Penrose arrived at Passages to assume his new command on 27 January and shortly after rode with Wellington to the mouth of the Adour to reconnoitre that stretch of the river and finalise the plan, the pair of them proceeding without any escort so as to attract no attention from the French. It was intended that the bridge would be created by positioning small coasting vessels and decked boats in the river and constructing a passageway by means of tightly stretched cables laid on these craft, on top of which would be placed planks for the troops to cross. Penrose considered that he could obtain most of the materials required from the transports, though he wrote to Keith on 8 February requesting 12-inch cables and six small anchors, along with chain, grapnels, spikes and forks. These were ready to sail from Cawsand Bay by the 21st, but in the event did not arrive in time for the actual bridging.

During mid-February there was hectic activity along the coast as the necessary vessels and equipment were found, though the bar across the Adour mouth meant that only craft with very shallow draughts could be used. The process was repeatedly harassed by the weather and at one point 24 vessels procured at St Jean de Luz were trapped there when the wind and tide threw up a mound of shingle at the mouth of its river. Wellington was obliged to employ some of his troops digging an opening to let them escape. By 20 February, however, the small harbour of Socoa, the chosen forward assembly point, was packed with the shipping of Penrose's miniature fleet. There was his flagship, the sloop *Porcupine* (24), the small brig *Lyra*, an armed schooner and ketch, a captured French boat armed with an 18-pounder carronade and manned by eleven volunteers from the transports, and five gunboats. The latter craft were each manned by only nine seamen, including an officer, their complements being filled by 50 artillerymen provided by the army. Alongside all of these were four small transports carrying materials for a boom to be placed above the bridge, as well as 46 chasse marées, each of about 10 tons displacement, carrying cordage and planks and which were to form the actual bridge. Unfortunately, during the 20th and 21st the whole was unable to leave Socoa because of the weather, and it was still pinned for much of the 22nd, one observer believing that if the gale had increased all the vessels would have been destroyed. However, by 5pm it had relented sufficiently for the cumbersome process of putting to sea to begin, they having 20 hours to sail the 14 miles to the Adour so as to cross the bar on the flood tide. Not all of them could be got out of Socoa in a single movement at night, and several went aground, a mortified Penrose writing on the 23rd that much of the day would have to be spent in reassembling the fleet. He was worried by the constant delays, particularly as the commander of Wellington's left wing, Lieutenant-General Sir John Hope, started ferrying his advanced guard across the river a few hours after the fleet departed Socoa. With no more than some pontoons and five small boats to establish and maintain the bridgehead, these troops, numbering about 700 men by nightfall, would be extremely vulnerable to any sustained French attack. In fact, one assault only was made, but the British were fortunately able to beat this off with the aid of rocket fire. Penrose's only consolation in this predicament was the appearance of two more brigs, the *Rolla* (16) and the *Martial* (14), to strengthen his command.[45]

Most of the fleet finally reached the mouth of the Adour during the morning of 24 February, the next hurdle being the negotiation of its treacherous bar, a narrow channel that was apt to shift in severe weather. A high surf was running, which made its entrance hard to find and in trying to discover it one boat, containing Captain O'Reilly of the *Lyra* (an officer newly promoted after his efforts at the siege of San Sebastian), was upset, though most of its occupants were saved. Two other boats did succeed in making the crossing but, with much of his fleet straggling and scattered, Penrose decided to wait six hours for the next high tide before trying to push the chasse marées intended for the bridge up-river; he considered that at that moment too many would be wrecked if the move were attempted.

By then Hope had managed to ferry 3000 men across the river and this figure had grown to 8000 by the evening of the 24th, the general becoming understandably anxious to see the bridge in place. Aware of these concerns, Penrose once more urged his command forward around noon, again the business of finding the entrance to the bar being difficult and dangerous. Two of the leading boats from the *Lyra* and the *Martial* were upset and their crews drowned, Captain Elliot of the *Martial* being one of them. A boat from one of the transports was also lost before a flag was placed on the shore indicating the most promising spot where the surf might be passed. Finally one of the chasse marées, manned by a British lieutenant, five seamen and a Spanish volunteer, succeeded in going through, the crew tied to its masts to stop being washed overboard. They were greeted by cheers from the troops on the bank and, rather more appreciated one may imagine, the reward of 50 guineas that had been put up for the first to cross. Following this came a prize boat armed with a small carronade and three gunboats, though one of these was beached immediately after the passage. The whole manoeuvre was rendered more difficult still because once over the bar the vessels had to avoid the beach which was immediately under their lee. The rest of the fleet then followed, one of the small transport brigs also being wrecked on the beach, though her cargo was saved. 'All those vessels, my Lord,' reported an exuberant Penrose, 'passed over this dangerous bar without Pilots, without a single British subject who had ever crossed it before, and with the aid of a man waving a small flag on the beach before them.' All told the operation cost the lives of 35 men, particularly unfortunate being Norman, the *Martial*'s assistant surgeon, who was rescued by a gunboat after Elliot's craft was overturned only to be crushed to death by the gunboat's 24-pounder when she then ran aground on the beach.

The construction of the bridge began on 25 February and was completed by the following afternoon despite the problems posed by a river running at seven knots. Selecting a point where the river was 270 yards wide, narrower than previously assumed, 30 chasse marées were anchored at stern and bow facing upstream, they being secured together by five hawsers linked through the vessels' capstans. On one bank these were tied to French heavy guns captured some months previously and on the other to capstans secured by large stakes and wedges. The whole structure, largely constructed by Royal Engineers brought in with the fleet, rose and fell with the tide and was protected from enemy attacks directed from up-river by a boom of floating spars and chains, the creation of which was left to naval personnel and was itself protected by gun-boats. However, Wellington's hope that the Adour estuary might be used as a harbour for his transports was thwarted by the extreme shallowness of the water over the bar: this was only nine feet at high tide and only the smallest of vessels could enter. Nevertheless the final construction was one of the finest pieces of military engineering during the Peninsular War and reflected immense credit on the individuals concerned. By the evening of the 26th Hope had 15,000 troops established across the river and was, by the day after, able to complete the investment of Bayonne.[46]

Also on 27 February, about 40 miles to the west of the new bridge, Wellington engaged Soult's main army at Orthez and after hard fighting drove it back towards Aire. Rather than pursue the defeated French, however, Wellington's next target was Bordeaux, a city whose capture would encourage the region's Royalists as well as offering the chance of using the Gironde for Allied supplies. An advanced force was able to take the city on 12 March, the French abandoning all their positions on the left bank of the Garonne. However, if Bordeaux's navigation was to be opened it would require the elimination of all French naval units in the Gironde and the securing of a number of riverine strongpoints. Wellington informed Penrose on the 17th that Bordeaux had fallen and pressed for a naval force to clear the river. Penrose had been anticipating such a request and had tried, unavailingly, to find people familiar with the Gironde's navigation. Failing this he had sent the *Lyra* on ahead to gather all the information she could about conditions in the river. He himself left Passages when weather permitted on 24 March, his squadron consisting of the *Porcupine*, *Kangaroo* (16), *Podargus* (14), *Martial* and *Vesuvius*, rendezvousing *en route* with the *Egmont* (74), *Andromache* (38), *Belle Poule* (38) and *Challenger* (18), which he took under his orders. The united squadron entered the Gironde on the 27th.[47]

Despite his dearth of local pilots, Penrose, now flying his flag from the more suitable *Egmont*, boldly ordered his vessels up river, ignoring heavy fire from an assortment of land batteries and causing the French great surprise. The squadron had proceeded only a short distance when they sighted the main French naval force in the area, the 74-gun *Regulus*, three brigs and a number of chasse marées, privateers and gunboats, all in the process of weighing. Penrose immediately gave the signal for a general chase as the enemy moved up river, the pursuit being maintained despite continuing fire from shore batteries until the

French sought refuge through a narrow, buoyed channel at Meschers. This position was guarded by a powerful battery reinforced by seamen from the *Regulus* herself and would need careful preparations before being approached. In the meantime the British seized four nearby chasse marées laden with wine, small arms and clothing, while Penrose gave orders for the masters of each of his vessels to take soundings. Next morning efforts were made to position the *Vesuvius* so that her high-trajectory fire might be brought to bear on the French, though this was thwarted when the wind brought on an ebb tide earlier than expected. Another attempt in the afternoon finally had to be abandoned when it was discovered that the shoals and the Falmont bank that protected the French vessels were much more extensive than shown on British charts. More successfully, a party of marines and seamen was landed to eliminate the artillery in the Fort de Grave, a strong work on the southern bank at the mouth of the Gironde. In all 22 pieces of heavy ordnance were destroyed or removed.

After some delay, Penrose also managed to get in contact with Lord Dalhousie, the Allied commander in Bordeaux. This offered the prospect of future co-operation between the two services, though for the moment Dalhousie's force was judged too weak to cross to the north bank of the river. To try and maintain communications as efficiently as possible, Penrose stationed his smaller vessels at intervals along the Gironde, ordering that soundings be taken all the time they were engaging in passing signals to and fro: blue-water sailors understandably tend to be nervous when confined to comparatively narrow rivers. Although the local inhabitants from the southern side seemed friendly, the British ships being frequently surrounded by a small fleet of craft sporting white Bourbon flags and during the evening of the 31st the *Egmont*'s purser acquiring the first supplies of locally-purchased fresh beef, a much less agreeable discovery came in the shape of Fort Blaye, a strongpoint situated 25 miles down river from Bordeaux. Penrose sent the *Porcupine*, the *Vesuvius* and two of his smaller brigs on a mission to occupy Paté Island, near to Blaye, preparatory to positioning the bomb vessel to bombard the fort. However, the island proved to be both stronger than anticipated, being defended by a large round tower, and within the range of Blaye's guns. Furthermore the latter, an old Vauban construction, was a fortress of great strength itself, well-armed and standing on top of a steep bank. Penrose wrote that it would require a regular siege as its garrison showed no sign of deserting the Bonapartist cause. When two naval officers were sent towards it under a flag of truce, their real motive being to gather information on the place, they were abruptly fired upon. Penrose fulminated about a 'rascally act' that was a 'disgraceful violation' of the normal customs of war, but in truth naval officers had resorted to this ploy to gain information on more than one occasion over the years and he had no real grounds for complaint when his ruse had been rumbled. *Vesuvius* now began to bombard the fort, her shells seeming to do some damage, but Blaye's commander, General Merle, refused to be intimidated and capitulate.[48]

This resistance was a major setback as the fort effectively served to keep the Gironde closed as a supply artery for Wellington's army, though elsewhere at least naval operations did enjoy a greater measure of success. On 2 April a small French flotilla was spotted standing down the river just above Poullaic, its intention evidently being to join the *Regulus* and her consorts. Captain Coode of the *Porcupine*, the senior British officer present, sent all the boats he could muster – four launches, two pinnaces, two barges, four cutters and a trio of gigs – to engage them. The French fired at their attackers but, when the British pressed on, ran their craft ashore some four miles away from Fort Blaye. The British also landed and, with the enemy reinforced by a body of about 200 soldiers, a sharp engagement ensued until the Royal Marines formed up and joined in the action, the French then retreating. The British lost 14 wounded and two more missing, a brig, three gunboats and an armed chasse marée being burned and another brig, six gunboats and three armed chasse marées being captured. Also seized was an Imperial barge.[49]

Farther down the Gironde, Penrose had been preparing his forces to strike at the *Regulus*, the British benefiting from the arrival of another 74-gun ship in the shape of the *Centaur*. The intention was for a body of almost 700 seamen and marines, drawn from the larger ships and led by Captain Harris of the

Belle Poule, to assault the landward battery guarding the anchorage during the night of 6–7 April. Simultaneously the *Egmont* would be laid alongside the *Regulus* and would try to silence her, the *Centaur* meanwhile remaining in reserve ready to aid either the *Egmont* or the landing party as required. Were the three French brigs to attempt to flee up river they were to be secured by the *Andromache* and the *Porcupine*. In the event, possibly anticipating the scale of the attack that was about to be launched against them, around midnight the French set fire to the *Regulus* and the brigs, all the warships being destroyed.

With the main target removed, Harris's landing force was instead sent to destroy the remaining French strongpoints on the northern bank between Blaye and its mouth at Point Courbe. During the 7–8th five positions were attacked and the detachment succeeded in destroying a total of 47 heavy guns and 17 mortars without the loss of a single man, the French retreating in a state of some demoralisation. These successes allowed Penrose to boast that he had cleared the river by land and water for a distance of 50 miles, though the vital obstruction maintained by Fort Blaye meant that the squadron still relied on dragoons to maintain its communications with Bordeaux.

The problem was solved only when news arrived that Napoleon had abdicated on 6 April. Word of this did not reach the south of France until the 11–12th (Wellington and Soult fought a sanguinary and pointless battle at Toulouse on the 10th) and Penrose could report shortly afterwards that Dalhousie and Decaen, the local French commander, had agreed to a suspension of hostilities. One aspect of this was that, while armed British vessels were not allowed up river, all merchant shipping could proceed past Blaye to Bordeaux without being stopped or searched.[50]

In this way did the Royal Navy's contribution to the Peninsular War come to an end.

*   *   *

There was to be no climactic finale to the Peninsular War for the Royal Navy. On both eastern and western coasts the conflict ended more with a whimper than a bang. Indeed throughout the long seven years of struggle there had been no Trafalgar-like triumph to draw attention to the extent of its efforts and this has perhaps been the primary reason for its neglect by historians of the war.

Yet the Peninsula provides an example of how naval power can have a profound strategic impact on a land campaign. It is too easy when considering this period to view the Navy merely as Britain's shield, protecting the country from invasion and guarding her trade. It could also be a sword for it was British naval power that enabled British armies to be transported to the Peninsula and then maintained and supported there for six years. The regular Spanish and Portuguese forces, who comprised the bulk of those fighting Napoleon, also heavily relied on British logistical support and so too on the Royal Navy. That this naval power could, as demonstrated at Corunna, evacuate any army facing disaster gave ministers in London a vital element of flexibility when deciding whether and to what extent they could commit troops to the region. Within the theatre of war itself the Allies enjoyed the ability to move soldiers and equipment rapidly by water, a facility largely denied to the French. This in turn made coastal strongpoints a much more serious headache for Napoleon's troops than they otherwise would have been. Most particularly, in the case of Cadiz it caused them a major setback that severely disrupted their operations in southern Spain.

In many ways the most striking feature that shines through from any study of any campaign is the sheer variety of tasks undertaken by naval personnel. Alongside all the obvious duties that one may have expected, such as convoy protection, coastal assaults and the interdiction of French movements, are a myriad of other endeavours. British sailors are to be found manning gunboats and batteries on the Tagus, ageing Spanish line-of-battle ships at Cadiz, and signal towers along the Lines of Torres Vedras. They built bridges, they hauled supplies inland, and they provided the muscle power to implement amphibious landings and withdrawals. When the Spanish squadron at Ferrol had to be moved it was British sailors who prepared the vessels for sea, also providing support for many of the Spanish warships on their ultimate voyages to safer havens such as Havana and the Balearics. British warships provided a constant and reliable postal service for Wellington's communications with London and other points, a provision whose normal swift efficiency contrasted starkly with the problems Napoleon had when it came to keeping in touch with events beyond the Pyrenees. Similarly crucial was the responsibility for moving the vast amounts of bullion that were endlessly demanded by Wellington as he tried to keep his army solvent and avoid the necessity of living off the land. Finally, naval vessels were given the burden of trying to supply arms and ammunition to the numerous guerrilla groups that operated within range of the coast, a job that was difficult, potentially dangerous and, for the captains concerned, often diplomatically demanding. In undertaking all of these tasks the sailors involved displayed a degree of professionalism and application which illustrated why the Royal Navy was such a potent force.

It has always been Wellington's army that has attracted the plaudits for its Peninsular achievements: Wellington's navy is every bit as deserving.

Notes

Abbreviations used in the notes

National Record Office files:

ADM	=	Admiralty
FO	=	Foreign Office
WO	=	War Office
NMM	=	National Maritime Museum
BL	=	British Library
WD	=	*The Dispatches of F M the Duke of Wellington, 1799–1818* edited by J Gurwood (London 1834–9)
WSD	=	*Supplementary Despatches, Correspondence and Memoranda of Field Marshal Arthur Duke of Wellington* edited by the Second Duke of Wellington (London 1858–72).

Introduction

1 Paul Kennedy, *The Rise and Fall of British Naval Mastery* (London 1991), pp59–60. He underplays the importance of the Peninsular War and misleadingly compares it to the North African campaigns in the Second World War.

2 H N Shore, 'The Navy in the Peninsular War', *The United Service Magazine*, Vol XLVII (New Style), (1912–14).

3 Sir Charles Oman, *A History of the Peninsular War*, 7 vols (Oxford 1902–30; reprinted London 1995–7).

4 Two examples of published accounts are P C Krajeski, *In the Shadow of Nelson: The Naval Leadership of Admiral Sir Charles Cotton, 1753–1812* (London 2000), and D D Horward, 'Admiral Berkeley and the Duke of Wellington: The Winning Combination in the Peninsula' in W B Cogar (ed), *New Interpretations in Naval History* (London 1989).

Chapter 1: Portugal 1807–8

1 *The Naval Chronicle* (London 1808), preface to Vol XX.

2 D R Ringrose, *Transportation and Economic Stagnation in Spain, 1750–1850* (Durham, NC 1970), pp3–17. J Marshall-Cornwall, *Marshal Massena* (London 1965), pp179–80.

3 ADM 109/106, Victualling Board to Liverpool (Secretary of State for War), 18 December 1809; and Bunbury (Under-Secretary of State for War) to Victualling Board, 30 December 1809. S G P Ward, *Wellington's Headquarters* (Oxford 1957), pp97–8. ADM 1/344, Admiral Berkeley to the Admiralty, 21

April 1812, No 117. G E Watson, 'The United States and the Peninsular War, 1808–1812', *Historical Journal*, Vol 19, No 4 (1976), pp870–1. C N Parkinson (ed), *The Trade Winds: A Study of British Overseas Trade during the French Wars, 1793–1815* (London 1948), p232.

4 The precise strengths of the Lisbon station, detailed at intervals of six months, can be found in ADM 8/96. For the extension of its limits and the arguments over the issue, see: ADM 2/1367, pp238–9; ADM 2/1373, pp268–78; and *WSD*, Vol VII, p46.

5 Warships off Cadiz from W L Clowes, *The Royal Navy* (London 1897–1903; reprinted 1996–7), Vol 5, p246. ADM 1/415, Vice-Admiral Purvis to the Admiralty, 10 November 1809, No 84; and same to same, 1 April 1810, No 133. ADM 1/422, Rear-Admiral Legge to the Admiralty, 9 January 1812, No 4. Squadron off Catalonia from NMM Codrington Papers, COD/5/5, Captain Codrington to Admiral Cotton, 10 May 1811. Overall strengths of the Mediterranean Fleet can be found in the ADM 8 series: unfortunately these list only the ships and not their stations.

6 ADM 1/138, Admiral Gambier to the Admiralty, 21 June 1808 for the initial force off the northern coast. ADM 1/141, same to same, 15 May 1809, No 345, and 1/144, Gambier to Captain Popham, 20 August 1810, for later force levels. For numbers in 1813 see ADM 1/154, Captain Collier to Admiral Keith, 4 September 1813. For Ferrol see ADM 1/138, Admiral Gambier to Rear-Admiral de Courcy, 21 July 1808, No 474; and Captain Hotham to Gambier, 30 July 1808.

7 ADM 2/1365, pp28–30. ADM 50/50, Sir Sydney Smith's journal.

8 FO 63/58, ff13–33.

9 D Francis, *Portugal 1715–1808* (London 1985), pp260–1 and 275. H N Shore, 'The Navy in the Peninsular War', *The United Service Magazine*, Vol XLVII (New Style), (1912–14), pp470–1. J W Fortescue, *A History of the British Army* (London 1899–1930), Vol VI, pp92–6.

10 Squadron's strength from ADM 50/50. Smith's career can be traced in Clowes, *op cit*, Vols 4 and 5. Nelson's comment from Sir R V Hamilton and J K Laughton (eds), *Recollections of James Anthony Gardner* (London 1996), p145n.

11 Shore, *op cit*, Vol XLVI (NS), pp468–9. ADM 2/1365, pp38–42. ADM 50/50, entries for 22 November 1807. ADM 1/19, Rear-Admiral Smith to Araujo, 22 November 1807. In September Copenhagen, despite Danish neutrality, had been bombarded into submission by a British force determined to secure control of its fleet. Smith felt unable to attempt a direct assault on Lisbon because he had no troops: ADM 50/50, entry for 22 November 1807.

12 Fortescue, *op cit*, Vol VI, pp99–100. Sir Charles Oman, *A History of the Peninsular War* (Oxford 1902–30; reprinted London 1995–7), Vol I, pp26–30.

13 Francis, *op cit*, p280. Oman, *op cit*, Vol I, p30.

14 Shore, *op cit*, Vol XLVI (NS), pp472–5. Francis, *op cit*, p282.

15 ADM 1/19, Smith to the Admiralty, 1 December 1807 (two despatches). Shore, *op cit*, Vol XLVI (NS), p475. Clowes, *op cit*, Vol 5, p233.

16 ADM 1/19, Rear-Admiral Smith to the Admiralty, 1 December 1807; and same to same, 6 December 1807. ADM 50/50, entry for 5 December 1807. Fortescue, *op cit*, Vol VI, p104n.

17 ADM 1/340, Admiral Cotton to the Admiralty, 7 September 1808, No 231.

18 For Russian hostility, see M S Anderson, *The Eastern Question, 1774–1923* (London 1974), pp40–1, Siniavin's squadron from Clowes, *op cit*, Vol 5, p233. ADM 2/1365, pp46–7.

19 ADM 1/339, Vice-Admiral Cotton to the Admiralty, 9 December 80; and same to same, 16 January 1808, No 16. *The Naval Chronicle*, Vol XXVII

(London 1812), p370. Cotton, who was promoted to full admiral on 28 April 1808, was a friend of Mulgrave, the Admiralty First Lord, a fact helping to explain his appointment to Portugal despite having recently declined the command of the Halifax station.

20 The warships off the Tagus were: *Hibernia* (120), *Alfred* (74), *Agamemnon* (64), *Defence* (74), *Ganges* (74), *Foudroyant* (80), *Conqueror*, *Plantagenet*, *Ruby* (64) and *Confiance*. Off Oporto were the *Raven* and *Cheerful*. With the convoy were the *Nymph* and *Nautilus*. ADM 1/339, Cotton to the Admiralty, 16 January 1808, No 16.

21 ADM 1/339, Cotton to the Admiralty, 24 January 1808, No 24; same to same, 25 January 1808, No 21 (the numbering of despatches was sometimes out of sequence); same to same, 31 January 1808, No 23; return of provisions required, 27 January 1808; Captain McKinley to Cotton, 15 February 1808 (two separate despatches); Cotton to the Admiralty, 21 February 1808, No 55; and same to same, 22 February 1808, No 58. *The Naval Chronicle*, Vol XXVII, p371.

22 ADM 1/339, Cotton to the Admiralty, 5 March 1808, No 69; same to same, 16 March 1808, No 77; same to same, 28 March 1808, No 89; same to same, 30 March 1808, No 91; same to same 27 April 1808, No 126; and same to same, 23 August 1808, No 223.

23 *Ibid*, Cotton to the Admiralty, 18 February 1808, No 48; same to same, 20 February 1808, No 52; same to same, 16 March 1808, No 77; same to same, 2 February 1808, No 30; and same to same, 21 April 1808, No 117. Squadron's strength on 1 July 1808 from ADM 8/96.

24 ADM 1/339, Captain Yeo to Cotton, 14 February 1808; Cotton to the Admiralty, 23 April 1808, No 120; and same to same, 25 May 1808, No 138. Clowes, *op cit*, Vol 5, pp415–6. Shore, *op cit*, Vol XLVI (NS), p592.

25 Junot's strength from Oman, *op cit*, Vol I, p283. ADM 1/339, Cotton to the Admiralty, 7 April 1808, No 102; and same to same, 16 May 1808, No 134. A Hayter (ed), *The Backbone: Diaries of a Military Family in the Napoleonic Wars* (Durham 1993), p157.

26 ADM 1/339, Cotton to the Admiralty, 3 June 1808, No 146; same to same, 9 June

1808, No 147; same to same, 11 June 1808, No 156; and same to same, 12 June 1808, No 157. ADM 1/340, same to same, 18 June 1808, no 163; and same to same, 28 June 1808, No 174. Hayter, *op cit*, p151. *The Naval Chronicle*, Vol XXVII, p374.

27 For the Portuguese rising see Oman, *op cit*, Vol I, pp208–12, ADM 1/340, Cotton to the Admiralty, 22 June 1808, No 169; same to same, 23 June 1808, No 178; same to same, 7 July 1808, no number; Bligh to Cotton, 9 July 1808; and Cotton to the Admiralty, 14 July 1808, No 195. WO 1/718, pp91–3, 95–6, 111–3 and 115–16. Hayter, *op cit*, pp166–7 and 172.

28 Ironically this had originally been assembled with the aim of attacking Spain's New World colonies, other forces also being prepared for an assault on the Balearic Islands.

29 WO 6/47, pp42–4. ADM 1/4208, List of transports assembled at Cork, 14 June 1808. Oman, *op cit*, Vol I, pp227 and 230n.

30 ADM 1/340, Cotton to the Admiralty, 9 July 1808, no number; and same to same, 3 August 1808, No 204. *WD*, Vol 4, p69. According to *Donegal*'s log, ADM 51/1880, the landings began on 27 July, but this was presumably just a small advanced party.

31 BL Add Mss 49482, Gordon Papers, f66, Lieutenant General Moore to Lieutenant-Colonel Gordon, 6 May 1808. Many of these vessels were normally employed moving coal from northern England to London.

32 ADM 1/340, Cotton to the Admiralty, 19 August 1808, No 216; and same to same, 21 August 1808, No 218,. WO 6/47, pp67–9. Sir J F Maurice (ed), *The Diary of Sir John Moore* (London 1904), Vol II, p254–5. Oman, *op cit*, Vol I, pp230 and 248.

33 *WD*, Vol 4, pp192–3. Quote from Shore, *op cit*, Vol XLVI (NS), p153.

34 *WD*, Vol 4, pp192–3. Sir R Henegan, *Seven Years Campaigning in the Peninsular and the Netherlands from 1808 to 1815* (London 1846), Vol I, pp12–14.

35 A L F Schaumann, *On the Road with Wellington*, edited by A Ludovici (London 1924), pp1–3. Shore, *op cit*, Vol XLVI, p155 quoting Baron Ompteda.

36 *WD*, Vol 4, pp70–2, 106 and 124. ADM 1/424, Wellington to Lieutenant-

General Maitland, 16 August 1812. ADM 1/340, Cotton to the Admiralty, 14 August 1808, No 214. Shore, *op cit*, Vol XLVI (NS), p157 quoting from Dr Neale's account.

37 *WSD*, Vol XIII, pp232–4.

38 Full details are in Oman, *op cit*, Vol I, appendix IX, pp625–8, though the convention is wrongly dated as 13 August rather than the 30th.

39 ADM 1/339, Cotton to the Admiralty, 25 January 1808, No 20; same to same, 8 February 1808, No 39; and same to same, 21 February 1808, No 54. In a despatch of 1 April 1808, No 96, Cotton admitted that all the reports he received about the Russians were vague and contradictory.

40 All the ramifications of the Cintra agreement are very well considered in R M Schneer, 'Arthur Wellesley and the Cintra Convention: A New Look at an Old Puzzle', *Journal of British Studies*, Vol 14, No 2 (Spring 1980), particularly pp107–8. Oman, *op cit*, Vol I, pp271–2, 284–5 and 291–300. Shore, *op cit*, Vol XLVII (NS), pp358–60. ADM 1/340, Cotton to the Admiralty, 4 September 1808, No 227. ADM 2/1365, pp246–51.

41 ADM 1/340, Cotton to the Admiralty, 12 September 1808, No 235; same to same, 18 November 1808, No 283; and same to same, 10 December 1808, No 295. ADM 2/1366, pp222–3.

Chapter 2: The Spanish Revolt, 1808–9

1 G L Newnham Collingwood (ed), *A Selection from the Public and Private Correspondence of Vice-Admiral Lord Collingwood* (London 1828), Vol II, p391.

2 The course of Napoleon's attempted absorption of Spain from Oman, *op cit*, Vol I, pp1–11 and 33–71; D G Chandler, *The Campaigns of Napoleon* (London 1967), pp603–11; J M Thompson, *Napoleon Bonaparte: His Rise and Fall* (Oxford 1969), pp240–5.

3 WO 6/185, pp6–13, 17–20, 22–4 and 27–31; and ADM 2/1365, pp207–10 for the British Government's plans and intentions for Spain. On the question of attacking Spanish colonies, see C D Hall, *British Strategy in the Napoleonic War, 1803–15* (Manchester 1992), pp98–9.

4 ADM 1/414, Purvis to the Admiralty,

29 May 1808, No 119; and same to same, 6 June 1808, No 122. Castlereagh's orders to Purvis of 4 June 1808 are in WO 6/185, pp36–9.

5 ADM 1/414, Purvis to the Admiralty, 11 June 1808, No 119; and same to same, 6 June 1808, No 122. Castlereagh's orders to Purvis of 4 June 1808 are in WO 6/185, pp36–9.

6 ADM 1/414, Purvis to the Admiralty, 29 May 1808, No 119; and same to same, 6 June 1808, No 122. Castlereagh's orders to Purvis of 4 June 1808 are in WO 6/185, pp36–9.

7 The best single-volume account of these operations, and of the whole war, is D Gates, *The Spanish Ulcer* (London 1986). Detailed accounts can be found in Oman, *op cit*, Vol I.

8 ADM 1/415, List of Spanish vessels ready for sea, 9 February 1809; Purvis to the Admiralty, 10 February 1809, No 39; same to same, 17 February 1809, No 40; Purvis to Berkeley, 24 February 1809; Purvis to the Admiralty, 21 March 1809, No 60; Collingwood to the Admiralty, 25 March 1809, No 69; Purvis to the Admiralty, 2 April 1809, No 76; and same to same, 10 November 1809, No 84.

9 ADM 1/414, Otway to Collingwood, 25 July 1808; and Collingwood to the Admiralty, 4 October 1808, No 226. ADM 52/4187, Log of HMS *Montagu*. Oman, *op cit*, Vol I, pp303n and 320–3. Oman says Reille lifted the siege of Rosas on 12 July, but this must be a mistake. Otway, who was there, dated his last despatch the 25th and spoke of Reille's withdrawal the same day.

10 D Thomas, *Cochrane* (London 1980), pp126–30; F Marryat, *Life and Letters of Captain Marryat* (London 1872), p46; C Lloyd, *Captain Marryat and the Old Navy* (London 1939), pp65–72. ADM 1/414, Cochrane to Collingwood, 31 July 1808. Both Thomas and Marryat say Cochrane took 95 prisoners from Mongat, though he says 71 in his despatch to Collingwood. ADM 2/1366, pp14–15. Oman, *op cit*, Vol I, p331.

11 Thomas, *op cit*, pp130–3. Marryat, *op cit*, p46. ADM 1/414, Brenton (*Spartan*) to Rear-Admiral Thornborough, 16 September 1808; and Collingwood to the Admiralty, 19 October 1808, No 234.

12 ADM 1/414, Bennet's reports to Collingwood for 22 November–4 December 1808; and Collingwood to the Admiralty, 1 December 1808, No 272. ADM 1/415, Cochrane to Collingwood, 5 December 1808. D Smith, *The Greenhill Napoleonic Wars Data Book* (London 1998), pp271–2. *The Naval Chronicle*, Vol XXI (London 1809), pp166–7 and 259–60. Thomas, *op cit*, pp134–42. Marryat, *op cit*, pp50–1. Oman, *op cit*, Vol II, pp42–57.

13 Marryat, *op cit*, pp59–63.

14 ADM 52/4508, Log of HMS *Hydra* for 1809. ADM 1/415, Collingwood to the Admiralty, 4 May 1809, No 93. Collingwood numbered the convoy at 16 vessels, though in his despatch to the Admiralty No 97 of 11 May Purvis spoke of no fewer than 30 supply ships and Frere, the British ambassador to Spain, spoke of 24 such vessels in a letter of 9 May. Collingwood may have been embarrassed by such a failure and keen to minimise its worth to the enemy, though to be fair to him the *Hydra*'s log also spoke of 16 merchant vessels and she was on the spot. See also Clowes, *op cit*, Vol 5, p278; and Oman, *op cit*, Vol III, p16.

15 ADM 1/415, Collingwood to the Admiralty, 1 November 1809, No 88; and Hallowell to Collingwood, 1 November 1809. Clowes, *op cit*, Vol 5, pp278–81.

16 ADM 1/415, Collingwood to the Admiralty, 1 November 1809, No 138.

17 ADM 2.1365, pp292 and 330.

18 *Ibid*, pp339 and 347–9. ADM 1/4208, Canning to the Asturian Envoys, 12 June 1808; and Canning to the Admiralty, 13 June 1808. ADM 1/138, Gambier to the Admiralty, 17 June 1808, No 466; same to same, 21 June 1808, no number; and Gambier to Rear-Admiral De Courcy, 21 July 1808, No 474.

19 Clowes, *op cit*, Vol 5, p421. ADM 1/138, Atkins to Gambier, 28 June 1808; same to same, 15 July 1808; and same to same, 24 July 1808.

20 ADM 1/138, Tower to Atkins, 18 August 1808.

21 The progress of the land campaigns around Bilbao can be traced in Gates and Oman, *op cit*, Vol I. ADM 1/139, Atkins to Gambier, 28 September 1808; and Gambier to the Admiralty, 14 October 1808, No 748.

22 ADM 1/139, Gambier to the Admiralty, 14 October 1808, No 748; Digby to Gambier, 15 October 1808; Gambier to the Admiralty, 4 December 1808, No 866; and same to same, 5 December 1808, No 868. ADM 2/1366, pp324–5. ADM 2/1367, pp26–7.

23 The rescue and transfer of the Spaniards can be followed in J Stewart, 'The Stolen Army', *Army Quarterly*, Vol 66 (1953), pp243–51. Oman, *op cit*, Vol I, pp367–75. A N Ryan (ed), *The Saumarez Papers* (London 1968), pp29–30, 36–7 and 39–40. ADM 2/1366, pp135–8. ADM 1/139, De Courcy to Gambier, 5 October 1808, No 728; and Digby to Gambier, 15 October 1808. Clowes, *op cit*, Vol 5, pp250–1, ADM 52/3861, Log of HMS *Racoon*. The government's view of how important the successful rescue of the Spaniards was is made clear by their rewarding of Keats with the Order of the Bath.

24 Gates, *op cit*, pp106–7. *WSD*, Vol XIII, p325. ADM 1/139, De Courcy to Gambier, 14 October 1808, No 747; De Courcy to the Admiralty, 24 October 1808, No 771; and same to same, 25 October 1808, No 772. BL Add Mss 49482, Gordon Papers, f167v. Shore, *op cit*, Vol XLVII (NS), No 1016 (July 1913), p486.

25 Gates, *op cit*, pp106–10. Also C Hibbert, *Corunna* (London 1961).

26 ADM 1/139, Gambier to the Admiralty, 10 November 1808, No 801; De Courcy to Gambier, 23 November 1808, No 847; and same to same, 25 November 1808, No 848.

27 ADM 1/139, De Courcy to Gambier, 1 December 1808, no number; and De Courcy to the Admiralty, 22 December 1808, No 903. ADM 2/1367, p31, 43–9 and 63–4. The Admiralty was fortunate that these events were occurring in the winter months when the fleet maintained in the Baltic had been withdrawn: this provided them with a reserve allowing the southwards redeployment to cover the emergency.

28 Oman, *op cit*, Vol I, pp563–4. Gates, *op cit*, pp110–1. Hibbert, *op cit*, p135. The latter says that the Navy did not like the idea of a Corunna evacuation, though this was not the case – see p68.

29 Hibbert, *op cit*, pp135–6.

30 *Ibid*, pp161–3. ADM 1/140, De Courcy

to the Admiralty, 13 January 1809, No 34. Shore, *op cit*, Vol XLVII (NS), pp488–9. NMM McKinley Papers, MCK/6(b), Rear-Admiral Hood to McKinley, 10 January 1809, and Supplement of 13 January 1809.

31 Oman, *op cit*, Vol I, pp582–94. Gates, *op cit*, pp112–4. Hibbert, *op cit*, pp169–91. Shore, *op cit*, Vol XLVII (NS), pp491–2.

32 Shore, *op cit*, Vol XLVII (NS), pp492–5. ADM 1/140, De Courcy to the Admiralty, 12 January 1809, no number; and same to same, 23 January 1809, No 48. *The Naval Chronicle*, Vol XXI (London 1809), pp83–4.

33 Hibbert, *op cit*, pp195–6. Shore, *op cit*, Vol XLVII (NS), pp496–7. ADM 1/140, De Courcy to the Admiralty, 23 January 1809, No 48. WO 1/229, p584.

34 ADM 1/140, De Courcy to the Admiralty, 23 January 1809, No 48; and same to same, 4 February 1809, No 88.

35 ADM 2/1367, pp188–9. ADM 1/141, Adam to Gambier, 10 March 1809; Mends to Gambier, 20 March 1809; Adam to Gambier, 1 April 1809; and Burton to Adam, 12 April 1809.

36 ADM 2/1368, pp162–3 and 200–1. ADM 1/141, Gambier to the Admiralty, 15 May 1809, No 345. Oman, *op cit*, Vol II, pp382 and 386–7.

Chapter 3: Portugal, 1809–12

1 ADM 1/342, Berkeley to the Admiralty, 26 March 1810, No 63.

2 ADM 1/340, Berkeley to the Admiralty, 25 December 1808, No 305. *Dictionary of National Biography*, Vol II (Oxford 1921), pp358–9. S C Tucker and F T Reuter, *Injured Honor: The Chesapeake-Leopard Affair, 22 June 1807* (Annapolis 1996), pp74–5. Clowes, *op cit*, Vol 4, pp380–388.

3 Tucker and Reuter, *op cit*, p74. B M De Toy, *Wellington's Admiral: The Life and Career of George Berkeley, 1753–1818* (Florida University PhD Thesis 1997), p602. This is by far the best examination and assessment of Berkeley to date.

4 Warwickshire Record Office, Letterbook of Admiral Berkeley, CR114A/616, p167. De Toy, *op cit*, pp466–7, 541 and 592. *WD*, Vol 8, p433.

5 ADM 2/1367, pp74–8 and 97–9.

6 ADM 1/341, Return of Transports in the Tagus, 20 December 1808;

Berkeley to the Admiralty, 16 January 1809, No 11; and same to same, 30 January 1809, no number. Oman, *op cit*, Vol II, p205.

7 ADM 1/341, Berkeley to the Admiralty, 26 January 1809, No 15; same to same, 28 January 1809, No 16; same to same, 11 February 1809, No 27; same to same, 12 February 1809, No 29; and same to same, 17 February 1809, No 32; Admiralty Office to Berkeley, 23 February 1809; Berkeley to the Admiralty, 1 March 1809, No 40; and same to same, 2 March 1809, No 42. ADM 2/1367, pp238–9 and 243–4.

8 Oman, *op cit*, Vol II, pp178–95, 223–49 and 263–4. ADM 1/341, McKinley to Berkeley, 29 March 1809. NMM, McKinley Papers, MCK/6(b), Coutts Crawford to McKinley, 21 March 1809. *The Naval Chronicle*, Vol XXI, pp49–52. Gates, *op cit*, pp138–42.

9 ADM 1/341, Bolton to Berkeley, 15 April 1809. WO 1/720, pp293 and 307. *WSD*, Vol VI, p230. Rear-Admiral A Phillimore, *The Life of Admiral of the Fleet Sir William Parker* (London 1876), Vol I, p372. Parker of the *Amazon* was a young captain still in his twenties who disliked Bolton and resented having to part with the marines from his ship: he doubted if the French even planned an attack in the first place.

10 *WSD*, Vol VI, p230. ADM 1/341, Berkeley to the Admiralty, 25 June 1809. NMM, McKinley Papers, MCK/6(d), Conde de Maceda to McKinley, 22 May 1809; Berkeley to McKinley, 2 June 1809 (two despatches); and same to same, 21 June 1809.

11 Oman, *op cit*, Vol II, pp283n and 286–9. Gates, *op cit*, pp149–51.

12 ADM 1/341, Berkeley to the Admiralty, 23 April 1809, No 96; same to same, 25 April 1809, No 99; same to same, 26 April 1809, No 101; and same to same, 4 August 1809, No 183. ADM 1/342, Berkeley to the Admiralty, 26 March 1810, No 63. ADM 2/1368, pp159–60. ADM 1/4210, War Office to the Admiralty, 12 May 1809. ADM 8/98, strength of Portuguese station, 1 July 1809.

13 Oman, *op cit*, Vol II, pp438–41. ADM 1/341, Berkeley to the Admiralty, 19 May 1809, No 120; and same to same, 23 May 1809, No 123. Warwickshire

Record Office, Letterbook of Admiral Berkeley, CR 114A/616, p260. Gates, *op cit*, pp151–5.

14 The Talavera campaign can be followed in detail in Oman, *op cit*, Vol II, pp422–600, and in a more concise form in Gates, *op cit*, pp173–90.

15 *The Naval Chronicle*, Vol XXI, pp438–9. ADM 1/1939, Hotham to Gambier, 24 June 1809, No 7. Hotham to Governor Garcia, 26 June 1809; Hotham to Gambier, 28 June 1809, No 9; and same to same, 6 July 1809, No 13. Phillimore, *op cit*, Vol I, pp384–6.

16 The movement of the Ferrol squadron can be traced in ADM 1/4211, Bagot (Under-Secretary at the Foreign Office) to the Admiralty, 10 July 1809. ADM 2/1369, pp31–4. ADM 1/1939, Hotham to the Admiralty, 29 July 1809. ADM 1/1940, Hotham to Gambier, 26 August 1809, No 23; same to same, 20 September 1809, No 27; same to same, 1 October 1809, No 29; and Statements of stores provided by British ships. ADM 1/2078, Linzee to the Admiralty, 29 August 1809; same to same, 12 September 1809; Linzee to Vargas, 2 September 1809; Vargas to Linzee, 3 September 1809; and the 'Details of the daily progress of work on the Spanish vessels' for August and September. ADM 1/341, Berkeley to the Admiralty, 30 July 1809, No 181; same to same, 4 August 1809, No 183; and same to same, 4 September 1809, No 17 (for some reason the numbering of despatches was restarted in the middle of August).

17 ADM 1/341, Berkeley to the Admiralty, 1 June 1809, No 127; same to same, 10 June 1809, No 143; same to same, 18 July 1809, No 172; and same to same, 13 September 1809, No 21. *WD*, Vol 4, pp41–2; and Vol 5, pp415 and 432–3.

18 Oman, *op cit*, Vol II, pp609–10 and, for a detailed description of the Lines, Vol III, pp419–36. Gates, *op cit*, pp222–3 from whom the quote is taken.

19 Oman, *op cit*, Vol III, appendix XIV, pp554–8 for Wellington's numbers in November 1810. ADM 1/342, Statement of shipping in the Tagus, 11 September 1809; Berkeley to the Admiralty, 10 February 1810, No 34; same to same, 24 February 1810, No 42; same to same, 27 February 1810, No 49; same to same, 25 March 1810, No 52;

same to same, 31 March 1810, No 58;
same to same, 4 April 1810, No 67; and
Re-embarkation schedule, 9 May 1810.
WD, Vol 5, pp583–4, Wellington's
quote on p584.

20 ADM 1/342, Berkeley to the Admiralty,
4 October 1810, No 229. ADM 8/99,
strength of Portuguese squadron, 1
November 1810.

21 NMM, Yorke Papers, YOR/2, Berkeley
to Yorke (First Lord of the Admiralty),
4 July 1810, letter No 14. ADM 1/342,
Berkeley to the Admiralty, 17 August
1810, No 190; and same to same, 27
November 1810, No 283. WO 1/808,
pp416–7.

22 Historic Manuscripts Commission,
*Report on the Manuscripts of Earl
Bathurst preserved at Cirencester Park*
(London 1923), pp148–9. NMM, Yorke
Papers, YOR/2, Berkeley to Yorke, 29
September 1810, letter no 120. *WSD*,
Vol VII, p32.

23 Leeds University Library, Brotherton
Collection, Mulgrave Papers Box VII,
19/29, Perceval to Mulgrave, 18
November 1808.

24 ADM 1/4212, Liverpool (Secretary of
State for War) to the Admiralty, 23
March 1810. ADM 2/1370, pp328, 338,
388–9, 394 and 396–7. R N Buckley, *The
Napoleonic War Journal of Captain
Thomas Henry Browne, 1807–1816*
(Army Records Society 1987), pp71–7
and 123–5. For an extended review of
the arguments in favour of converting
warships, with marginal comments
indicating why they were resisted, see
Perceval's memorandum cited in note
23 above.

25 *WD*, Vol 6, p196. H N Shore, 'The
Navy and the lines of Torres Vedras',
United Service Magazine, Vol XLII
(NS) (1910–11), pp11–12.

26 ADM 1/342, Berkeley to the Admiralty,
18 October 1810, No 230. ADM 1/343,
same to same, 24 January 1811, No 339.
Shore, *op cit*, Vol XLVIII (NS), p8.
Oman, *op cit*, Vol III, p440. *WD*, Vol 6,
p497. Wellington acknowledged the
sterling work of the flotilla on 20
October, see p527. The quote on Saint-
Croix comes from Oman.

27 H N Edwards, 'The Diary of
Lieutenant C Gilmor, RN – Portugal –
1810', *Journal of the Society for Army
Historical Research*, Vol 3 (1924),
pp149–60.

28 ADM 1/342, Berkeley to the Admiralty,
10 November 1810, No 258; and same
to same, 22 November 1810, No 266.
WD, Vol 6, pp570 and 631; and Vol 7,
p3, 7–8 and 114. Oman, *op cit*, Vol III,
pp462, 467, 470–1 and 477–8. Gates, *op
cit*, pp236–9.

29 ADM 1/342, Berkeley to the Admiralty,
16 November 1810, No 261; same to
same, 14 December 1810, No 291; and
same to same, 27 December 1810, No
300. ADM 1/343, same to same, 5
January 1811, no number. Warwickshire
Record Office, Letterbook of Admiral
Berkeley, CR 114A/616, pp168–9 and
172. *WD*, Vol 6, pp601–2; and Vol 7,
pp70 and 77. ADM 2/1371, pp110–11.

30 Shore, 'Torres Vedras', *op cit*, pp12–13.
ADM 1/343, Berkeley to the Admiralty,
15 March 1811, No 408.

31 ADM 1/343, Return of Transports, 28
March 1811; Berkeley to the Admiralty,
12 April 1811, No 434; same to same, 25
May 1811, No 493; and same to same,
15 June 1811, No 523. ADM 2/1371,
pp353–4; and ADM 2/1372, pp141–2
and 175. *WD*, Vol 7, pp379, 386 and
504; and Vol 8, p168.

32 ADM 1/343, Berkeley to the Admiralty,
7 May 1811, No 475; and same to same,
28 June 1811, No 218. ADM 1/344,
same to same, 24 January 1812, No 22;
and same to same, 18 April 1812, No 97.
ADM 2/1373, pp194–5. ADM 2/1374,
pp193–4. *WD*, Vol 8, p347.

33 ADM 1/343, Berkeley to the Admiralty,
6 July 1811, No 224; same to same, 5
August 1811, No 249; Lieutenant
Geddes to Berkeley, 4 August 1811; and
Lieutenant Brown to Berkeley, 5
August 1811. *WD*, Vol 7, pp635–6.
Oman, *op cit*, Vol IV, pp267–8, 383,
408, 419–20 and 438–9. Gates, *op cit*,
pp326–40.

34 ADM 1/343, Berkeley to the Admiralty,
3 November 1811, No 310.

35 ADM 1/344, Berkeley to the Admiralty,
10 April 1812, No 90. Oman, *op cit*, Vol
V, p224. W Seymour, *Great Sieges of
History* (London 1991), p126.

Chapter 4: Convoys, Bullion and Arms

1 Sir R V Hamilton (ed), *Letters and
Papers of Admiral of the Fleet Sir T
Byam Martin* (London 1898), Vol II,
p409.

2 ADM 1/342, Disposition of the Lisbon squadron, 8 September 1810. B Lavery, *Nelson's Navy* (London 1989), p305 considers that convoys 'did not use an unduly large proportion of naval resources', though this does not allow for periodic escorting and accounts for only permanent assignments.

3 ADM 7.64, Convoy list.

4 ADM 1/346, Rear-Admiral Linzee to the Admiralty, 19 March 1813, No 20.

5 *WD*, Vol 5, pp487 and 497; Vol 6, pp15, 39–40 and 64. ADM 109/107, Admiralty to Victualling Board, 20 June 1810.

6 *WD*, Vol 6, pp382, 411 and 445–6.

7 *Ibid*, Vol 9, pp131–2; and Vol 10, pp104–5, 459 and 508. Oman, *op cit*, Vol 6, p569. Ward, *op cit*, pp97–8.

8 ADM 109/106, Bunbury (Under Secretary for War) to the Victualling Board, 30 December 1809.

9 Lavery, *op cit*, p305. Parkinson, *op cit*, pp81–3.

10 ADM 1/4515, Dyson to the Admiralty, 11 January 1813; and same to same, 23 January 1813.

11 Statistics from F Crouzet, *L'Economie Britannique et le Blocus Continental, 1803–15* (Paris 1958), appendix II, table 1, p883. E F Heckscher, *The Continental System* (London 1922) produces different figures detailing 'real' trade values, but the importance of Iberian markets after 1809 are similarly indicated.

12 R Davis, *The Rise of the English Shipping Industry* (Newton Abbot 1972), pp228–31. ADM 1/341, Berkeley to the Admiralty, 26 April 1809, No 101.

13 Parkinson, *op cit*, pp84 and 231–2.

14 Lavery, *op cit*, p307.

15 For the problems of the convoy escort see NMM, CAR/102/2, Papers of Captain Carteret, Carteret to the Admiralty, 26 December 1813. ADM 1/422, Legge to the Admiralty, 19 April 1812, No 31.

16 ADM 1/346, Captain Buck to Linzee, 14 February 1813. ADM 1/478, Captain Cumby to Vice-Admiral Keats, 20 December 1813. ADM 1/341, Captain King to Martin, 2 June 1813. Sir R V Hamilton, *The Recollections of James Anthony Gardner* (London 1906). Lavery, *op cit*, pp307–9.

17 ADM 1/342, Berkeley to the Admiralty,

5 July 1809, No 161. ADM 1/343, same to same, 13 September 1811, No 229. ADM 1/625, Captain Braimer to Vice-Admiral Thornborough, 20 March 1813.

18 Lavery, *op cit*, p310.

19 ADM 51/2707, Log of HMS *Phipps*.

20 Francis, *op cit*, pp261–2 for the *Apollo*'s disaster. ADM 1/478, Cumby to Keats, 20 December 1813. ADM 52/3861, Log of HMS *Racoon*.

21 *WD*, Vol 10, p273. C S Forester, *The Age of Fighting Sail* (London 1970), pp70–1.

22 ADM 1/416, Captain Bullen to Cotton, 14 June 1810; and Captain Pringle to Cotton, 19 June 1810. ADM 7/46, p61. ADM 1/344, Legge to Martin, 6 July 1812. Clowes, *op cit*, Vol 5, p504n.

23 P Crowhurst, *The French War on Trade. Privateering 1793–1815* (Aldershot 1989), pp145 and 149. ADM 1/421, Lieutenant-Colonel Green to Pellew, 1 August 181; and Penrose to Lieutenant-General Campbell, 3 September 1811.

24 ADM 1/422, Captain Phillips (*Onyx*) to Legge, 17 January 1812. ADM 1/423, Captain Osborne (*Fearless*) to Legge, 24 May 1812.

25 ADM 1/423, Captain Usher to Penrose, 30 April 1812. Clowes, *op cit*, Vol 5, pp503–4.

26 ADM 1/419, Captain Price to Keats, 27 May 1811 (two despatches); Captain Shepheard to Keats, 5 June 1811; and Captain Thomas to Legge, 8 July 1811.

27 ADM 1/423, Captain Adam to Pellew, no date (evidently May 1812), No 14; and Usher to Penrose, 27 May 1812. ADM 1/424, Report of Lieutenant Gibbs, RE, 15–21 August 1812.

28 Figure from D J Starkey, E G Van Eyck van Neshiga and J A De Moor, *Pirates and Privateers* (Exeter 1997), p170, no 32.

29 These examples are from *WD*, Vol 6, p33; Vol 8, pp73 and 198; and Vol 11, p356. Others can be found.

30 J M Sherwig, *Guineas and Gunpowder* (Cambridge, Mass 1969), p2234

31 *Ibid*, p255. *WSD*, Vol VII, p35.

32 ADM 2/1366, pp16, 21, 34–5, 127–8, 131–2 and 343.

33 *WSD*, Vol VI, pp556–7; and Vol VII, p197. *WD*, Vol 4, p475; Vol 5, p97; Vol 6, pp156–7 and 220; and Vol 7, p432. ADM 1/416, Berkeley to Rear-Admiral

Pickmore, 25 June 1810; and Pickmore to the Admiralty, 2 July 1810, No 186.

34 *WSD*, Vol VII, p510.

35 ADM 1/414, Collingwood to the Admiralty, 20 June 1808, No 139.

36 *WSD*, Vol VII, pp9 and 510. ADM 1/418, Keats to the Admiralty, 21 December 1811, No 78. For Cockburn see J Pack, *The Man who Burned the White House* (Hampshire 1987), pp132–5 and ADM 1/418, Keats to the Admiralty, 10 March 1811, No 19.

37 Pack, *op cit*, pp135–7. ADM 1/418, H Wellesley to Keats, 19 April 1811.

38 The correspondence concerning this can be followed in ADM 1/418, see particularly Bardaxi to H Wellesley, 29 January 1811; Keats to the Admiralty, 23 March 1811, no number; same to same, 29 March 1811, No 40; and same to same, 31 March 1811, No 41.

39 BL Add Mss 57393, Herries Papers, fv–f 53–4 (provisional folio order).

40 *WSD*, Vol VIII, p735.

41 C J Esdaile, *The Spanish Army in the Peninsular War* (Manchester 1988), p140. Sherwig, *op cit*, p237n.

42 AO 3/126/4, Return of the Corunna depot, 1812.

43 ADM 1/422, Captain Adam to Pellew, 15 January 1812.

44 *Ibid*, Captain Barton to Pellew, 24 December 1811; and same to same, 15 January 1812.

45 *Ibid*, Codrington to Pellew, 2 February 1812. ADM 1/426, Adam to Pellew, 25 May 1813.

46 ADM 2/1368, pp4–6. *WSD*, Vol VI, p230. B Hall, *op cit*, Vol III, pp6–12, 74–9 and 102–19. NMM, McKinley Papers, MCK/6(c), Captain Capel to McKinley, 9 April 1809; and same to same, 21 April 18009.

47 ADM 2/1369, p100.

48 AO 3/126/4, Return of the Corunna depot, 1812.

49 ADM 2/1371, pp128–30. ADM 1/146, Captain Christian to Cotton, 26 August 1811; this is an extremely long despatch that contains a great deal of interesting information on the guerrillas of northern Spain. One authority, quoting a Spanish source, estimates that by 1812 there were 38,520 guerrillas in Spain operating in 22 different groups: see Esdaile, *op cit*, p161.

Chapter 5: Cadiz and the Eastern Coast, 1810–14

1 ADM 1/420, Pellew to Codrington, 22 July 1811.

2 *The Naval Chronicle*, Vol XXIII, pp 147–8. Marshall, *op cit*, Vol II, p140. H G Thursfield (ed), *Five Naval Journals, 1789–1817* (London 1951), p372. ADM 1/417, Keats to the Admiralty, 23 August 1810, No 286. Lady Jane Bourchier (ed), *Memoirs of the Life of Admiral Sir Edward Codrington*, (London 1873), Vol I, pp171–3. ADM 1/422, Legge to the Admiralty, 8 March 1812, No 21.

3 Oman, *op cit*, Vol III, pp145–7.

4 The Cabinet's intentions and fears are clearly set out in despatches from Castlereagh to Dalrymple, the Governor of Gibraltar: see WO 6/185, pp23–30.

5 ADM 1/416, Purvis to the Admiralty, 12 February 1810, No 44; and same to same, 22 February 1810, No 59. Oman, *op cit*, Vol III, p148 says the Spanish force from Ayamonte was the first reinforcement to reach the city: Purvis's despatch says otherwise.

6 Smith, *op cit*, p389.

7 ADM 2/1369, pp380–2. ADM 1/416, List of warships at Cadiz, 12 April 1810.

8 J Donaldson, *Recollections of the Eventful Life of a Soldier* (London 1847), pp61–4, 71 and 78. Oman, *op cit*, Vol III, pp 147 and 318–9. *WSD*, Vol XIII, p403. ADM 1/416, Purvis to the Admiralty, 11 February 1810, No 43; same to same, 22 February 1810, No 59; same to same, 26 February 1810, No 78; and same to same, 12 March 1810, No 83.

9 Bomb vessels were specialised ships designed to engage land targets with explosive and incendiary shells. Amidships was a bed containing two heavy mortars that could be traversed to fire at a high angle for longer range. These weapons could shell targets up to a range of 4000 yards, the actual firing being, from 1804, the responsibility of the newly-established Royal Marine Artillery. See C Ware, *The Bomb Vessel* (London 1994). The siege of Cadiz was to witness the constant use of such vessels.

10 Oman, *op cit*, Vol III, p320. *WSD*, Vol VI, p513; and Vol XIII, p403. ADM

1/416, Vice-Admiral Purvis to the Admiralty, 19 April 1810, no number; and same to same, 23 April 1810, No 136. ADM 51/2915, Log of HMS *Thunder*, 12–22 April 1810. Thursfield, *op cit*, pp370–1.

11 ADM 1/416, Pickmore to the Admiralty, 11 June 1810, No 174. ADM 51/2915, Log of HMS *Thunder*, 26 April–4 May.

12 Oman, *op cit*, Vol III, pp231–2. Donaldson, *op cit*, p67. ADM 1/416, Pickmore to the Admiralty, 31 May 1810, No 166.

13 ADM 1/416, Purvis to Pickmore, 16 March 1810; and Pickmore to the Admiralty, 21 June 1810, No 156.

14 *Ibid*, Purvis to the Admiralty, 12 March 1810, No 83; Purvis to Pickmore, 16 March 1810; and Purvis to the Admiralty, 23 April 1810, No 136. ADM 1/417, List of Spanish vessels at Cadiz, 1 August 1810. Oman, *op cit*, Vol III, p321.

15 ADM 1/416, Purvis to Pickmore, 16 March 1810; and Pickmore to the Admiralty, 11 June 1810, No 174. ADM 7/42, pp1–4.

16 For the saga of events at Cartagena, see ADM 1/418 for Rowley's activities in August–September 1810, and ADM 1/419, 420 and 422 for events in 1811–12. Also ADM 7/44, p93 for Cotton's views.

17 The eventual movements of the warships from Cadiz can be followed in ADM 1/417 and ADM 7.43, p123, with particular voyages recounted in Pack, *op cit*, pp132–3 and Bourchier, *op cit*, Vol I, pp178–85. Admiralty worries are clearly shown in ADM 2/1370, pp163–6 and 445–6.

18 ADM 2/1370, pp151–5. *WSD*, Vol VI, pp556–7, 566 and 580; the comment from Wellesley is on p566. ADM 1/416, Keats to the Admiralty, 30 July 1810, No 260, corner note.

19 ADM 1/416, Keats to the Admiralty, 30 July 1810, No 260; and Pickmore to the Admiralty, 9 May 1810, No 143.

20 *Ibid*, Keats to the Admiralty, 6 August 1810, No 271; and same to same, No 275. Smith, *op cit*, says that in the summer of 1811 the French Cadiz flotilla contained 1456 men, p389.

21 ADM 1/417, Keats to the Admiralty, 23 August 1810, No 286; same to same, 31 August 1810, No 311; and same to

same, 17 September 1810, No 322. ADM 2/1371, pp39 and 41–3.

22 ADM 1/417, Keats to the Admiralty, 24 October 1810, No 339; and same to same, 27 October 1810, No 341. ADM A/419, Keats to the Admiralty, 13 April 1811, No 49, an extensive despatch answering Admiralty questions about the service of small vessels at Cadiz.

23 ADM 1/417, Keats to the Admiralty, 6 October 1810, No 314; same to same, 2 November 1810, No 365; and same to same, 3 November 1810, No 366. ADM 1/418, same to same, 26 November 1810, No 67. ADM 51/2595, Log of HMS *Milford*, October–November 1810. Marshall, *op cit*, Vol III, Part 1, pp130–4.

24 ADM 1/417, Keats to the Admiralty, 16 November 1810, No 379. ADM 1/418, Keats to Cotton, 24 November 1810; Keats to the Admiralty, 26 November 1810, No 67; same to same, 10 December 1810, No 73; same to same, 16 December 1810, No 77; and same to same, 7 January 1811, No 9. ADM 51/2595, Log of HMS *Milford*, November–December 1810. Marshall, *op cit*, Vol III, Part 1, pp134–6,

25 Marshall, *op cit*, Vol III, Part 1, p136. For the strategic implications of Soult's Estremaduran campaign see Oman, *op cit*, Vol IV, pp29–31 and 93–4.

26 ADM 1/417, Keats to the Admiralty, 22 December 1810, No 79; same to same, 13 January 1811, No 12; and same to same, 5 February 1811, No 18. ADM 1/418, Keats to Cotton, 20 February 1811, No 20; same to same, 28 February 1811, No 25; same to same, 7 March 1811, No 27; and same to same, 7 March 1811, No 28. Marshall, *op cit*, Vol III, part 1, pp137–40. For the land campaign see Oman, *op cit*, Vol IV, pp98–130 and Gates, *op cit*, pp249–52.

27 ADM 1/418, Keats to the Admiralty, 24 March 1811, No 26; and same to same, 24 March 1811, No 37. Oman, *op cit*, Vol IV, pp377–92, particularly pp381–6 for the crucial resistance of the Spaniards in the Allied line.

28 ADM 1/421, Legge to the Admiralty, 22 November 1811, No 37. ADM 1/422, same to same, 9 January 1812, No 4; same to same, 8 March 1812, No 21; and same to same, 2 May 1812, No 39. ADM 1/417, Keats to the Admiralty, 12 September 1810, no number.

29 Oman, *op cit*, Vol IV, pp444–5 and 475–6.

30 WO 1/402 details British operations in southern Spain at this time, see particularly pp445–77 and 533–44. Also Oman, *op cit*, Vol IV, pp593–4; and Vol V, pp109–29. Gates, *op cit*, pp277–80.

31 ADM 1/423, Legge to the Admiralty, 16 July 1812, No 61; and same to same, 18 July 1812, No 34. ADM 1/424, same to same, 26 August 1812, no number.

32 Krajeski, *op cit*, pp172–3. R N W Thomas, 'British Operations on the Coast of Catalonia, 1808–11' in A D Berkeley (ed), *New Lights on the Peninsular War. International Congress on the Iberian Peninsula. Selected Papers 1780–1840* (British Historical Society of Portugal 1991), p51. Oman, *op cit*, Vol III, p290–9, 311–2 and 500–1. ADM 7/42, pp28–9.

33 ADM 2/1370, pp349–50. ADM 7/42, pp28–9.

34 Bourchier, *op cit*, pp188–91. ADM 7/43, p356. ADM 1/419, Adam to Cotton, 25 March 1811.

35 ADM 1/418, Rogers to Cotton, 12 December 1810; and same to same, 15 December 1810. Marshall, *op cit*, Vol II, p844. Oman, *op cit*, Vol IV, p241 wrongly states that the action took place on 25 December and that the attackers came from 'frigates'. For Fane's successful operations in the summer, see Krajeski, *op cit*, pp164–5.

36 ADM 1/419, Codrington to Cotton, 24 April 1811. ADM 1/421, Codrington to Pellew, 20 July 1811; and Buck to Codrington, 25 July 1811. ADM 1/422, Adam to Pellew, 15 January 1812; and Codrington to Lacy, 18 February 1812.

37 Oman, *op cit*, Vol IV, pp490–6. NMM, Codrington papers, COD/5/5, Cotton to Codrington, 18 April 1811; same to same, 22 April 1911; and Bullen (*Cambrian*) to Codrington, 19 April 1811. ADM 1/419, Cotton to the Admiralty, 24 April 1811, No 87. Marshall, *op cit*, Vol II, pp598–9.

38 Bourchier, *op cit*, pp206–8. NMM, Codrington Papers, COD/5/5, Codrington to Cotton, 30 April 1811; and Codrington to Campoverde, 3 May 1811. ADM 51/2817, Log of HMS *Blake*, 3–4 May 1811. Oman, *op cit*, pp494–6.

39 Tarragona's siege from: Bourchier, *op cit*, pp218–30. ADM 1/419, Codrington to Cotton, 15 May 1811; same to same, 15 June 1811; same to same, 16 June 1811; and same to same, 23 June 1811. ADM 51/2187, Log of HMS *Blake*, May–June 1811. NMM, Codrington Papers, COD/5/5, Bullen to Codrington, 8 May 1811; Memorandum on supplies moved to Tarragona, ? May 1811; Rear-Admiral Fremantle to Codrington, 19 May 1811; and Cotton to Codrington, 22 May 1811. Oman, *op cit*, Vol IV, pp496–527. Gates, *op cit*, pp296–301.

40 ADM 1/420, Minute from Codrington, 6 July 1811; Codrington to Adam, 1 July 1911; Adam to Codrington, 10 July 1811; Codrington to Pellew, 18 July 1811; same to same, 23 August 1811; and Pellew to H Wellesley, 10 August 1811. Bourchier, *op cit*, pp254–6.

41 ADM 1/420, Lieutenant Colonel Green to Codrington, 17 July 1811; Codrington to Green, 26 July 1811; Green to Pellew, 6 August 1811; Pellew to Green, 31 July 1811; and Green to Pellew, 23 August 1811. ADM 1/421, Pellew to Codrington, 30 July 1811; Codrington to Pellew, 2 August 1811; and Pellew to H Wellesley, 10 August 1811.

42 ADM 1/420, Codrington to Pellew, 22 August 1811. ADM 1/421, Thomas (*Undaunted*) to Pellew, 2 September 1811; same to same, 21 October 1811; and Green to Pellew, 10 October 1811.

43 ADM 1/421, Major-General Roche to Pellew, 16 August 1811; and Pellew to Roche, 4 September 1811.

44 Oman, *op cit*, Vol V, pp25–46. ADM 1/421, Adam to Pellew, 29 July 1811.

45 Oman, *op cit*, Vol V, pp58–73. ADM 1/422, Eyre (*Magnificent*) to Pellew, 27 November 1811; Barton to Pellew, 24 December 1811; same to same, 15 January 1812; and Adam to Pellew, 30 January 1812.

46 ADM 1/422, H Wellesley to Bardaxi, 23 January 1812; and Adam to Pellew, 19 March 1812. Oman, *op cit*, Vol V, p611.

47 ADM 1/420, Codrington to Pellew, 12 July 1811. ADM 1/421, Pellew to H Wellesley, 10 August 1811. ADM 1/422, Pellew to the Admiralty, 8 February 1812, No 14; and same to same, 15 March 1812, No 36. For examples of ministerial efforts to employ the troops on Sicily during 1808–12, see Marquess of Londonderry (ed),

Memoirs and Correspondence of Viscount Castlereagh (London 1848–53), Vol VI, p475; and WO 6/38, pp2–6. For Mulgrave's rage at Bentinck's obstructionism see BM Add Mss, Bathurst Papers, BM 57, Vol 6, Mulgrave to Bathurst, no date (certainly after March 1812). *WSD*, Vol VII, p301.

48 ADM 1/422, Rear-Admiral Hallowell to Pellew, 11 March 1812; and Pellew to the Admiralty, 15 April 1812, No 59.

49 ADM 1/423, Pellew to the Admiralty, 23 July 1812, no number; Lieutenant-General Maitland to Pellew, 31 July 1812; Hallowell to Pellew, 2 August 1812; Pellew to Maitland, 2 August 1812; Hallowell to Pellew, 3 August 1812; and same to same, 10 August 1812. ADM 1/424, Hallowell to Maitland, 3 September 1812; and Pellew to the Admiralty, 12 September 1812, No 185. WO 1/812, p127. *WSD*, Vol VII, p378. Bourchier, *op cit*, p284.

50 Oman, *op cit*, Vol V, pp347–8 and Gates, *op cit*, p363 both make the point.

51 ADM 1/423, Hallowell to Pellew, 24 August 1812; same to same, 2 September 1812; same to same, 15 September 1812; and same to same, 19 October 1812. Oman, *op cit*, Vol V, p610.

52 ADM 1/424, Bathurst to Hallowell, 24 August 1812; same to same, 26 August 1812; same to same, 29 August 1812; Hallowell to Pellew, 18 August 1812; and Peyton (*Thames*) to Hallowell, 30 September 1812. Oman, *op cit*, Vol VI, pp163–4.

53 NMM, Codrington Papers, COD/5/7, Account of ordnance supplied to the Spaniards from 30 May 1812 to 7 February 1813. ADM 1/424, Codrington to Pellew, 27 September 1812, No 21. At the end of 1811, in response to repeated local requests for arms, Pellew was sent 15,000 muskets to be distributed in eastern Spain as he saw fit: ADM 2/1373, p267.

54 ADM 1/425, Codrington to Pellew, 6 February 1813. Bourchier, *op cit*, pp305–6.

55 *WD*, Vol 10, pp104–5 and 156. ADM 1/426, Zehnfenning (Green's successor as military agent in Catalonia) to Pellew, 9 May 1813. Oman, *op cit*, Vol VI, p277.

56 ADM 1/426, Lieutenant-General Murray to Pellew, 2 June 1813; Hallowell to Pellew, 4 June 1813; and same to same, 10 June 1813. Oman, *op cit*, Vol VI, p499.

57 ADM 1/426, Hallowell to Pellew, 14 June 1813; same to same, 19 June 1813; Murray to Pellew, 14 June 1813; Hallowell to H Wellesley, 13 June 1813; Peyton to Adam, 13 June 1813; and Adam to Pellew, 4 July 1813.

58 *Ibid*, Adam to Pellew, 24 July 1813. Oman, *op cit*, Vol VII, pp81–8 and 96–109.

59 ADM 1/427, Pellew to the Admiralty, 15 October 1813, No 260. ADM 1/428, Hole to Vice-Admiral Pickmore, 20 October 1813; Dilkes to Bathurst, 15 January 1814; and same to same, 23 January 1814.

Chapter 6: The Northern Coast, 1810–14

1 *WSD*, Vol VII, pp439–40.

2 ADM 2/1369, p100. ADM 1/142, Gambier to the Admiralty, 24 October 1809, No 91. ADM 1/143, Proby (*Amelia*) to Gambier, 24 April 1810 for an example of naval attacks on the French supply line.

3 ADM 1/143, Parker to Gambier, 8 February 1810. Oman, *op cit*, Vol III, pp217–20.

4 ADM 1/143, Aylmer to Mends, 9 July 1810; and Mends to Gambier, 11 July 1810. Marshall, *op cit*, Vol II, p949. Oman, *op cit*, Vol III, p486, numbers Parker's force at a thousand: Mends, who should have known, gives half that in his despatch.

5 ADM 1/144, Mends to Gambier, 25 July 1810; Gambier to Popham, 20 August 1810; and Popham to Gambier, 9 September 1810. H Popham, *A Damned Cunning Fellow* (Tywardreath 1991), p194.

6 ADM 1/144, Mends to Gambier, 30 September 1810; same to same, 14 October 1810; same to same, 31 October 1810; same to same, 6 November 1810; and same to same, 8 December 1810. Oman, *op cit*, Vol III, p486–7, is considerably in error about the expedition: it was not commanded by Popham, it did not include a marine battalion (the Admiralty was ready to commit one but it was too long in preparing), 600 lives were lost rather than 800, and Mends mentions the loss of only the Spanish vessels.

7 ADM 1/146, Rouget to Bessières, 18 March 1811. For the French garrisons, see Oman, *op cit*, Vol IV, pp462–3 and 641.

8 ADM /145, Collier to Gambier, 20 April 1811, No 11. ADM 1/146, Tobin to Gambier, 16 June 1811, No 4.

9 ADM 1/145, Collier to Gambier, 29 April 1811, No 13. ADM 1/146, Tobin to Gambier, 23 June 1811, No 5; and same to same, 20 July 1811, No 8. ADM 1/147, Collier to Gambier, 23 August 1811, No 9. Oman, *op cit*, Vol IV, p641.

10 ADM 1/146, Collier to Gambier, 12 August 1811, No 4.

11 *Ibid*, Collier to Gambier, 12 August 1811, No 5; and same to same, 18 August 1811, No 6.

12 ADM 1/147, Tobin to Collier, 22 August 1811; Collier to Gambier, 20 August 1811, No 7; same to same, 21 August 1811, No 8; same to same, 24 August 1811, No 10; and same to same, 30 August 1811, No 11.

13 *Ibid*, Collier to Cotton, 30 September 1811, No 6; same to same, 4 October 1811, No 8; same to same, 14 October 1811, No 9; same to same, 20 October 1811, No 11; same to same, 14 November 1811, No 12; same to same, 16 November 1811, No 14; same to same, 1 December 1811, No 21; and Christian and Collier, 8 November 1811.

14 See Oman, *op cit*, Vol V for a detailed review of the situation in Spain in the spring of 1812.

15 ADM 2/1373, pp228–30. C Lloyd, *The Keith Papers*, edited by Vol III (London 1955), pp265–8.

16 There is only one full-length biography of Popham, its title being indicative of the man: see Popham, *op cit*, note 5.

17 ADM 1/149, Popham's diary for 6–21 June. NMM, Malcolm Papers, MAL/2 MS 60/088, pp74–6.

18 ADM 1/149, Popham's diary for 22–28 June. Popham, *op cit*, pp199–200. NMM, Malcolm Papers, MAL/1 MS 60/038, pp101–3. British Library Loan 57, Vol 108, Melville Mss, ff82–3, Popham to Melville, 14 July 1812.

19 ADM 1/150, Popham to Keith, 31 July 1812, No 40. Popham, *op cit*, pp201–2. NMM, Malcolm Papers, MAL/1 MS 60/038, pp113–7. Oman, *op cit*, Vol V, pp554–5.

20 ADM 1/150, Popham to Keith, 4 August 1812, No 42; Report on Santander by the masters of the *Venerable*, *Medusa* and *Rhin*, 4 August 1812; Return of provisions brought by the *Diadem*, 4 August 1812; and Popham to Keith, 31 August 1812, No 73.

21 For Guetaria's value see ADM 1/149, Collier to Keith, 30 March 1812; and Collier to Douglas, 18 May 1812. Also *WD*, Vol 9, pp464–5.

22 NMM, Malcolm Papers, MAL/1 MS 60/038, p90. Popham, *op cit*, pp203–5. There is a flurry of letters between Popham and Mendizabal about Guetaria in ADM 1/150, with the sailor's account of the failure in Popham to Keith, 25 September 1812, No 85.

23 Detailed accounts of these operations can be found in Oman, *op cit*, Vol V, pp504–48 and 567–82; and Vol VI, pp1–20. See Gates, *op cit*, pp343–66 for a more concise version.

24 Oman, *op cit*, Vol VI, pp21–49. ADM 1/150, Popham to Keith, 26 July 1812, No 36.

25 *WD*, Vol 10, pp450, 453, 464–6, 471 and 491. Shore, *op cit*, Vol XLVIII (NS), pp234–5. Popham, *op cit*, p206. ADM 1/150, Popham to Keith, 7 October 1812, No 101; same to same, 8 November 1812, No 122; and same to same, 20 November 1812, No 128.

26 *WD*, Vol 9, pp570–4, quote on p574. Despite his successes Popham was not reappointed to the Spanish command in the following year and received no recognition for his efforts in 1812. He was surprised by this, particularly as he believed he had Wellington's support. One may wonder if the general's graceless letter after Burgos played a part in this, though it should also be noted that Keith had doubts about Popham's capacity to work well with the Spaniards and that may have been a factor. See Popham, *op cit*, pp212–3 and Lloyd, *op cit*, p284.

27 *WD*, Vol 9, p495. Lloyd, *op cit*, pp284–5. ADM 2/1375, pp188–9 and 307–8. See ADM 1/150 and 151 for Popham's attempts to organise an attack on Santona and also his fluctuating views on the likelihood of success. Bouverie's orders for the winter can be found in ADM 1/152, Popham to Bouverie, 20 December 1812.

28 ADM 1/153, Bloye (*Lyra*) to Keith, 13 May 1813. Oman, *op cit*, Vol VI, pp252–74. Smith, *op cit*, p419.

29 *WD*, Vol 10, pp104–5 and 334. Sir R V Hamilton (ed), *Letters and Papers of Admiral of the Fleet Sir T Byam Martin*, Vol II (London 1898), p316. Lloyd, *op cit*, p290. Oman explains Wellington's plans for 1813 in *op cit*, Vol VI, pp299–313.

30 *WD*, Vol 9, pp349 and 461. *WSD*, Vol VII, pp439–40, quote from p440. One may reflect on what Wellington's response would have been had the Admiralty tried to give him advice on the disposition of his forces.

31 *WD*, Vol 10, pp273, 360–1 and 459.

32 *WSD*, Vol VIII, pp145–7.

33 Lloyd, *op cit*, p293. Hamilton, *op cit*, p355. Oman, *op cit*, Vol VI covers the Vittoria campaign in great detail: pp299–556. A briefer account can be found in Gates, *op cit*, pp383–92.

34 *WD*, Vol 10, pp461–2, 509 and 544–5. Lloyd, *op cit*, pp294–5. Shore, *op cit*, Vol XLVIII (NS), pp354–5. Oman, *op cit*, Vol VI, p569.

35 ADM 1/154, Collier to Keith, 6 July 1813, No 30; and Biscayan Deputies and Consulate of Bilbao to Collier, 6 July 1813. *WSD*, Vol XIV, p220.

36 *WD*, Vol 10, pp458–9, 495, 509 and 522–3. Oman, *op cit*, Vol VI, pp566–86. ADM 8/96.

37 *WD*, Vol 10, pp561–2; and Vol 11, pp17–19.

38 ADM 2/1377, pp286–97. Lloyd, *op cit*, pp295–6 and 300–1. WO 1/733, pp5–36. *WSD*, Vol VIII, pp223–5. Hamilton, *op cit*, pp354–5. Oman, *op cit*, Vol VI, pp567–8 only briefly alludes to the dispute and, while providing no analysis, completely takes Wellington's part. Melville he dismisses as a person of 'complete insignificance'.

39 ADM 1/154, Collier to Keith, 6/7 August 1813, No 42; same to same, 25 August 1813, No 50; Memorandum from Collier to the squadron, 26 August 1813; Collier to Keith, 27 August 1813, No 51; same to same, 30 August 1813, No 53; Memorandum from Collier to the squadron, 30 August 1813; and Collier to Keith, 1 September 1813, No 54. Oman, *op cit*, Vol VII, p10–36 and 58–62.

40 Hamilton, *op cit*, pp394–5, 397–400, 404–11 and 414. ADM 1/154, Collier to Keith, 4 September 1813 (wrongly numbered 55).

41 ADM 1/154, Collier to Keith, 21 September 1813, No 67; same to same, 17 October 1813, No 75; and same to same, 31 October 1813, No 83. *WD*, Vol 11, p211.

42 ADM 1/155, Collier to Keith, 11 October 1813, No 76; same to same, 1 November 1813, No 85; and same to same, 19 November 1813, No 93. ADM 1/156, Collier to Keith, 17 January 1814, No 10; and same to same, 23 January 1814, No 12.

43 ADM 1/155, Campbell (*Lyra*) to Collier, 10 October 1813. *WD*, Vol 11, pp211–2, 402–3 and 406. Lloyd, *op cit*, pp305–9. *WSD*, Vol VI, p689.

44 Shore, *op cit*, Vol XLVIII (NS), p617. Clowes, *op cit*, Vol V, p537. ADM 1/155, Collier to Keith, 1 November 1813, no number. *WD*, Vol 11, pp285, 296, 387, 406 and 493.

45 ADM 1/156, Rear-Admiral Penrose to Keith, 8 February 1814, No 16; same to same, 9 February 1814, No 17; same to same, 14 February 1814, No 19; same to same, 21 February 1814, No 23; same to same, 23 February 1814, No 24; and Keith to Penrose, 21 February 1814. Shore, 'Peninsular War', *op cit*, Vol XLVIII (NS), pp622–5; and Shore, 'The Navy and Wellington's Army', *The United Services Magazine* (1914) Vol XLVIII (NS), pp26–8: this is the same extended article that has already been cited but for some reason, to the confusion of the historian and librarian alike, altered its title for the later parts of its publication. Oman, *op cit*, Vol VII, pp332–3. Buckley, p259.

46 ADM 1/156, Penrose to Keith, 25 February 1814, no number; same to same, 28 February 1814, No 28; and O'Reilly to Penrose, 26 February 1814. Buckley, *op cit*, pp260–4. Oman, *op cit*, Vol VII, pp336–8. Shore, 'Wellington's Army', *op cit*, Vol XLVIII (NS), pp28–32.

47 For Orthez and the occupation of Bordeaux, see Oman, *op cit*, Vol VII, pp356–95; and Gates, *op cit*, pp454–8. For Penrose's initial movements, see *WD*, Vol 11, p588. Reverend J Penrose, *Lives of Vice-Admiral Sir Charles Vinicombe Penrose and Captain James Trevenen* (London 1850), p31.

48 ADM 1/156, Penrose to Keith, 27

March 1814, No 48; same to same, 28 March 1814, No 49; same to same, 29 March 1814, No 50; same to same, 2 April 1814, No 52; same to same, 4 April 1814, No 55; and Penrose to Coode (*Porcupine*), 30 March 1814. J Penrose, *op cit*, pp32–5. Oman, *op cit*, Vol VII, p400.

49 ADM 1/156, Coode to Penrose, 2 April 1814. Shore, 'Wellington's Army', *op cit*, Vol XLVIII (NS), p114.

50 ADM 1/156, Memorandum from Captain Bingham (*Egmont*), 4 April 1814; Penrose to Keith, 7 April 1814, No 57; same to same, 9 April 1814, No 60; same to same, 11 April 1814, No 61; same to same, 16 April 1814, No 65; and Harris to Bingham, 9 April 1814.

Bibliography

Unpublished primary sources

PUBLIC RECORD OFFICE, KEW
ADM 1/138–158, Channel Fleet in letters.
ADM 1/339–346, Lisbon station in letters.
ADM 1/414–428, Mediterranean Fleet in letters.
ADM 1/4208–12, War Office to Admiralty correspondence.
ADM 1/1939, 1940 and 2078, correspondence from Captains Hotham and Linzee.
ADM 1/478, 625 and 4515, assorted correspondence relating to convoys.
ADM 2/1366–1379, Admiralty out letters.
ADM 7/42–46, letterbook of Admiral Cotton.
ADM 7/64, convoy lists.
ADM 8/96–98, vessels serving on the Lisbon station, 1808–13.
ADM 52/1866, log of HMS *Port Mahon*.
ADM 52/1880, log of HMS *Donegal*.
ADM 52/2114, log of HMS *Amelia*.
ADM 52/2707, log of HMS *Phipps*.
ADM 52/2915, log of HMS *Thunder*.
ADM 52/3861, log of HMS *Racoon*.
ADM 52/4508, log of HMS *Hydra*.
ADM 52/2187, log of HMS *Blake*.
ADM 109/106–7, Victualling Board out letters.
WO 1/717–733, War Office to Admiralty correspondence.
FO 63/58, Portuguese alliance.
AO 3/126/4, report on the depot at Corunna, 1812.

NATIONAL MARITIME MUSEUM, GREENWICH
CAR/102/2, Captain Carteret's papers.
COC/11, Captain Cockburn's papers.

KEI/35/1/3 and 37/1, Admiral Keith's papers.
MCK/6(b), (c) and (d), Captain McKinley's papers.
YOR, Secretary Yorke's papers.

BRITISH LIBRARY, LONDON
British Library Add Mss.
BM Loan 57, Vol 108, Melville papers.
38325–6, Liverpool papers.

WARWICKSHIRE RECORD OFFICE, WARWICK
CR 114A/616, letterbook of Admiral Berkeley.

Printed primary sources

Gurwood, J (ed), *The Dispatches of F M the Duke of Wellington, 1799–1818*, 12 vols (London 1834–9).

Hamilton, Sir R V (ed), *Letters and Papers of Admiral of the Fleet Sir T Byam Martin*, Vol II (London 1898).

Lloyd, C (ed), *The Keith Papers*, Vol III (London 1955).

Londonderry, Marquess of (ed), *Memoirs and Correspondence of Viscount Castlereagh*, 12 vols (London 1848–53).

Newnham Collingwood, G L (ed), *A Selection from the Public and Private Correspondence of Vice-Admiral Lord Collingwood*, 2 vols (London 1828).

Stewart, Sir W, *Cumloden Papers*, 2 vols (Edinburgh and London 1871).

Wellington, Second Duke of (ed), *Supplementary Despatches, Correspondence and Memoranda of Field Marshal Arthur Duke of Wellington*, 15 vols (London 1858–72).

SECONDARY SOURCES

Anderson, H S, *The Eastern Question, 1774–1923* (London 1974).

Berkley, A D (ed), *New Lights on the Peninsular War. International Congress on the Iberian Peninsula. Selected papers 1780–1840.* (London 1991).

Bourchier, Lady J, *Memoirs of the Life of Admiral Sir Edward Codrington*, 2 vols (London 1873).

Buckley, R N, *The Napoleonic War Journal of Captain Thomas Henry Browne, 1807–1816* (London 1987).

Chandler, D G, *The Campaigns of Napoleon* (London 1967).

Clowes, W L, *The Royal Navy*, 6 vols (London 1897–1903).

Cogar, W B (ed), *New Interpretations in Naval History* (London 1989).

Crawford, A, *Reminiscences of a Naval Officer* (London 1999).

Crouzet, F, *L'Economie Britannique et le Blocus Continental, 1803–15* (Paris 1958).

Crowhurst, P, *The French War on Trade. Privateering 1793–1815* (Aldershot 1989).

Davis, R, *The Rise of the British Shipping Industry* (Newton Abbot 1972).

Dixon, C, 'To Walk the Quarter Deck: the Naval Career of David Ewen Bartholomew', *Mariner's Mirror*, Vol 78, No 3 (August 1992).

Donaldson, J, *Recollections of the Eventful Life of a Soldier* (London 1947).

Edwards, H N, 'The Diary of Lieutenant C Gillmore, RN – Portugal 1810', *Journal of the Society for Army Historical Research*, Vol 3 (1924).

Esdaile, C J, *The Spanish Army in the Peninsular War* (Manchester 1988).

Forester, C S, *The Age of Fighting Sail* (London 1970).

Fortescue, J W, *A History of the British Army*, 10 vols (London 1899–1930).

Francis, D, *Portugal, 1715–1808* (London 1985).

Fullom, S W, *The Life of Sir Howard Douglas* (London 1863).

Gates, D, *The Spanish Ulcer* (London 1986).

Glover, M, *The Peninsular War* (Newton Abbot 1974).

Hall, B, *Fragments of Voyages and Travels*, 2 vols (Edinburgh 1832).

Hall, C D, *British Strategy in the Napoleonic War, 1803–15* (Manchester 1992).

Hamilton, Sir R V and J K Laughton, *Recollections of James Anthony Gardner* (London 1996).

Hayter, A (ed), *The Backbone. Diaries of a Military Family in the Napoleonic War* (Durham 1993).

Heckscher, E F, *The Continental System* (London 1922).

Henegan, Sir R, *Seven Years Campaigning in the Peninsula and the Netherlands from 1808 to 1815*, 2 vols (London 1846).

Herries, E, *Memoir of the Public Life of the Right Hon John Charles Herries*, 2 vols (London 1880).

Hibbert, C, *Corunna* (London 1961).

Horward, D D, 'British Seapower and its Influence upon the Peninsular War (1808–1814)', *Naval War College Review*, Vol 31 (1978).

James, W, *The Naval History of Great Britain*, 6 vols (London 1837).

Kennedy, P, *The Rise and Fall of British Naval Mastery* (London 1991).

Kincaid, J, *Adventures in the Rifle Brigade and Random Shots from a Rifleman* (London 1981).

Krajeski, P C, *In the Shadow of Nelson. The Naval Leadership of Admiral Sir Charles Cotton, 1753–1812* (London 2000).

Lavery, B, *Nelson's Navy* (London 1989).

Lewis, W A (ed), *A Narrative of my Professional Adventures, 1790–1839* by W H Dillon, 2 vols (London 1956).

Lloyd, C, *Captain Marryat and the Old Navy* (London 1939).

Ludovici, A (ed), *On the Road with Wellington* by A L F Schaumann (London 1924).

Marcus, C J, *A Naval History of England. The Age of Nelson* (London 1971).

Marshall, J, *Royal Naval Biography*, 3 vols (London 1824).

Marshall-Cornwall, J, *Marshal Massena* (London 1965).

Marryat, F, *Life and Letters of Captain Marryat* (London 1872).

Maurice, Sir J F (ed), *The Diary of Sir John Moore*, 2 vols (London 1904).

Naval Chronicle, Vols XVIII–XXXI (London 1807–14).

Oman, Sir C, *A History of the Peninsular War* 7 vols (Oxford 1902–30; reprinted London 1995–7).

Pack, J, *The Man Who Burned the White House* (Hampshire 1987).

Parkinson, C N (editor), *The Trade Winds: A Study of British Overseas Trade during the French Wars, 1793–1815* (London 1948).

Penrose, J, *Lives of Vice-Admiral Sir Charles Vinicombe Penrose and Captain James Trevenen* (London 1850).

Phillimore, A, *The Life of Admiral of the Fleet Sir William Parker* 2 vols (London 1876).

Popham, H, *A Damned Cunning Fellow* (Tywardreath 1991).

Rait, R S, *The Life and Campaigns of Hugh, First Viscount Gough, Field Marshal*, 2 vols (London 1913).

Ringrose, D R, *Transportation and Economic Stagnation in Spain, 1750–1850* (Durham, NC 1970).

Seymour, W, *Great Sieges of History* (London 1991).

Sherwig, J M, *Guineas and Gunpowder* (Cambridge, Mass 1969).

Shore, H N, 'The Navy in the Peninsular War', *The United Services Magazine*, Vols XLVI–XLVIII New Style (1912–14).

——, 'The Navy and the Lines of Torres Vedras', *The United Services Magazine*, Vol XLII New Style (1910–11).

Smith, D, *The Greenhill Napoleonic Wars Data Book* (London 1998).

Starkey, D J, Van Eyck van Hershiga, E G and De Moor, J A, *Pirates and Privateers* (Exeter 1999).

Thomas, D, *Cochrane* (London 1980).

Thompson, J M, *Napoleon Bonaparte: His Rise and Fall* (Oxford 1969).

Thursfield, H G (ed), *Five Naval Journals, 1789–1817* (London 1951).

Ward, S G P, *Wellington's Headquarters* (Oxford 1956).

Ware, C, *The Bomb Vessel* (London 1994).

Watson, G E, 'The United States and the Peninsular War, 1808–1812', *Historical Journal*, Vol 19, No 4 (1976).

Unpublished thesis

De Toy, B M, *Wellington's Admiral: The Life and Career of George Berkeley, 1753–1818* (University of Florida PhD thesis, 1997).

Index